DISABLED PEOPLE IN BRITAIN
AND DISCRIMINATION

COLIN BARNES has a hereditary visual impairment and
for seven years attended special schools. He studied
special education needs at Huddersfield Polytechnic and
in 1989 obtained his Ph.D. at Leeds University. He is a
co-editor of the international journal *Disability, Handicap and Society* and is principal research officer for the
British Council of Organizations of Disabled People.

what the law said
what the impact to the
learner?
is prevelant (because... -
of that
references)

COLIN BARNES

Disabled People in Britain and Discrimination

A Case for Anti-Discrimination Legislation

WITH A NEW UPDATED FOREWORD AND
ADDITIONS TO THE BIBLIOGRAPHY

HURST & COMPANY, LONDON

*in association with the
British Council of Organizations of Disabled People*

To Hil

CONTENTS

v

TABLES

FOREWORD TO THE SECOND IMPRESSION

Today, in contrast to two and a half years ago when this book was first published, debates about disability – particularly among politicians and in some parts of the media – have shifted dramatically from purely medical concerns to human rights issues and the role of legislation. Discrimination against disabled people is now widely understood as a major social problem that can only be solved by statutory means. We will look at the reasons for this unprecedented transformation, and at recent Government proposals to eliminate discrimination – proposals that fall far short of what is needed.

As this study shows (see Chapters 1 and 9), disabled people in the United Kingdom have been actively engaged in a struggle for equal rights and opportunities for almost three decades. This book forms an integral part of that struggle. Unlike most studies of disablement, both in Britain and overseas, it is based on what has become known as the 'social model of disability'. This is a theoretical construct developed during the 1970s and '80s by such disabled writers as Paul Abberley, Ken Davis, Vic Finkelstein, Paul Hunt and Mike Oliver to explain disabled people's oppression.

Traditional explanations of disabled people's individual and collective disadvantage rest upon the assumptions of the 'medical model of disability'. This approach maintains that impairment has such a traumatic physical and/or psychological impact upon individuals that they are unable to achieve a reasonable quality of life by their own efforts. It is a perspective that is now recognised as an inadequate basis for understanding disablement.

The 'social model of disability', on the other hand, shifts the emphasis away from individuals with impairments towards restricting environments and disabling barriers. Hence, disabled people are prevented from securing a standard of living comparable to that of non-disabled people by a comprehensive and pervasive system of economic and social barriers increasingly referred to as social oppression or institutional discrimination. This book provides a mass of quantitative and qualitative evidence in support of this perspective. It has demystified the social model of disability and brought it into the 'real world'. In short, it provides clear empirical support for a group of theorists whose work has hitherto been dismissed or ignored by mainstream academics, professionals and policy-makers.

Equally important, the research on which these book is based poses a direct challenge to traditional approaches to disability research production. Unlike previous studies in this field it was conceived and conducted by disabled people – only two of the twelve people involved in the research process were non-disabled. It was also carried out under the direction of an organisation controlled and run by disabled people themselves – the British Council of Organisations of Disabled People (BCODP) – rather than an established research institution or university, and it achieved a level of accountability and participation unrivalled for this type of project (see Preface and Acknowledgements). Consequently, it set standards against which other disability-related research might be judged.

Furthermore, since this book's publication the BCODP and its member-organisations have successfully conducted research on a whole range of disability-related issues. These include: disabling imagery and the media, self-operated personal assistance schemes, housing and disabled people, independent living for disabled people, and direct payments for disabled people with personal assistance needs – issues which, by and large, have been ignored by established research institutions.

Moreover, in 1992 the BCODP organised two residential seminars to introduce newcomers to the notion of independent living and personal assistance. These remarkable events brought together over 100 disabled people with 'severe' physical impairments from all over Britain to discuss and develop strategies for living independently and employing personal assistants. Given the environmental barriers faced by this particular section of the disabled community (see Chapter 7) this is no mean achievement and something which had never been attempted before in Britain.

This heightened self-confidence and activity from within the disabled people's movement has also stimulated more individuals with impairments to come together to form their own organisations, and to participate actively in the struggle for equal rights and opportunities. Since 1991 there has been a 20 per cent growth in the number of organisations which constitute the BCODP. There has also been a significant increase in the numbers of disabled people willing to fight for their rights through direct action and political demonstrations.

Two recent examples are particularly noteworthy. On 28 March 1994 Sir Jimmy Savile – a well-known British disc jockey who received his knighthood for charity work – was scheduled to open a garden for 'the disabled' costing more than £40,000 in Leeds City station – a station which is only partly accessible to people with mobility-related impairments. The ceremony was disrupted by 300 disabled activists some of whom handcuffed themselves to a waiting Intercity train destined for London. As a result, the train was delayed for thirty-five minutes while British Rail officials cut the protesters free. Subsequently, the city's traffic was brought to a halt for a further thirty minutes because the demonstrators occupied a major junction in the city centre after leaving the station. On 9 July 1994 over 3,000 disabled people from all over Britain attended a 'Rights Now' rally in Trafalgar Square, London.

The 1990s have witnessed an increase in international activity too. In April 1992 Disabled People's International (DPI), the international counterpart of the BCODP, held its third world congress in Vancouver, Canada. It coincided with the organisation of 'Independence 92' in recognition of the end of the United Nations Decade of Disabled People. It was attended by 4,000 delegates from over 120 countries, half of them from developing countries.

On 3 December 1993 the Parliament of the European Union in Brussels was given over to almost 500 disabled people from all parts of Europe to discuss the human rights situation of disabled Europeans. A year earlier France added its name to the growing list of countries which now have anti-discrimination legislation for disabled people, and the Government of the Republic of Ireland made a firm commitment to do the same in that country before 1995.

In Britain, in addition to and probably because of these events, the campaign for anti-discrimination legislation has been bolstered by the active involvement of most of the 'traditional' disability organisations controlled and run by non-disabled people. Until this point the commitment of many of these organisations to disabled people's rights had not gone beyond the stage of discussions; today they are providing much-needed resources, both human and financial. While their motives might be intrinsically different from those of the BCODP (see Chapter 9) their support must be welcomed if only because of the extent of institutional discrimination experienced by disabled people, which remains largely unchanged since this book was written.

As mentioned earlier, although today there is no dispute about the extent of discrimination against disabled people, this was not the case two and a half years ago. At the start of 1992 the British Government still denied that discrimination against disabled people was a major problem. Although this book was completed in July 1991 it was only formally launched on Monday 27 January 1992. On the following Friday, 31 January, in a House of Commons debate on the Civil Rights (Disabled Persons) Bill introduced by the Labour MP Alf Morris – the tenth attempt to get anti-discrimination legislation through Parliament (for details of previous attempts see Appendix) – the Conservative Government's Minister for Disabled People, Nicholas Scott, admitted for the first time: 'Discrimination against disabled people is widespread.'

But while the Government was forced to concede that discrimination is a major problem, it was not prepared to allow a Bill to go through Parliament to deal with it. Putting business interests before those of the disabled population, ministers argued that Britain could not afford such a policy. They went on to suggest that discrimination could be overcome by policies of education and persuasion rather than by regulation and enforcement.

However, since the Bill had cross-party support, the Government had to resort to underhand tactics in order to prevent it from being put to the vote. Consequently, its passage was successfully blocked by the Conservative MP for Kingswood, Robert Haywood, by the use of a filibuster, i.e. he continued speaking until the deadline for the vote had passed. It is some consolation to note that Robert Haywood's reward for talking out the Bill was to lose his Parliamentary seat later that year in the 1992 general election. Indeed, disabled activists played a crucial role in his defeat by publicly drawing attention to his part in the Bill's demise at every opportunity during the election campaign.

Since then there have been three other attempts to get an anti-discrimination Bill on to the statute books, and all of them have been thwarted in one way or another by the Government's use of dubious and undemocratic Parliamentary procedures. The Labour peer, Baroness Lockwood, picked up the Alf Morris Bill and successfully steered it through the House of Lords in 1992. It returned to the Commons on 26 February 1993, but after a five-hour debate during which it again received cross-party backing, the Conservative whip Andrew Mackay followed Government instructions and cried 'Object', thus preventing the Bill from progressing further. Similar tactics were used to wreck an identical Bill for Northern Ireland five months later.

But the Civil Rights (Disabled Persons) Bill re-emerged in the House of Commons with the sponsorship of Dr Roger Berry, who had replaced Robert Haywood as Labour MP for Kingswood. It received its second reading unopposed on 11 March 1994. Yet despite an assertion by the Prime Minister, John Major, a few days later that he hoped the Bill would reach the 'Committee stage', his Government again prevented its progress on its return to the House at the Report stage. When it appeared before the Commons on 6 May the Bill was effectively killed off by eighty-two minor amendments tabled by Conservative backbench MPs: James Clappison,

Edward Leigh, Lady Olga Maitland, Richard Spring and Michael Stern. It transpired later that these amendments were drafted by Parliamentary Counsel on the instructions of Nicholas Scott, the Minister for Disabled People.

Roger Berry's Civil Rights (Disabled Persons) Bill was finally laid to rest on Friday 15 July when Nicholas Scott reiterated the Government position that it failed to take account of the interests of the business community, and that the expense of implementing it would prove insupportable. Instead, he proposed five steps to supplement a long-term policy of tackling discrimination through education, persuasion and increasing awareness. Meanwhile, in a Government re-shuffle announced on Wednesday 20 July, Scott's long tenure of office came to an end, and he was replaced by the young and newly-promoted William Hague.

The five proposals are outlined in 'A Consultation on Government Measures to Tackle Discrimination Against Disabled People' (July 1994), and it can be predicted that they would achieve relatively little. The areas for discussion include employment, housing, the provision of goods and services, financial services and the establishment of a disablement advisory body.

First, in opposition to the views of disabled people and their organisations, the Government have finally made it clear that they intend to scrap the employment quota scheme. This is no real surprise since it has not supported the scheme since the 1950s. Instead, it is to initiate a process of 'consultation', notably with employers (*sic*), on the right to 'non-discrimination' – with the emphasis on direct discrimination – and on the limits to 'reasonable access' in the workplace. As Chapter 4 clearly shows, disabled peopled face a whole range of attitudinal and environmental problems in the labour market which will definitely not be solved through consultation.

Secondly, they propose extending building regulations to include new houses and flats. This is a welcome development since there is a chronic shortage of accessible homes in the United Kingdom. However, there is no indication of what these extended regulations will cover or when they will come into force, or indeed whether they will apply to all newly-constructed houses or only to those built by certain sections of the housing market, e.g. by housing associations. Moreover, since Britain's house-building programme is currently stagnant, especially where council housing – the main source of accommodation for disabled people – is concerned, and is unlikely to pick up in the next few years, the new regulations are unlikely to make a significant difference to the present situation (see Chapter 7).

Thirdly, a statutory right of non-discrimination in the provi-
on of goods and services is to be introduced. Again a welcome
development, but this does not extend to inaccessible premises,
spurious interpretations of health and safety regulations, or inac-
cesible transport systems. In other words, the bulk of Britain's high
streets, shopping centres and leisure facilities will remain out of
bounds to disabled people. Additionally banks, building societies
and insurance companies will be encouraged to develop and produce
voluntary 'codes of good practice' for staff dealing with disabled
people. Again this is aimed at eliminating direct rather than indirect
discrimination. As this study makes clear, voluntary policies have
hitherto had only a marginal effect on public attitudes or behaviour.

Finally, the Government intends to set up an 'advisory' body: 'the
National Disability Council, to monitor discrimination, advise
ministers and help draw up even more codes of good practice. The
Government-appointed council will include members of existing
committees, people from disability organisations and 'organisations
representing business and employers'.

Recent research by the 'Right Now' campaign, known up till 1994
as the Voluntary Organisations for Anti-Discrimination Legislation
(VOADL – see Chapters 1 and 9), provides substantial evidence
that the Government has significantly overestimated the cost of
implementing the Civil Rights (Disabled Persons) Bill. The Government produced a hugely inflated figure of £17 billion with which to
justify their case and frighten Conservative MPs. The Report 'What
Price Civil Rights?' draws on research from both within Britain and
outside – notably from the United States where anti-discrimination
legislation, the Americans with Disabilities Act, came into operation
in 1990.

As this book shows by means of numerous examples, these
policies will not solve the problem of discrimination against disabled
people. This is because, like racism, sexism, heterosexism and other
forms of prejudice, discrimination against disabled people is institutionalised in the very fabric of British society. It encompasses direct,
indirect and passive discrimination, and its roots reach down into
the very foundations of Western society. It is evident in our abortion
laws, our education system, the labour market, the benefit system,
the health and social support services, the built environment (housing, transport and public buildings), the leisure industry,
the media and the political system. It cannot be eradicated with
ill-thought-out piecemeal policies such as those outlined in the
Government's 'Consultation', but requires firm and decisive action
such as that proposed in Chapter 10.

Institutionalised discrimination against disabled people is unlikely to disappear in the foreseeable future. As the author of this book, which provides a comprehensive analysis of this phenomenon and is thus a starting-point for anyone wishing to understand and contribute to its eventual elimination, I want nothing more than to see the day when it can have its category re-assigned from 'social policy' to 'social history'. That remains the book's purpose.

August 1994 COLIN BARNES

An additional 29 titles are included in the Bibliography (pages 255–6).

PREFACE AND ACKNOWLEDGEMENTS

This study was conceived, sponsored and written with the full cooperation of disabled people and their organisations, in particular the British Council of Organizations of Disabled People (BCODP). From its inception in 1989 the project has been under the direction of Dr Mike Oliver, Reader in Disability Studies at Thames Polytechnic, London. Its development has been closely monitored by a research advisory group chaired by Jane Campbell (London Boroughs Disability Resource Team and deputy chair of BCODP) which included Stephen Bradshaw (Executive Director of the Spinal Injuries Association), Caroline Glendinning (Haldsworth's Research Fellow in the Department of Social Policy at the University of Manchester), Mike Oliver and Richard Wood (Director of BCODP).

Initially the project was jointly funded by Charity Projects and the Joseph Rowntree Memorial Trust. But since 1 January 1991, it has been supported solely by the latter. Research facilities were provided by the Department of Social Policy and Sociology at the University of Leeds.

My involvement with the project did not begin until 1 January 1990, following my appointment as principal research officer for BCODP. However, although I have been involved in disability issues and disability research for the past 10 years my interest in the subject is not simply academic, it stems from personal experience. I was born with an hereditary visual impairment and spent the first seven years of my statutory education in special schools, first in a residential institution for 'blind' and 'deaf' children, and later in a segregated unit for partially sighted children. My father spent almost his entire working life in sheltered employment and my mother experienced mental illness resulting in her temporary hospitalisation — shortly after I had been directed into a residential school by the local education authority.

The first five months of 1990 were spent studying previous research on disability and accumulating data from a variety of secondary sources. In addition, I had a number of detailed discussions with several major figures within the disability movement in order to ascertain their views on how the project should proceed and what form it should take. These included Ken Davis (Derbyshire Coalition of Disabled People), John Evans (Hampshire Coalition of Disabled People and Chairman of BCODP), Vic Finkelstein (Open University), Rachel Hurst (Greenwich Association of Disabled People and Disabled People's International) and Philip

Mason (Hampshire Coalition of Disabled People).

In May 1990 a detailed plan of the proposed document was produced. This was then circulated to each member of the advisory group and discussed in detail at an advisory group meeting held on 7 June. The proposal was accepted and the production of the document began.

In order to ensure accountability throughout the project, as each chapter was written a primary draft of it, accompanied by an invitation for comment, was submitted to the ten people mentioned above, Peter Large of the Disablement Income Group, and Linda Ward of the Joseph Rowntree Memorial Foundation. Subsequently, each draft along with any received comments were discussed thoroughly at monthly advisory group meetings before any amendments were made.

BCODP's member-organisations were constantly kept up to date on the project's progress via the literature normally circulated by the BCODP management committee. I also delivered verbal reports on research developments at each of the BCODP council meetings during 1990/1. The Committee of Voluntary Organizations for Anti-Discrimination Legislation (VOADL) was also kept informed in the same way.

On 31 December 1990, a preliminary copy of the proposed document was sent to each of the above along with a further invitation for comment. Amendments were made during March 1991, and the finished document was submitted for publication in April 1991.

Unlike previous studies of disability this book does not provide detailed case studies documenting the isolated experiences of individual disabled people. This was a conscious decision on the part of the research advisory group and myself. This is because such an approach tends to focus the reader's attention primarily upon individual disabled people, and not upon the discriminatory policies and institutionalised practices which create disability; the very opposite of what this book seeks to achieve.

After reading this book it might be argued that important areas within the context of disability have not been given the attention which they deserve. This is particularly pertinent with regard to the level of discrimination experienced by disabled members of the gay community, ethnic minorities, and women with impairments. Unfortunately this was unavoidable for two principal reasons. First, the general aim of the project was to establish conclusively that people with impairments experience discrimination every day of their lives – regardless of sexual preference, ethnic background or gender. Secondly, the research was conducted at a point in time when a vast amount of information in the general area of disability was being produced which could not have been excluded from this analysis. This inevitably meant that some material had to be excluded.

I accept full responsibility for this and any other shortcomings which might be apparent in this document. However, I would hastily point out that this study should not be seen as a definitive statement on institutional discrimination against disabled people, but rather as a stimulus for other research in this hitherto neglected but crucially important area.

Acknowledgements

This book could not have been written without the enthusiasm, help and cooperation of all those mentioned above, as well as countless individuals currently involved in the struggle for disabled people's rights

Special thanks must also go to Sarah M. Barnes for her computing expertise, Len Barton for his helpful comments on the chapter on education, Henry Enns for writing the foreword, Christopher Hurst for his editorial advice, Roland Hurst for his continued support, Mary Lance for her proof-reading abilities, Geoff Mercer for providing research facilities at Leeds, Jenny Morris for her contribution to the section on housing, and the Royal Association for Disability and Rehabilitation (RADAR) for a small grant at the project's inception.

July 1991   COLIN BARNES

ABBREVIATIONS

AA	Attendance Allowance
AA	Automobile Association
ABTA	Association of British Travel Agents
ACE	Access Committee for England
ACE	Advisory Centre for Education
ADL	Anti-Discrimination Legislation
AFE	Advanced Further Education
ALAC	Artificial Limb and Appliance Centre
ASABH	Association of Spina Bifida and Hydrocephalus
ATC	Adult Training Centre
BBC	British Broadcasting Corporation
BCODP	British Council of Organizations of Disabled People
BDA	British Deaf Association
BMA	British Medical Association
BRU	Broadcasting Research Unit
BSI	British Standards Institute
CAB	Citizens Advice Bureau
CAE	Centre for an Accessible Environment
CEH	Centre on Environment for the Handicapped
CIL	Centre for Integrated/Independent Living*
CORAD	Committee on Restrictions against Disabled People
CSDP	Chronically Sick and Disabled Persons Act
CSIE	Centre for Studies on Integration in Education
DA	Disability Alliance
DAA	Domestic Assistance Addition
DAS	Disability Advisory Service
DBC	Deaf Broadcasting Council
DCC	Derbyshire County Council
DCDP	Derbyshire Coalition of Disabled People
DDA	Disabled Drivers' Association
DE	Department of Employment
DES	Department of Education and Science
DHA	District Health Authority
DHSS	Department of Health and Social Security
DIG	Disablement Income Group
DLA	Disability Living Allowance
DoE	Department of the Environment
DoH	Department of Health
DPI	Disabled People's International

*In Britain, 'Integrated' is used by some organisations and 'Independent' by others. The latter is the standard usage in the United States.

DPTAC	Disabled Persons Transport Advisory Committee
DRO	Disablement Resettlement Officer
DRS	Disablement Resettlement Service
DSA	Disabled Students' Allowance
DSA	Disability Services Authority
DSS	Department of Social Security
DT	Department of Transport
DTWO	Department of Transport and the Welsh Office
DWA	Disabled Working Allowance
ERC	Employment Rehabilitation Centre
ERS	Employment Resettlement Services
ES	Employment Services
ESN(M)	Educationally Subnormal (Moderate)
ESN(S)	Educationally Subnormal (Severe)
FE	Further Education
FSS	Family Support Services
GCE	General Certificate of Education
GCSE	General Certificate of Secondary Education
GLAD	Greater London Association for Disabled People
GMCDP	Greater Manchester Coalition of Disabled People
GP	General Practitioner [medical]
HCIL	Hampshire Centre for Independent Living
HD	Health Districts
HE	Higher Education
HMI	Her Majesty's Inspectors
HMSO	Her Majesty's Stationery Office
HPI	Handicapped Pupils Form
ICA	Invalid Care Allowance
ICIDH	International Classification of Impairment, Disability and Handicap
ILEA	Inner London Education Authority
ILF	Independent Living Fund
ILM	Independent Living Movement
ILS	Independent Living Scheme
INSET	In-Service Education and Training
IQ	Intelligence Quotient
IVB	Invalidity Benefit
LA	Local Authority
LADC	Leeds Access for the Disabled Committee
LEA	Local Education Authority
LRT	London Regional Transport
MA	Mobility Allowance
MP	Member of Parliament
MSC	Manpower Services Commission

NACABx	National Association of Citizens Advice Bureaux
NACEDP	National Advisory Council for the Employment of Disabled People
NCC	National Consumer Council
NCIVB	Non-Contributory Invalidity Benefit
NFER	Nuffield Foundation for Education Research
NHS	National Health Service
NTA	Non-Teaching Assistant
NUT	National Union of Teachers
OPCS	Office of Population, Censuses and Surveys
PA	Personal Assistant
PHAB	Physically Handicapped and Able-Bodied
RADAR	Royal Association for Disability and Rehabilitation
RICA	Research Institute for Consumer Affairs
RNIB	Royal National Institute for the Blind
RNID	Royal National Institute for the Deaf
SAD	Sisters Against Disability
SCPR	Social and Community Planning Research
SDA	Severe Disablement Allowance
SE	Special Education
SEN	Special Educational Needs
SERPS	State Earnings-Related Pension Scheme
SIA	Spinal Injuries Association
SJAC	Silver Jubilee Access Committee
SKILL	The National Bureau for Students with Disabilities
SOCS	Self Operated Care Scheme
SPS	Sheltered Placement Scheme
SSD	Social Services Departments
SSP	Statutory Sick Pay
TA	Training Agency
TUC	Trades Union Congress
UN	United Nations
UPIAS	Union of Physically Impaired Against Segregation
VSW	Visiting Social Worker
VOADL	Voluntary Organizations for Anti-Discrimination Legislation
WHO	World Health Organization
YDU	Young Disabled Unit
YT	Youth Training
YTS	Youth Training Schemes

1

INTRODUCTION

Throughout the 1980s there was a growing campaign to persuade the British Government to introduce anti-discrimination legislation in order to enable disabled people to participate fully in the mainstream economic and social life of society. Increasingly, disabled people and organisations controlled by them have come to play an active role in this campaign. During the decade there were several attempts to get this legislation on to the statute books (see Appendix), but hitherto successive governments have successfully prevented the introduction of these bills, arguing that there is little if any evidence of widespread discrimination against disabled people.

Behind the opposition to anti-discrimination legislation lie the assumptions of the traditional individualistic medical view of disability, which explains the difficulties faced by disabled people in their daily lives as individually-based functional limitations. This leads to the assertion that there are few specific examples of discrimination against disabled people. Neither of these arguments corresponds with the experience of a growing number of disabled people and their organisations, who argue that most problems faced by disabled people are socially created and that discrimination is an everyday occurrence.

The data used are both quantitative and qualitative and were collected from a variety of secondary sources, many from government departments such as the Office of Population, Censuses and Surveys (OPCS), the Department of Education and Science (DES) and Employment Services (ES). Moreover, in order to add weight to the campaign for the implementation of anti-discrimination legislation, the book focuses on areas for which the government has direct responsibility, notably education, employment, income, the built environment, transport, housing, health and community services.

Definitions and Terminology

Increasingly in recent years disabled people have come to recognise that the term 'disability' represents a complex system of social restrictions imposed on people with impairments by a highly discriminatory society. To be a disabled person in modern Britain means to be discriminated against. Hence this book adopts a twofold classification of disability and impairment based on that first

1

proposed by Disabled People's International (DPI) in 1981. DPI is the first international organisation controlled and run by disabled people (Driedger, 1989).

Impairment is the functional limitation within the individual caused by physical, mental or sensory impairment.

Disability is the loss or limitation of opportunities to take part in the normal life of the community on an equal level with others due to physical and social barriers.

The difference between these definitions and those proposed by DPI is that DPI uses the terms 'disability' and 'handicap' in place of 'impairment' and 'disability', because of their wider currency at the international level. In some languages direct translations of the word 'impairment' have a profoundly negative meaning.

This terminological change was considered necessary because of the role language plays in the creation of disability. In the same way that ethnic minorities and women have identified the power of language in the promotion of racism and sexism, so disabled people have become sensitive to the way words perpetuate discrimination. To counter linguistic discrimination, disabled people have actively promoted their own definitions, as above. Consequently, although officially used by Harris (1971), the terms 'impairment' and 'disability' were applied to similar concepts to those above by the Union of the Physically Impaired Against Segregation (UPIAS) in 1976. Hence their use and meaning are becoming widely recognised by the majority of organisations of and organisations for disabled people, an increasing number of professionals, as well as some sections of the general public.

In addition, while 'impairment' may be attributable to a number of social causes (Abberley, 1986), its meaning is now almost universally accepted (Martin, Meltzer and Elliot, 1988; Wood, 1981). To begin to refer specifically to individually-based functional limitations as 'disability' at this stage would undermine what limited progress has already been made in establishing the latter as social restriction. Finally, historically the term 'handicap' has associations of 'cap in hand' and begging and until recently was used extensively of people with learning difficulties. It implies that their impairment is permanent and that they will almost certainly remain dependent throughout their lives (Young, 1987); thus its use is no longer acceptable to many disabled people.

It follows then that 'disabled people' is used here to refer to all those with impairments, regardless of cause, who experience disability as social restriction,

. . . whether those restrictions occur as a consequence of inaccessible built environments, the inability of the general population to use sign language, the lack of reading material in braille or hostile public attitudes to people with non-visible disabilities (Oliver, 1990, p. vii).

Discrimination therefore is not simply a question of specific examples of individuals discriminating against disabled people, although this is not an uncommon view. This book sets out to demonstrate that discrimination is institutionalised within the very fabric of British society.

Following recent studies of sex and race relations in Britain (Banton, 1983; Ginsburg, 1988; Gregory, 1987; McCrudden, 1981; Nanton, 1990), institutional discrimination is evident when the policies and activities of public or private organisations, social groups and all other types of organisation in terms of treatment and outcome result in inequality between disabled people and non-disabled people.

Institutional discrimination is embedded in the work of contemporary welfare institutions, and is present if they are systematically ignoring or meeting inadequately the needs of disabled people compared with able-bodied people. It is also present if agencies are regularly interfering in the lives of disabled people as a means of social control in ways, and/or to an extent, not experienced by able-bodied people. It is therefore a descriptive concept related to outcome.

We are concerned with a particularly pervasive and comprehensive form of institutional discrimination which operates both in society generally and in the state, and is supported by history and culture. It incorporates the extreme forms of prejudice and intolerance usually associated with individual or direct discrimination, as well as the more covert and unconscious attitudes which contribute to and maintain indirect and/or passive discriminatory practices within contemporary organisations. Examples of the influence of institutional discrimination on social policy include the way the education system is organised, and the operation of the labour market, both of which are influenced by government and both of which perpetuate the disproportionate economic and social disadvantage experienced by disabled people. It is evident therefore that within this frame of reference direct, indirect and passive discrimination are not easily distinguishable concepts but are intertwined in most contexts.

Anti-Discrimination Legislation and Legislation relating to Disabled People

This book was produced against the paradoxical situation of a growing awareness of the importance of the principles of equal human rights throughout the world, notably in Eastern Europe and South Africa, and a definite retreat from those principles as applied to disadvantaged groups in Britain. For example, despite the moral liberalisation of the late 1960s and early 1970s, the principle of sexual conformity has recently been officially reaffirmed by Parliament with the introduction of Section 28 of the Local Government Act of 1988 (Colvin and Hawksley, 1989; Evans, 1989). Although the notion of equal rights for women and ethnic minorities was endorsed in statute in the 1970s, government support for this legislation during the 1980s was conspicuous by its absence (Lester, 1987), and consequently women's weekly earnings still average around two thirds of those of their male equivalents (McDowell, 1989). In addition, the Policy Studies Institute's influential *Third Survey of Black and White Britain* shows conclusively that racial minorities suffered disproportionately during the economic recession of the early 1980s (Brown, 1985).

In contrast to the situation of women and ethnic minorities, however, the principle of equality for disabled people has never been enshrined in law by the British Parliament, thus indicating the relative importance attached to notions of equal opportunities for disabled people by successive British governments, as well as the double discrimination encountered by members of the gay community, women and black people who have impairments (Campling, 1981; Conference of Indian Organizations, 1987; Lesbian and Gay Committee, 1990; Lonsdale, 1990; McDonald 1991; Morris, 1989; RAD, 1991). Indeed, because of the size and nature of the task at hand it would be impossible to deal with this issue as fully as it deserves within our present context, but the disproportionate levels of discrimination experienced by these groups should be borne in mind.

Hitherto British legislation relating to disabled people has been *ad hoc*, piecemeal and grossly inadequate. In the field of education, for example, the benefits of integrating disabled children into mainstream schools have been acknowledged in statute since the 1944 Education Act (the only children not included were those with 'severe mental handicaps' living in long-stay hospitals, for whom responsibility was not transferred from the health service to the education authorities until 1970). It was subsequently endorsed by the 'Warnock Report on Special Educational Needs' (1978) and in the 1981 Education Act. But because of loopholes in both the 1944 and 1981 Acts, there was a steady increase in the number of children in segregated schools until the mid-1980s, and later improvements have been only marginal (Swann, 1988, 1991). Moreover, there is now a growing realisation among teachers and parents that the Conservative Government's Education Reform Act (1988) is likely to make the process of integration more rather than less difficult.

With employment, while the 1944 Disabled Persons (Employment) Act acknowledged the right to paid work for disabled people, unemployment among them has remained high compared to that among able-bodied people. The recent Government-sponsored OPCS surveys of disability found that only 34 per cent of disabled people under pension age living at home were working (Martin, White and Meltzer, 1989). Yet rather than reinforce the quota scheme introduced in 1944 to ensure that disabled people can find work, in keeping with the demands of most disabled people's organisations, the present administration still favours policies of 'education' and 'persuasion' (DE, 1990; ES, 1988; *Hansard*, 1990), although these strategies are expensive and proven failures. The futility of these and similar policies will be examined in detail in the final chapter.

The link between disability, unemployment and poverty is well known. Although they seriously underestimate the size of the problem (Thompson *et al.*, 1989, 1990; DA, 1990), the OPCS surveys provided further evidence of the enormous gap between the weekly incomes of disabled people and able-bodied people (an average of £39 per week at 1988 prices), yet there has been a decisive retreat from the idea of a state-funded comprehensive disability income during the 1980s.

This is evident with the recent shift from statutory to discretionary provision in the state-funded benefit system (Glendinning, 1990; Lynes, 1988), the increased emphasis by Government on the role of the voluntary sector in this area (HMSO, 1990), and the failure by ministers to include disabled people and their organisations in policy-making. For example, since the OPCS surveys were announced in 1984 the Government has promised on several occasions that the results would be followed by a thorough and extensive review of disability benefits. It also promised full consultation with disabled people's organisations throughout that review. The last of the six OPCS surveys was published in July 1989. The Government published its proposals in the form of a White Paper titled *The Way Ahead: Benefits for Disabled People* on 10 January 1990. The Bill which will implement those proposals appeared just one day later. 'A Bill is not a consultative document' (DA, 1990).

The Book's Focus

This book marks another stage in the growing international campaign to secure equal rights for disabled people. In Britain the roots of this campaign can be traced back to the nineteenth century with the formation in the 1890s of the British Deaf Association and the National League of the Blind (Pagel, 1988). The movement took hold in the post-1945 years with the formation of the Disabled Drivers Association (DDA) in the 1940s (Campbell, 1990), the struggles for independence by disabled inmates in residential institutions in the 1950s and early 1960s (Mason, 1990), and the setting up of the Disablement Income Group (DIG) by two disabled women in 1965 (DIG, 1985). The proliferation of disability organisations during the 1970s and the lack of progress in securing an adequate disability income resulted in the formation of an umbrella organisation known as the Disability Alliance (DA) in 1975.

Both DIG and the DA have mainly concerned themselves with the financial needs of disabled people, an approach rooted in the assumption that disabled people are economically and socially dependent on the rest of society. It also perpetuates that myth by ignoring the causes of that dependence, namely the systematic exclusion of disabled people from mainstream economic and social life (UPIAS, 1976). The majority of organisations of disabled people favour a broader approach.

From the mid-1970s onwards organisations of disabled people such as UPIAS, formed in 1974; the Liberation Network, which functioned mainly through the publication of the magazine *In From the Cold* between 1979 and 1983, and the early disabled women's movement Sisters Against Disability (SAD), have all shared the same basic goals of removing negative discrimination in all its forms and securing equal rights for disabled people. Similar goals were later adopted by the British Council of Organizations of Disabled People (BCODP) after its inception in 1981. A member of DPI, BCODP is an association of over eighty organisations controlled and run by disabled people. These range from small groups working on single issues to national organisations with huge memberships.

The campaign for equal status for disabled people grew in stature during the 1980s with the formation in 1985 of the Voluntary Organizations for Anti-Discrmination Legislation (VOADL) committee. This was significant in the struggle for equal rights for disabled people in Britain because it signified a decisive coming together of organisations of disabled people, such as BCODP, along with the more traditional organisations for disabled people like the

Royal Association for Disability and Rehabilitation (RADAR), for the sole purpose of getting anti-discrimination legislation on to the statute books.

This book represents the latest in a long line of studies which, to varying degrees, have all outlined the extent and effects of institutional discrimination against disabled people. Two notable examples are the Silver Jubilee Access Committee (SJAC) report *Can Disabled People Go Where You Go*? (1979) and the report of the Committee on Restrictions against Disabled People (CORAD, 1982), the first because it drew attention to a 'number of blatant acts of discrimination against disabled people', and caused the then Labour Government to set up CORAD under the chairmanship of Peter Large, himself a disabled person, who had chaired the SJAC committee. CORAD is important because it saw the problem of discrimination in a structural, or institutional, context. It looked at a wide range of issues such as access to public buildings, transport systems, education, employment and entertainment. It made important recommendations for improving public attitudes toward disabled people. It also called for the introduction of anti-discrimination legislation to secure disabled people's rights by law.

However, unlike other studies which have looked at these issues in detail, the present one is the first to be conceived, sponsored and written with the full cooperation of disabled people and their organisations. The project was originally conceived by members of the VOADL committee in 1989, and it was subsequently agreed that it should be under the control of an advisory group set up and chaired by BCODP with a representative from VOADL and a research supervisor, Dr Mike Oliver, Reader in Disability Studies at Thames Polytechnic, London. The advisory group was controlled by disabled people and all its members had a history of working both professionally and voluntarily with other disabled people.

Arguments for Anti-Discrimination Legislation

Besides organisations of and organisations for disabled people, there is evidence of support for anti-discrimination legislation from the Trades Union Congress (TUC) (Willis, 1989), lawyers (Palmer and Poulton, 1987), and a substantial majority of the general public (Outset, 1987).

The denial of equal rights for disabled people cannot be morally justified when other disadvantaged groups have protection under the law, no matter how inadequate that protection may be. It is also becoming increasingly apparent that to make as many as 6.2 million people financially and socially dependent through institutionalised discrimination is economically untenable, particularly since the 'demographic time bomb' could cause that number to increase (*Skills Bulletin*, 1989).

Because of the unprecedented decline in births and the increased life-span of the British population it is currently estimated that by the end of the century one person in six will be above retirement age. There is little doubt that the incidence of disability increases with age (see Martin, Meltzer and Elliot, 1988). This has obvious implications for the British economy in terms of the national infrastructure — the built environment, housing stock, transport systems, health and community-based services etc. — as well as creating serious skill shortages in the labour force (*Labour Market Quarterly Report*, 1990; *Skills Bulletin*, 1989).

Similar demographic changes are occurring in many western-type democracies throughout the world, and a number have already adopted legislation proscribing discrimination against disabled people. These include the United States, Canada, Australia and New Zealand. Indeed, Government responsibility for securing equal rights for disabled people was stated in the United Nations (UN) World Programme of Action Concerning Disabled People, which was adopted by consensus in the UN General Assembly in 1982. To provide a framework for implementing the Programme of Action the General Assembly proclaimed a UN Decade of Disabled Persons from 1983 till 1992.

The UN Programme of Action outlines a global disability strategy aimed at preventing disability, and realising the full potential of disabled people. It explicitly recognises the right of all human beings to equal opportunities and is an important extension of the concept of human rights (UN, 1988). Similar recommendations have been made by the Commission of the European Community and the Council of Europe (Expert Seminar, 1989), although most member-states already have the right of equal treatment for disabled people in specific areas, particularly employment, stipulated in law (Commission of the European Communities, 1988).

General Outline

Before discussing the extent of discrimination encountered by disabled people in modern Britain it is important to understand why that discrimination exists. Chapter 2 therefore focuses on the philosophical and cultural roots of discrimination, and the discriminatory policies of the past, and shows how they influence contemporary British institutions and attitudes.

Each of the subsequent chapters deals with one of the seven basic human rights which were identified by DPI in 1981, often denied to disabled people, but considered essential for their full participation in modern society. These include the right to education, employment, economic security, services, independent living, culture and recreation, and the right to influence (DPI, 1981).

Chapter 3 looks at education. It includes an examination of Government legislation and its implications for disabled children, parents and professionals, data on the numbers of children in segregated provision, an evaluation of the limitations of segregated provision, an appraisal of the barriers to mainstream education systems for disabled children at the primary, secondary and tertiary levels.

Discrimination in employment is discussed in Chapter 4. Attention is focused on unemployment and underemployment among disabled people; forms of direct and indirect discrimination in employment; government policy since the 1944 Disabled Persons (Employment) Act, notably registration, the quota scheme and the controversy over its implementation; and the role of Disability Resettlement Officers (DROs), Employment Services (ES), Disability Advisory Service (DAS), training schemes and sheltered workshops.

By looking at the financial circumstances of disabled people, including those with and without paid work, Chapter 5 shows how disabled people are economically and socially marginalised by the present welfare system which not only keeps them in relative poverty but also ensures their dependence on others, notably unpaid helpers (usually women) and professionals.

Chapter 6 examines health and community-based services for disabled people, in particular the ideologies of 'care' and the notion of 'rehabilitation', current health and social support services for disabled people with reference to community-based facilities, gaps in provision and the role of professionals.

Chapter 7 addresses the question of independent living in relation to housing, transport and the built environment. It includes a brief appraisal of official policy in each of these areas since 1945, and of the current situation regarding access to housing, transport systems and the environment. The data show that despite relatively minor improvement in each of these areas in the late 1980s, physical barriers remain central to the general oppression of disabled people in contemporary Britain.

To demonstrate how disabled people are excluded from mainstream social and leisure pursuits, Chapter 8 compares the recreational activities of disabled people with those of able-bodied people, and demonstrates how the culture and leisure industries contribute to discrimination.

Chapter 9 focuses on the numerous ways in which disabled people are prevented from participating in the democratic process both in politics generally and in organisations which purport to represent their interests. It contains subsections on the barriers to integration in conventional politics, and the degree of influence disabled people have within state and voluntary charities and organisations of disabled people. The data show that hitherto only the latter have given disabled people any real opportunity to exercise control over their own lives.

The conclusion discusses the gradual but significant shift from rights-based to needs-based policies for disabled people since the 1939–45 war and makes a number of recommendations. These include a call for comprehensive anti-discrimination legislation, the implementation of an all-inclusive Freedom of Information Act and the adequate funding and resourcing of organisations controlled and run by disabled people, since it is they and only they who are equipped to safeguard disabled people's rights.

2

A BRIEF HISTORY OF DISCRIMINATION AND DISABLED PEOPLE

To appreciate fully the extent and complexity of the discrimination experienced by disabled people in modern Britain an understanding of history is critical. Consequently the main objectives of this chapter are to draw attention to the philosophical and cultural foundations of discrimination; to outline briefly the discriminatory practices and policies of the past; and to show how they have influenced current British attitudes and institutions.

Early Influences

To pinpoint precisely the origins of society's attitudes toward disability and disabled people would be almost impossible. Among the many suggestions that have been made is the view that our perceptions of impairment and disability are coloured by a deep-rooted psychological fear of the unknown, the anomalous and the abnormal (Douglas, 1966). It is widely acknowledged, however, that our perceptions of normality are partly if not wholly determined by others through learning and the natural transmission of ideology and culture. Here ideology and culture both refer to a communally accepted set of values and beliefs which influences the perceptions of individuals. It provides in advance some basic categories and a set of rules in which ideas and values are formed. Above all, 'it has authority, since each is induced to assent because of the assent of others' (Douglas, 1966). While individual perceptions and ideas vary slightly, cultural concepts are usually more rigid.

Some writers have suggested that cultural intolerance of disability and disabled people can be explained by reference to the economy. For example, our distant ancestors lived in such a harsh environment that there was little opportunity to support individuals with impairments who could not take care of themselves (Thomas, 1982), but with the advent of relatively stable communities able to produce an economic surplus through the development of agriculture, such an analysis becomes difficult to sustain. Indeed there is sufficient historical and anthropological evidence to show that there is no universal approach to disability, either in the way disabled people are perceived or in the way societies respond to them (see Hanks and Hanks, 1980; Oliver, 1981, 1990). Consequently explanations which

11

rely solely on the economy are untenable; cultural factors must be considered also.

In the cultural precursors to our own society, however, there is evidence of a consistent bias against disability and disabled people which has only recently been seriously challenged. Examples can be found in religion, Greek philosophy and European drama and art since well before the Renaissance.

In the Old Testament much of Leviticus is devoted to a reiteration of the physical and mental perfections deemed necessary for all aspects of religious ritual (Lev. 21. 16–20). Indeed, only lately have people with learning difficulties been allowed to receive some sacraments in the Roman Catholic Church. Moreover, while the ancient Greeks and Romans placed a high priority upon the care of those injured and subsequently disabled in battle, they were enthusiastic advocates of infanticide for sickly or deformed children. In Sparta these policies were demanded by law (Tooley, 1983).

Throughout the Middle Ages disabled people were the subject of superstition, persecution and rejection. Haffter (1968) has pointed out that in medieval Europe disability was associated with evil and witchcraft. Deformed and disabled children were seen as 'changelings' or the Devil's substitutes for human children, the outcome of their parents' involvement with the black arts or sorcery. The *Malleus Maleficarum* of 1487 declared that these children were the product of the mothers' intercourse with Satan. The idea that any form of physical or mental impairment was the result of divine judgement for wrongdoing was pervasive throughout the British Isles in this period. And the association between disability and evil was not limited to the layman. Protestant reformer Martin Luther (1483–1546) proclaimed that he saw the Devil in a profoundly disabled child. If these children lived, Luther recommended killing them. They were the focus of a mixture of emotions which embodied guilt, fear and contempt.

William Shakespeare's *Richard III* illustrates clearly the attitudes that would be experienced by someone born into a world which placed a high premium upon physical normality:

> *Cheated of feature by dissembling nature,*
> *Deformed, unfinished, sent before my time*
> *Into this breathing world, scarce half made up,*
> *And that so lamely and unfashionable*
> *The dogs bark at me as I halt by them.*

Shakespeare portrays Richard as twisted in both body and mind. Since he cannot succeed as a lover because of his deformity he is determined to succeed as a villain. This essentially distorted and inherently negative view of disabled people is evident in a great deal of literature and art, both classical and popular, and continues to be produced today (see Gartner and Joe, 1987).

Mental and physical impairments were also primary targets for amusement and ridicule during the Middle Ages. And Thomas' (1977) analysis of the joke books of Tudor and Stuart England reveals the extent of this dimension of the discrimination encountered by disabled people. Besides references to the other so-called timeless universals of 'popular' humour such as foreigners, women, and the clergy, there are many jokes about impairment and disabled people:

> Every disability from idiocy to insanity to diabetes and bad breath was a welcome source of amusement, 'we jest at a man's body that is not well proportioned', said Thomas Wilson, 'and laugh at his countenance . . . if it be not comely by nature'. A typical Elizabethan joke book contains 'merry jests at fools' and merry jests at 'blind folk'. While some of the tricksters' pranks are brutal to the extreme. (Thomas, 1977, pp. 80–1).

Visits to Bedlam were also a common form of amusement for the socially well placed and the practice of keeping 'idiots' as objects of entertainment was prevalent among the aristocracy (Ryan and Thomas, 1980). As we shall see later, disabled people are still the focus for much of what passes as comedy.

Until the seventeenth century those disabled people who were rejected by their families, along with other disadvantaged groups such as the sick, the elderly and the poor, relied almost exclusively on the haphazard and often ineffectual tradition of Christian charity and alms-giving for subsistence. They were rarely gathered together under one roof, however. Despite disenfranchising them from religious ceremony, Christianity, in keeping with the other major western religions, has always acknowledged a responsibility for disabled people. Individuals with severe impairments were usually admitted to one of the very small medieval hospitals in which the sick and bedridden poor were gathered. But the ethos of these hospitals was ecclesiastical rather than medical; they were dedicated to 'care' rather than 'cure' (Scull, 1984).

During the sixteenth century the wealth and power of the Church was greatly reduced because of a series of unsuccessful political confrontations with the monarchy. There was also a steady growth in the numbers of people seeking alms. This was due to several factors, including a growth in the population after a period of stagnation and depletion due to plagues, the beginnings of the commercialisation of agriculture, successive poor harvests, and an influx of immigrants from Ireland and Wales (Stone, 1985). Hence the fear of 'bands of sturdy beggars' preyed on the minds of local magistrates, who demanded a response from the central authority, namely the Crown (Trevelyan, 1948). To secure their allegiance, the Tudor monarchs were forced to make economic provision for people dependent upon charity. Consequently the Poor Law of 1601 marks the first official recognition of the need for state intervention in the lives of disabled people.

A general suspicion of those claiming alms, however, had already been formally established with the statute of 1388 which mandated local officials to discriminate between the 'deserving' and 'undeserving' poor. But although people with impairments were among the 'deserving poor', there was little attempt to separate them from the rest of the community. On the contrary, every effort was made to keep them within the local environment.

Although there was some parochial variation in the actual level of benefit, there was a degree of uniformity in the way disabled people were treated. The lion's share of resources was directed toward domestic or 'household relief' for people who were regarded as unable to work and were confined to the home. Funds were frequently provided to individuals and families willing to accept responsibility for people considered to be incapable of looking after themselves. Major changes to this essentially non-segregationist policy did not begin to be discussed or implemented until the nineteenth century.

However, a clear insight into society's general attitude toward disabled people during this period can be gleaned from an essay written by William Hay in 1754. Born in 1695, Hay was a typical gentleman of the period, a country squire, a Justice of the Peace and a Member of Parliament. He wrote an autobiographical essay titled *Deformity* one year before his death, which is in essence a heartfelt philosophical analysis of disability: a subject of which he had personal experience.

Hay describes himself as barely 5 feet tall with a back 'bent in my mother's womb'. His essay is an outline of the socio-psychological difficulties he experienced because of his impairment. He believed it had caused him to be bashful, uneasy and unsure of himself. He was extremely conscious of his personal appearance and considered himself very fortunate to have been born into a social class where a high emphasis was placed on good manners and politeness. This prevented any 'gentleman' from making derogatory remarks concerning his stature. He noted, however, how the gentle 'friendly' teasing of his close friends contrasted sharply with the treatment of disabled people by society at large, 'where insolence grows in proportion as the man sinks in condition' (Hay, 1754, quoted in Thomas, 1982, p. 62).

Industrialisation and After

Throughout the eighteenth and nineteenth centuries the policy of segregating severely disabled people into institutional settings slowly increased and was subsequently extended to other disadvantaged groups. Although the term 'institution' can be used to refer to a variety of social organisations ranging from the family to a university, it refers here to 'any long term provision of a highly organized kind on a residential basis with the expressed aims of 'care', 'treatment' or 'custody' (Jones and Fowles, 1984, p. 207). They include hospitals, asylums, workhouses and prisons.

One explanation for this important break with the past links it to the breakdown of early forms of state welfare in the face of large-scale urban industrialisation and the inevitable spread of poverty which followed (Mechanic, 1964). But the impetus to build institutions came before the growth of cities and was more pronounced in rural communities (Ingelby, 1983). A variation on this theme, however, suggests that the widespread incarceration of disabled people is directly attributable to the transition from agriculture and cottage-based industries to the large-scale factory-type system:

> The speed of factory work, the enforced discipline, the time keeping and production norms — all these were a highly unfavourable change from the slower, more self-determined and flexible methods of work into which many handicapped people had been integrated (Ryan and Thomas, 1980, p. 101).

Although such arguments tend to play down the general antipathy which surrounded disability before the Industrial Revolution, it is clear that the economic and social conditions created by the new system compounded the difficulties faced by disabled people. First, a family dependent upon waged labour alone could not provide for its members during economic depression, so that large groups of dependents were created by industrialisation. Secondly, the system of Poor Law relief which had survived since Elizabethan times was directly at odds with the ascending free market economy. Waged labour made the distinction between the able-bodied and the non-able-bodied poor crucially important, since parochial relief to the able-bodied poor interfered with labour mobility.

Segregating the poor into institutions, on the other hand, had several advantages over domestic relief; it was efficient, it acted as a major deterrent to the able-bodied malingerer, and it could instil good work habits into the inmates (Ingelby, 1983). These conclusions are clearly reflected in the Report of the Poor Law Commission and the Poor Law Amendment Act of 1834. The 1834 reforms introduced three new principles for state welfare policy: national uniformity, denial of relief outside an institution, and deterrence as the basis for setting the levels of welfare benefits.

Uniformity of provision was considered important in order to discourage potential workers from moving from one parish to the next in search of better benefits. Moreover, since aid was set at subsistence level only, uniformity would encourage people to move where the work was in the search for a better standard of living. As early as 1722 Parliament had granted local authorities the right to refuse benefit or outdoor relief to anyone unwilling to enter a workhouse, but the 1834 Poor Law reforms expressly endorsed it, although this instruction was never fully implemented.

Deterrence was evident in the principle of 'least eligibility' whereby a pauper's situation should be less comfortable than that of an 'independent labourer of the lowest class' before benefits could be granted. The workhouse was intended to be as unpleasant as possible so that no-one would enter it willingly. Families were broken up, inmates were made to wear specific uniforms, there were no recreational facilities and socialising was strictly forbidden in working hours. Routines were rigidly enforced and food was limited to what was considered necessary for survival and work.

Besides the horrors of institutions, described so vividly in the novels of Charles Dickens, the nineteenth century was also significant for an upsurge of Christian morality and humanitarian values which were to have a profound effect upon the lives of disabled people. A mixture of religious altruism and conscience, this spirit of Victorian patronage put an end to the widespread practice of infanticide for disabled children, which had hitherto been the rule rather than the exception (Tooley, 1983). It also stimulated some Victorians to question seriously the harsh treatment meted out to people who were generally considered incapable of finding work. When combined with the institutionalised mistrust of people claiming charity, these philanthropic ideals set in motion a process of differentiation which not only separated disabled people from other disadvantaged sections of the community, but also divided them up into specific categories and groups, with differing treatment for each group. The legacy of this policy remains with us today.

From the outset the Poor Law Commission decreed that the workhouses should separate the incarcerated population into four different groupings, namely able-bodied males, able-bodied females, children, and the 'aged and infirm'. It was intended that the latter, or those perceived as the 'deserving poor', were to be housed in different buildings and accorded different treatment. In the following years these categories were refined still further. Aided by the burgeoning medical profession, Poor Law Officials developed four specific categories for dealing with the non-able-bodied poor. They were the 'sick', the 'insane', 'defectives', and the 'aged and infirm' (Stone, 1985).

The term 'sick' described people with acute, temporary or infectious diseases. This group often automatically qualified for outdoor relief if it was available. But where incarceration was deemed necessary, separate accommodation was usually provided, although the conditions in these facilities were rarely better than those in the workhouse. Illness and impairment could not be seen as a route to better treatment, or it would discourage the poor from making provision for the future, and thus undermine the prevailing philosophy of self-reliance.

The 'insane' were singled out for special treatment from the outset. Despite the difficulties of definition and diagnosis, there was already a universal recognition of the 'problem' posed by people with mental illness. There were two main strategies for dealing with it. People termed 'idiots', 'lunatics', 'mad', 'mentally infirm', or 'suffering from diseases of the brain' (Scull, 1978) were either admitted to an asylum or boarded out on contract to families willing to be held responsible for them.

Several private asylums had been established in the seventeenth century. But the public outcry over the atrocious conditions in many of these establishments, brought to light by Evangelical reformers, forced the Government into setting up a state-run system in 1845. It is important to note, however, that the cruelty accorded to people perceived as mentally ill inside institutions was often no worse than that which they encountered in the community at large (Roth and Kroll, 1986).

Until 1871 Poor Law officials had no right to detain citizens in an institution against their will, but this did not apply to people termed insane. Prior to the Lunacy Legislation of 1845, the certification of insanity was the responsibility of local lay officials. Following that date confirmation of mental illness was valid only if a doctor was involved. This change has been attributed to doctors' assertions that mental illness had physiological causes and was responsive to medical treatment, and their successful struggle for control within private and public institutions (Scull, 1984). Once defined as mentally ill an individual could be detained on a doctor's recommendation and moved from one institution to another against her/his will. Doctors still retain this power (DHSS, 1987). Hence, 1845 can be seen as the start of the medical profession's subsequent domination of all aspects of disability.

The term 'defectives' was used to describe people with sensory impairments such as blindness, deafness and the lack of speech. After 1903 people with epilepsy and children termed 'mentally subnormal' were also added to this category. Although members of this group were still liable to be put into an institution, and their treatment therein was no different from that of other inmates, they were frequently singled out for special attention by Victorian philanthropists and charities. Many of the charities which exist today were founded during this period. For example, the British and Foreign Association for Promoting the Education of the Blind (now known as the Royal National Institute for the Blind [RNIB]) was formed in 1863 (RNIB, 1990).

'Aged and infirm', the oldest of the four categories, referred to people with chronic illness and/or permanent impairments. While there was little official controversy over their eligibility for outdoor relief, more often than not they too were directed into an institutional setting.

Towards the end of the nineteenth century the pressures to incarcerate people classified as belonging to one of these categories increased dramatically. First, the transition from relatively light industries such as textiles to the much heavier capital goods industries like iron, steel and the railways, in what has been called the 'second phase of industrialization' (Hobsbawn, 1968), further emphasised the importance of physical fitness as a criterion for finding work among working people. Secondly, welfare policies, particularly with regard to outdoor relief, were severely tightened during the 1870s and 1880s due to escalating costs because of rising unemployment after a decade of economic depression which began with the severe winter of 1860/1. This put more pressure on local authorities to apply the 'workhouse test' to anyone seeking aid. Thirdly, there was a further expansion of segregated institutions for the non-able-bodied poor following another set of public scandals and government enquiries exposing the appalling conditions in workhouses (Stone, 1985). The number of disabled people consigned to these establishments rose accordingly, and did not begin to fall until the 1950s (Scull, 1984).

Ideological legitimacy for the intensified oppression of disabled people during the eighteenth and nineteenth centuries can be found in the ascendant egocentric philosophies of the period, which stressed the rights and privileges of the individual over and above those of the group or state, in relation to property rights, politics and culture (Macfarland, 1978). 'Scientific' authenticity was forthcoming in 1859 with the publication of Charles Darwin's *On the Origin of Species*.

Based on Darwin's observations during his voyages on the *Beagle*, this study outlines his monumental theory of evolution, which places great emphasis upon the process of natural selection, the survival of the fittest, the notion that evolution is progress, and that progress is inherently beneficial. It had an understandable appeal to a society dominated by a relatively small elite of property-owning, self-interested, 'rational' individuals who welcomed any opportunity to justify their newly-acquired wealth, status and power. It was quickly adapted from the biological domain to apply to human societies (see Russell, 1948).

What later became known as 'Social Darwinism' dispelled and allayed the qualms of the rich about not helping the disadvantaged by assuring them that the latter's sufferings were the inevitable price of progress, which could only be resolved through the struggle for existence. Endorsed by a number of eminent intellectuals and academics of the period, these ideas were to have significant political and social repercussions throughout nineteenth- and twentieth-century Europe, and indeed the world.

Out of the general tendency to apply Darwin's theories to human affairs emerged the Eugenics movement. Concerned mainly with what they saw as racial degeneration through the birth of disabled children, the Eugenicists reiterated ancient fears that disabled people were a serious threat to British and European society. The work of Galton (1869), Dugdale (1910) and Goddard (1912) reinforced traditional myths that there were genetic links between physical and mental impairments, crime, unemployment and other social evils (see Sapsford, 1981). The stated aim of the Eugenicists was to improve the British race by preventing the reproduction of 'defectives' by means of sterilisation and segregation.

In 1896 the National Association for the Care and Control of the Feeble-Minded was set up as a pressure group for the lifetime segregation of disabled people. During the 1910 general election it campaigned vigorously on these issues. In the following two decades Eugenic fears were further endorsed by the invention and widespread use of Intelligence Quotient (IQ) tests in British schools. Their inventors, the French psychologists Binet and Simon, and principal advocates, notably the psychologist Cyril Burt, asserted confidently that intelligence is innate and that the majority of defectives were ineducable. Moreover, despite the fact that there are serious doubts about the validity of IQ-type tests as objective measures of intelligence (since they measure only a comparatively small range of human qualities, the nature of which is culturally determined [Tomlinson, 1981]) similar techniques are used today to separate the 'normal' from the 'subnormal'.

Eugenic fears were prevalent throughout the 1920s and 1930s. For example, the Report of the Departmental Committee on Sterilization chaired by Lord Brock recommended legislation to ensure the 'voluntary' sterilisation of 'mentally defective women' (Ryan and Thomas, 1980). Although such legislation was never actually passed in Britain (unlike America, where sterilisation became compulsory in a number of states), this has not prevented many such operations being carried out under various forms of coercion. Only recently a 36-year-old 'voluntary' patient in a mental hospital, who was described as 'mentally handicapped', was sterilised without her consent after she had developed a relationship with a male patient which 'probably' involved sexual intercourse or 'something close to it' (Morgan, 1989). The operation was justified on the grounds that the woman would be unable to cope with pregnancy or motherhood.

Eugenic ideals reached their logical conclusion during the 1939–45 war with the extermination of between 80,000 and 100,000 disabled people by the Nazis (Wolfensberger, 1980). But while the atrocities of the Nazi death camps put an end to the overt persecution of disabled people throughout Europe, there remains tacit support for comparable ideas among some sections of the British population, notably supporters of the National Front (Ryan and Thomas, 1980).

Moreover, research on human foetuses has recently been officially sanctioned by Parliament, partly on the basis that it might prevent the birth of disabled children (*Hansard*, 1990c). It is not uncommon, although rarely discussed openly, for some doctors with the compliance of parents to allow 'severely' impaired babies to die if the impairment is unexpected (Shearer, 1981). And it is considered socially acceptable for British women to have an abortion if there is any 'substantial risk' that the unborn child will be 'seriously handicapped' (HMSO, 1989), although 'seriously handicapped' is rarely defined. In addition, disabled children are more likely to be abandoned by their parents than their able-bodied peers, they have less chance of being adopted (Burrell, 1989), and they are more prone to physical and sexual abuse (Kennedy, 1989; Watson, 1989).

The Impact of the Welfare State

With the inception of the welfare state during the 1940s, official policy with regard to disabled people moved away from the extremes of earlier epochs in favour of a more overtly paternalistic approach. This can be explained with reference to a number of factors, including the humanitarian influence of the Victorian philanthropists, the general concern felt toward disabled ex-servicemen during and after the 1914–18 and 1939–45 wars, the changing political climate, and the prospect of a buoyant economy.

A number of welfare and training schemes had been set up for war casualties after the 1914–18 conflict. An expansion of these and similar facilities was recommended by the Tomlinson Report of 1941 (Schlesinger and Whelan, 1979). Moreover, the economic and social upheavals brought about by the depression of the 1930s, in conjunction with the need for national unity during and immediately after the 1939–45 war, stimulated among many politicians a concern for welfare programmes which had hitherto been absent (Doyal, 1980).

This resulted in a flurry of legislation which was to have a significant impact on the lives of disabled people. Indeed the first Act of Parliament to treat disabled people as a single group was the Disabled Persons (Employment) Act of 1944. As well as attempting to ensure that employers employed disabled people, this Act made provision for a variety of rehabilitation services and vocational training courses. The 1944 Education Act stated that every child should receive education suitable for her/his age, ability and aptitude, and obliged local education authorities to provide special educational treatment for those thought to need it. The National Health Service Act 1948 provided for the acute medical needs of disabled people, and made it possible for local authority health departments to provide any medical aids necessary to enable disabled people to live in their own homes. Finally, the National Assistance Act of 1948 made some provision for meeting the financial needs of disabled people, and mandated local authorities to provide residential facilities and services for people 'who are substantially and permanently handicapped by illness, injury or congenital deformity' (quoted in Oliver 1983).

Since the late 1950s there has been a concerted attempt by successive governments to reduce the numbers of people living in segregated institutions by expanding community-based services. The origins of the use of the phrase 'community care' can be found in the Report of the Royal Commission on Mental Deficiency of 1954–7, which considered the problems arising from outdated mental hospitals and the stigma associated with in-patient treatment. Although there was no precise definition given, subsequent government statements and documents on services for disabled people have increasingly used the term. It should be noted, however, that the phrase has different meanings for different groups of people and is discussed in more detail in Chapter 6.

The shift toward community-based services took a more decisive turn in 1961 when the Government announced its decision to halve the number of beds in mental hospitals, a move which prompted a number of critics to argue that the motives behind this change in policy were economic rather than humanitarian. One commentator, Titmuss, challenged the Government to refute this allegation, but there was no official reply. In 1962 the Ministry of Health published *A Hospital Plan*. This was followed one year later by *Health and Welfare: The Development of Community Care*, generally referred to as *The Community Care Blue Book*.

These two documents provided a sketchy outline of plans for community-based services, including proposals for increases in the numbers of general practitioners, home helps, district nurses, health visitors, sheltered housing schemes and sheltered workshops. Provision was intended for four specific groups, namely mothers and children, the elderly, 'the mentally disordered' and the 'physically handicapped' (Jones *et al.*, 1983).

Around this time a number of critical investigations into institutional life by social scientists was published (see for example Barton, 1959; Goffman, 1961; Miller and Gwynne 1972; Townsend 1967). In addition, there was a spate of sensational public expositions by the national press of the cruelty and harsh treatment manifest in institutions for 'the elderly' and 'the mentally ill'. All were subsequently investigated and in one particular case, the Ely enquiry, criminal proceedings were brought against hospital personnel (Jones *et al.*, 1983).

As a result of these enquiries, public and in some cases professional confidence in the services provided in long-stay hospitals and similar establishments was again seriously undermined. Local authority services, on the other hand, remained relatively unscathed and underdeveloped. Consequently the pressure to reduce the numbers of people in institutions run by the health service intensified while local authorities were encouraged to expand their facilities accordingly.

There was little agreement as to what services should be provided or where the money to fund the expansion should come from. Extensive variation characterised provision at the local level and budgets were already stretched due to two main factors. The first was the rising expectations of the general population after the setting up of the welfare state, and the second a steady increase in the numbers of 'dependent' people after the 1939–45 war. These included children, people over retirement age, and disabled people.

In an effort to develop and rationalise social service provision at the local level, the Government set up a commission of enquiry which published its findings in 1968. The Seebohm Report is generally considered a watershed in the development of community-based services for disabled people. Among its principal conclusions were the recommendations that local authorities should accumulate data relating to the nature and size of the problems associated with disability; and that they should develop and/or expand services in conjunction with those already provided by the health service and the voluntary sector. These recommendations were subsequently incorporated into the Local Authority Act 1970 and the Chronically Sick and Disabled Persons Act 1970. The establishment of social service departments in their present form quickly followed.

In conjunction with provision for the other main dependent groups, the new departments were responsible for social services for disabled people. These included the provision of social workers, occupational therapists, residential and day centre facilities, holidays, meals on wheels, respite services, and disability aids and adaptations. This resulted in the situation where almost every aspect of life for a disabled person had its counterpart in a profession or voluntary organization. Indeed one study estimated that there could be as many as twenty-three professional helpers involved in the life of one disabled person (Brechin and Liddiard, 1981).

Clearly the positive effects of this expansion are that the majority of disabled people now have more access to, relatively, more services and, on the whole, are less likely than, say, before the 1939–45 war to be consigned into a segregated residential setting. On the other hand, the organisation of these services risks their being sucked into a 'culture of dependence' which is predicated upon the assumption that individuals with impairments are people who are helpless and unable to make their own decisions and to choose for themselves the aids and services they need (Shearer, 1981). This is largely due to the fact that the majority of professionals and service-providers adhere either explicitly or implicitly to the traditional individualistic medically-influenced definitions of disability (Oliver, 1983; Sutherland, 1981; Davis 1986).

From the late 1950s onwards there has been a general tendency by government agencies to reduce the various categories of disability into one all-embracing conceptual framework. This revision was more pronounced in the 1960s, when it became clear that there were insufficient data available to facilitate the proposed expansion of services and to cost the development of new social security benefits. Accordingly the Office of Population, Censuses and Surveys (OPCS) was contracted by the Government to undertake a national disability survey. Findings were published by Harris in 1971 (Harris, 1971).

Harris used functional assessments of disability based on a threefold distinction between impairment, disability and handicap. Similar work was completed by Wood in 1981 (Wood, 1981) for the World Health Organization (WHO). Known as the International Classification of Impairment, Disability and Handicap (ICIDH), Wood's model was used in the second OPCS disability survey carried out during the 1980s (Martin, Meltzer and Elliot, 1988).

This approach remains close to medical classifications of disease. It conserves the notion of impairment as abnormality in function, disability as not being able to perform an activity considered normal for a human being, and handicap as the inability to perform a 'normal' social role (Oliver, 1990). Clearly this model is based upon assumptions about mental and physical normality. It assumes that disability and handicap are caused by psychological or physiological abnormality or impairment, and therefore the impairment is the primary focus of attention.

The first major problem with this approach is that psychological and physical normality and subsequently impairments are not easily defined. Definitions are dependent upon temporal, cultural and situational factors. For example, although homosexuality was considered normal by the ancient Greeks, until very recently it was perceived as a mental illness in many western societies. A male adult less than 5 feet tall might be construed as having a physical impairment in modern Britain, although he might be physiologically healthy.

Secondly, the human being is perceived as flexible and alterable while the physical and social environments are assumed to be fixed and unalterable. This is clearly unrealistic since historically humans have always moulded the environment to suit their needs rather than the other way round. Thirdly, since psychological and physical impairments are presented as the cause of disability and handicap, it follows that they should be cured by psychological or medical intervention. People with impairments become objects to be treated, changed, improved and made normal.

While medical intervention for treating illness and disease may be quite appropriate, from the perspective of the disabled person it is quite inappropriate for treating disability.

> In the past especially, doctors have been too willing to suggest medical treatment and hospitalization, even when this would not necessarily improve the quality of life for the person concerned. Indeed, questions about the quality of life have sometimes been portrayed as an intrusion upon the medical equation (Brisenden, 1986, p. 176).

Fourthly, because it is assumed that disabled people must adapt to a hostile environment, they are subjected to all kinds of emotional pressure in the process of adaptation. Those who succeed are sanctified and held up as exemplars of individual will and effort, while the majority who do not are referred to as passive, apathetic or worse (Reiser and Mason, 1990). This has obvious negative psychological implications, which can and often do compound impairment.

Fifthly, these definitions tend to present impairment, disability and handicap as static states. Apart from being inaccurate (Oliver, 1990), this approach creates artificial distinctions and barriers between disabled people and the rest of society (Zola, 1981) which, at best, prolong ignorance and misunderstanding and, at worst, nourish and sustain ancient fears and prejudices.

In short, these definitions not only help to create and perpetuate discrimination in all its forms but also waste valuable resources, both human and financial, 'on a grand scale' (Davis, 1986). Indeed, the fact that disabled people were excluded from participating in a meaningful way from the process of constructing these schemes is an indication of institutional discrimination by professionals. Above all, it is a waste of the most valuable resource of all, namely the perceptions of people who experience disability every day of their lives. It is not surprising therefore that these models are being rejected by a growing number of disabled people and their organisations, including the British Council of Disabled People (BCODP) and Disabled People's International (DPI).

Finally, Oliver (1990) has demonstrated that there is a far more sinister dimension to these schemes. His comparison of two sets of questions relating to the same topics illustrates the point. The first is based on the official individualised definition of disability and was used in the recent OPCS surveys, while the second is constructed on the basis of a social definition.

What complaint causes your difficulty in holding, gripping or turning things?

Have you attended a special school because of a long-term health problem or disability?

Does your health problem/disability prevent you from going out as often or as far as you would like?

Does your health problem/disability affect your work in any way at present?

These questions effectively reduce the problems that people with impairments face in their daily lives to their own personal inadequacies or functional limitations, and could have been reformulated as follows:

What defects in the design of everyday equipment like jars, bottles and tins causes you difficulty in holding, gripping or turning them?

Have you attended a special school because of your education authority's policy of sending people with your impairment to such places?

What are the environmental constraints which make it difficult for you to get about in your immediate neighbourhood?

Do you have problems at work because of the physical environment or the attitudes of others?

To understand why the first set of questions is intimidating for individual disabled people it is important to know something about the actual research process. In the OPCS surveys, for example, individuals with impairments were visited in their own home by official 'expert' researchers. They were asked a specified sequence of formal questions and there was no opportunity to clarify or discuss their answers. It is hardly surprising then that

> . . . .by the end of the interview, the disabled person has come to believe that his or her problems are caused by their own health disability problems rather than by the organization of society. It is in this sense that the process of the interview is oppressive, reinforcing onto isolated, individual disabled people the idea that the problems they experience in every day living are a direct result of their own inadequacies or functional limitations (Oliver, 1990, p. 12).

Conclusion

It is plain from the above discussion that although economic factors are significant in explaining social responses to and the experience of disability, cultural considerations are equally important. It is also evident that the philosophical and ideological foundations upon which discrimination against disabled people is justified are well entrenched within the core institutions of society.

The data show that there was substantial discrimination against disabled people in Britain prior to industrialisation, but it was relatively fragmented and took many forms. The economic and social upheavals which accompanied industrial development, however, precipitated discrimination becoming institutionalised throughout society. Indeed, the growing importance of economic rationality, individualism and medical science during this period contributed to and compounded ancient fears and prejudices, and provided intellectual justification for relatively more extreme discriminatory practices, notably the systematic removal of disabled people from the mainstream of economic and social life.

Since the 1939–45 war, however, there has been a general 'softening' of attitudes and a definite attempt to reverse this policy and integrate people with impairments into the community. To facilitate this goal there has been a rapid expansion of community-based services in both the state and private sectors, and a subsequent proliferation of professional helpers. While the positive effects of these developments are not in doubt, it is clear that they rest upon basically traditional perceptions of impairment and disability. Discrimination has not disappeared; it has simply been transformed into more subtle and less obvious forms.

3

EDUCATION

According to the Fish Report, *Educational Opportunities for All* (ILEA, 1985), the aims of education for all children and young people include the achievement of responsible personal autonomy and full participation in the communities in which they live. In practice this usually means employment and a relatively autonomous lifestyle. The type of education that the overwhelming majority of young people with impairments receive does not provide them with the skills and opportunities to achieve either.

Institutional discrimination against disabled people is ingrained throughout the present education system. The data show that most of the educational provision for disabled children and students remains basically segregative, is dominated by traditional medically-influenced attitudes, and commands a low priority within the education system as a whole. As a result, rather than equipping disabled children and young people with the appropriate skills and opportunities to live a full and active adult life, it largely conditions them into accepting a much devalued social role and in so doing condemns them to a lifetime of dependence and subordination. In addition, by producing dependence in this way it helps to create the negative stereotypes by which all disabled people are judged, and therefore a firm basis for the justification of institutional discrimination in society at large.

This chapter is divided into two main parts. The first looks at Government legislation in this area since the 1939–45 war, and considers its implications for education and disabled people. The second examines educational provision for children and students with impairments in special schools, the mainstream sector, and further and higher education.

Legislation and Education

Following the gradual establishment of mass education since the late nineteenth century, a corresponding system of mainly segregated 'special' facilities for pupils and young people with impairments soon emerged. From the 1890s onwards successive government documents presented special provision as a necessary adjunct to mainstream education because of its appropriateness for individuals whose needs were/are considered different from the rest of the

community, and because of the need to remove potentially disruptive or difficult pupils and students from the normal classroom in
order to maximise efficiency. Moreover, in the same way that services for disabled people generally had come to be dominated by
medical thinking, so too had special education. Similar considerations are applicable to special education in the late twentieth
century.

The 1944 Education Act Up till the 1944 Education Act, mainstream education, like special education, was not really considered
a major area for government intervention. Most schools, both
mainstream and special, were run by private or church charities
under the supervision of local government boards. The 1939–45
war, however, changed this situation. Recruits to the armed forces
were tested for general ability, and the authorities were startled by
the results, which showed widespread ignorance. Concern about
post-war economic recovery prompted the Government to rethink
its education policy.

Hitherto most British children attended 'elementary' school until
the age of fourteen. Secondary schools existed but parents had to
pay, so children from poorer backgrounds were almost all restricted
to the former. Less than 2 per cent of the population went to university. The Education Act of 1944 initiated several major changes,
including free secondary education for all, the raising of the school-
leaving age to fifteen, and a stated commitment to equality of
opportunity in education. The idea of equality, however, did not
extend to children with impairments.

As a result of the Act, most local education authorities (LEAs)
adopted academic selection as a method of deciding secondary
school placement. Selection at the age of eleven, the age of transition from primary to secondary school, was supposed to sort out
the academically able from the less able. Results from the 'Eleven
plus' examination determined whether children went to Grammar
Schools or Secondary Modern Schools. A minority who did 'well'
were able to attend the former while the remainder had little choice
but to go to the latter.

To make sure the new system would work, it was considered
essential to weed out as many children as possible who might inconvenience or obstruct its implementation; selection by ability sanctioned selection by disability. Hence, LEAs were instructed to make
separate provision for children with an impairment of 'body or
mind'. A set of categories for disabled children was produced.
'Partially sighted' and 'partially deaf' children were to be separated
from those termed 'blind' and 'deaf'; 'delicate', 'epileptic', 'diabetic'

and 'physically handicapped' were the main categories considered educable, whilst 'defective' children became 'educationally subnormal [ESN]', Two further categories added to the list for separate provision were 'speech defect' and 'maladjusted' (Tomlinson, 1982).

In view of the cost involved in providing separate facilities for such a variety of impairments, it was suggested that children with less severe 'handicaps' could be educated in mainstream schools, either in segregated facilities or 'normally'. But since such a policy would mean a reduction of pupils in the existing special school system, and conflicted with the desire to remove 'problem' children from the 'ordinary' classroom, it was never fully developed. As the Ministry of Education put it:

> Anyone who has known children in any of the categories will agree that the varieties of education offered in ordinary primary and secondary schools do not meet their needs (Ministry of Education, 1946, quoted in Tomlinson, 1982, p. 50).

Children considered ineducable were passed on to the health service and were designated 'severely subnormal'.

Despite the rhetoric of help and individual needs emanating from LEAs and professionals, it was widely acknowledged that some parents, particularly those of children labelled ESN, would need coercing into accepting that their children would be excluded from the mainstream sector. Hence, a certificate signed by a doctor could be used to coerce non-compliant parents. The Handicapped Pupils Form (HPI) had to be completed to secure compulsory attendance at a special school.

The category that expanded most in the immediate post-war period was that of ESN. The number of children in ESN schools doubled between 1947 and 1955 from 12,060 to 22,639, with a further 27,000 awaiting placement. Over two-thirds of the children termed 'handicapped' in the 1960s experienced 'mild' educational subnormality (ESNM). It has since been suggested that teachers were using this label to remove children who posed problems in both learning and behavioural terms from mainstream classrooms (Tomlinson, 1982).

Tomlinson (1982) has reported that during the 1960s 'aphasic' children (children who have communication difficulties), 'dyslexic' children (children who experience problems interpreting the printed character), 'autistic' children (children who have difficulty tuning in to 'normal' human wavelengths), 'psychologically crippled' children (children stressed by modern living conditions) and 'socially handicapped' children (children of the poor) were all recommended for special education.

In 1970 children who hitherto had been viewed as ineducable and designated 'severely subnormal' after 1959 were integrated into the special education system. The Mental Health Act of 1959 had suggested that these children should receive education and training but the 1970 Education (Handicapped Children) Act made this compulsory. The DES report *The Last To Come In* was decidedly positive about the proposed integration of children previously termed ineducable with those who were designated ESN. This created a further distinction, with the former referred to as 'ESN severe' or ESN(S) as opposed to ESN(M) for the latter.

The DES report on special education of April 1973 re-examined the categorisation and education of children with impairments. It was critical of the use of categories of handicap but did little to implement their abolition. A shift of emphasis was evident in DES Circular 2/75, which introduced new forms to replace HPI. An educational approach to assessment was now deemed preferable to a medical one, although medical concerns were still considered important. Special education (SE) forms 1–4 were intended to replace HP forms 2–4. Form SE 1 was completed by a teacher, SE 2 by a medical officer, SE 3 by a psychologist and SE 4 — a summary — by a psychologist or an LEA adviser. The views of parents or children were not considered important enough to warrant documentation.

In 1976 the Labour Government incorporated a section on special education in the 1976 Education Act, which was intended to implement comprehensivisation (the introduction of comprehensive schools supposed to accommodate all children regardless of academic ability) in England and Wales. Section 10 of the Act was included as a substitute for Section 33(ii) of the 1944 Education Act, a clause which was intended to change the legal emphasis of special education treatment in special schools to provision for all categories of disabled children in the mainstream sector. Section 10 stated that children should be educated in special schools only if they could not receive adequate tuition in 'ordinary' schools, or if the cost of that instruction would cause 'unreasonable public expenditure' (Tomlinson, 1982).

Although the shift toward comprehensive education implied an end to segregation for disabled children, there was little evidence during the 1970s that these schools were any better than their predecessors at integrating children who required 'special treatment' (HMSO, 1979). Founded upon egalitarian principles, comprehensive schools were envisaged as catering for all children regardless of gender, class, race or ability. In the event, however, reactionary fears among politicians, teachers and some sections of the general public over declining educational standards meant that the majority of comprehensives stuck to streaming, setting and banding rather than mixed-ability teaching. Section 10 of the 1976 Act was never implemented on economic grounds (Tomlinson, 1982).

The Warnock Report 1978.   The Warnock Report (1978) followed, and again, like its antecedents, it presented special provision as a helpful variant of mainstream schooling. Composed of twenty-seven professionals, only one of whom was a parent of children with impairments, the Warnock Committee stated that at least 20 per cent of the school population would need some form of special educational provision at some stage during the education process. Moreover, because this problem had been evident in mainstream schools for several years, since comprehensivisation there had been a steady growth in remedial classes in the mainstream sector. The Committee suggested that special provision should be met within these schools with the help of advisory and support services. Also, moves toward integration were encouraged.

The Report recommended the abolition of statutory categories of handicap in favour of a broader concept of 'special educational needs' (SEN). Educationally subnormal children and children classed as 'remedial' were to be termed children with 'learning difficulties'. Disruptive children who had hitherto been placed on an *ad hoc* basis in a variety of settings were now to come officially within the realm of SEN, under the heading 'children with emotional or behavioural difficulties'. The importance of provision below the age of five was stressed, as well as the need for continued education after sixteen, the statutory school-leaving age.

The committee also recommended that all teachers should be helped to an awareness of SEN through in-service training. Other professionals involved in this area — for example, health visitors, nursery nurses, educational psychologists and social workers — should also receive similar tuition. In addition, the Committee acknowledged the needs and anxieties of parents of children with SEN. But their views were not given priority; the Committee endorsed the idea of a 'partnership' between them and the professionals.

While the publication of the Warnock Report is generally perceived as something of a 'milestone' (ILEA, 1985) in the history of special education, in the main it does not move away from the traditional view of disabled children and young people, nor from conventional wisdom with regard to their education. While the demedicalisation of the labelling of disabled individuals within the educational context must be viewed positively – as Micheline Mason noted wryly, 'my special child' sounds infinitely better than 'my little invalid' (Reiser and Mason, 1990) – it represents little more than a cosmetic exercise. The concept of SEN retains the assumption that people categorised in this way are somehow 'less than human'. The emphasis is still on the inadequacy of the individual: it is s/he who is different; it is s/he who is at fault; and, most importantly, it is s/he who must change.

The Committee did not seriously question the general philosophy and organisation of the education system, although by implication it acknowledged that it is incapable of meeting adequately the educational needs of up to a fifth of its users. Their solution to the problem of SEN was a further expansion of professionally dominated support services. Within the present educational context this can only reinforce the perceived difference between pupils and students with SEN and the rest of the school population, as well as the general view that people with impairments are incapable of looking after themselves without professional help.

But perhaps the most glaring indictment of the Warnock Committee's position with regard to SEN and the role of disabled people within the community can be found in its discussion of what it terms 'significant living without work':

> The problem of how to accept life without employment and how to prepare for it, faces people with a variety of disabilities, including those who are of the highest intelligence but very severely handicapped . . . We believe that the secret of significant living without work may lie in handicapped people doing far more to support each other, and also in giving support to people who are lonely and vulnerable (Warnock Report, 1978, p. 202).

Although the Committee acknowledged the economic, social and psychological significance of paid employment for individuals within our society (see Chapter 4), it is clear that it had accepted unequivocally the orthodox view that disabled people would be excluded from the workplace. This has salient implications for the perpetuation of this myth. The most obvious of these is that professionals, themselves in secure employment, will determine when a child is young that s/he is unsuitable for paid work. The child's subsequent education will be organised accordingly. This results in a self-fulfilling prophecy, producing a 'downward spiral in professionals' expectations' about the child's potential for achievement (Kent and Massie, 1981). It is not surprising therefore that during the 1980s there has been a proliferation of life and leisure skills teaching for children and students with SEN throughout the education system.

Two pieces of legislation implemented those elements of the Warnock Report that the Government accepted. The 1980 Education Act provided parents with more information about SEN and about schools, although it was clear where the Government's priorities lay in terms of policies of integration:

> In present economic circumstances there is no possibility of funding the massive educational resources . . . which would be required to enable every ordinary school to provide an adequate education for children with serious educational differences (DES, 1980, quoted in Tomlinson, 1982, p. 54).

The 1981 Education Act initiated what are now generally seen as major changes in this area.

The 1981 Education Act.   The 1981 Education Act became law on 3 April 1983 (Swann, 1989). Under Section 1, SEN are defined in terms of children who have a significantly 'greater' learning difficulty than the majority of children of a similar age, or children with an impairment or impairments preventing them from making 'effective use' of mainstream provision within the local area. Special educational provision in relation to a child over two years means services which are additional to or somehow different from those provided generally for children of the same age in schools maintained by the LEA. For children under two years the Act covers educational provision of any kind.

Under the Act LEAs in England and Wales have a 'duty' to identify, assess and provide full-time free education for all children with SEN from the age of two to the end of compulsory schooling and up to 19 if they remain in school. LEAs must also provide facilities for children with SEN from birth. Local health authorities are compelled to tell LEAs and parents if they believe a child has, or may have, SEN, once s/he starts school at the age of five. Moreover, following a formal assessment an LEA may issue a child with SEN with a 'statement'. This document describes the child's particular needs and recommends how they should be met. If the child leaves school at sixteen and goes on to college, LEAs are still bound to provide free full-time education, but the 'additional protection' provided by the Act is lost.

The Act underlines the importance of professionals, particularly doctors, educational psychologists, speech therapists, physiotherapists, occupational therapists, health visitors, school nurses *et al.*, in the determination of SEN. It formally abolishes the categories of handicap, although it does not rule out their use. 'Diagnostic terms' may be necessary in the 'attainment of support services' (see DES, Circular 22/89, 1989).

Legally, however, parents have more involvement in the assessment of their child's needs. They can demand an assessment if they feel that these are not being met, and the LEA is bound to respond. Parents have access to more information and, theoretically at least, a larger say in the type of education to be provided, and where it should take place. They can contribute written information to the assessment process, and they have rights of appeal if they do not like the provision being proposed. The Act also suggests that the child's feelings should be considered during the examination process.

Although the 1981 Education Act clearly recognises the discriminatory policies of the past and, like its predecessors, endorses the general principle that children with impairments and learning difficulties should be educated in mainstream schools, it sets conditions for integration which allow LEAs to continue to segregate at will. It states that a child with SEN may be integrated into an 'ordinary' school so long as this is compatible with the child 'receiving the special education' that s/he requires; the 'provision of efficient education for the children with whom s/he will be educated'; and 'the efficient use of resources' (HMSO, 1981).

Children and young people with SEN are still perceived as different from the rest of the school population. Whilst all schools are expected to assess children's abilities and to provide written profiles, reports or statements of their educational needs and progress, LEAs are bound by law to mark pupils with SEN out for special treatment through the assessment and 'statementing' process.

While it may be argued that assessment and statementing in relation to SEN is a form of affirmative action, it can also be used to place children and young people with SEN in separate groups, classes or schools. Although lip-service is paid to the notion of parental and children's rights, education within the mainstream sector for a child with SEN is still not a right in the same way that it is for able-bodied children or children who do not experience learning difficulties. Integration is provisional, and is acceptable only as long as it does not interfere with the smooth running of the mainstream sector. It is a privilege which can be awarded or withdrawn by LEAs at will.

The procedures for assessing SEN required by the 1981 Act are highly discriminatory and complicated, and take time. One study estimated that the full assessment process can last as long as 67 weeks (ILEA, 1985). This can have serious negative implications for a child's education.

The process takes time because more people are expected to provide information, because parents are consulted more and because they are given time to consider their response. Apart from the unnecessary anxiety caused for the entire family by this process, due to the uncertainty of its outcome, it will almost certainly exacerbate any educational difficulties experienced by the child. Local authorities are not compelled to provide additional educational provision until the full assessment process is complete. Assessment can and should provide special equipment and/or additional help for access to the curriculum where appropriate, and any delay in providing that help can seriously damage a child's educational progress. Only recently a twelve-year-old girl missed the whole of her first year of secondary education due to the time taken in appealing against an unsatisfactory reassessment (*Contact*, 1990).

Since comprehensive assessment procedures are not an everyday occurrence within the British education system, parents are at a considerable disadvantage once the process is set in motion, whether they instigate it themselves or whether it is instigated by the LEA. The actual assessment procedure, the language used by professionals and the location of the examinations are generally highly discriminatory, and put the child being examined and her/his family under unnecessary social and psychological pressure. This can only make their difficulties worse (see for example ACE, 1988).

This is especially so for children and families who do not use English as their first language. The Fish Report (ILEA, 1985) noted how little progress has been made in establishing assessment procedures to identify SEN which take account of cultural and racial differences where English is not the language of the home and which are easily understood by parents. These families experience a double disadvantage in the assessment process and the disproportionately high number of children from ethnic and racial minority backgrounds in special schools (see Tomlinson, 1985; Barton, 1986) may be seen as an indication of the importance of this point.

Cultural and ethnic considerations did, however, prompt the Government to include an amendment in Circular 22/89 (DES, 1989) stating that for children whose 'mother tongue is not English', a lack of competence must not be equated with learning difficulties. It is important to note, however, that this statement does not apply to children with hearing impairments whose 'mother tongue' would be sign language. The culture and language of the deaf community continue to be ignored by the Department of Education and Science (DES).

Given these difficulties, parents should clearly be provided with as much information about assessment and SEN as possible. A succession of government documents, particularly Section 8 of the 1980 Education Act, the accompanying Education School Information Regulations 1981 and DES Circular 1/83, set out just what information LEAs should publish in relation to assessment and SEN. They must provide in an accessible form detailed information on the arrangements and policies for identifying children with SEN and for involving parents, policies which have been designed to promote 'frankness and openness on all sides'. There is, however, a large body of evidence to show that LEAs do not provide parents with the appropriate information (ILEA, 1985; Rogers, 1986, 1986a; Meltzer, Smyth and Robus, 1989).

In response to a growing concern expressed by parents over the lack of data emanating from LEAs in this area, the Centre for Studies on Integration in Education (CSIE) analysed the material put out by 66 out of the 104 LEAs in England and Wales. Thirty-four authorities chose not to submit their publications for analysis. The survey showed that most LEAs omit to mention or explain key aspects of the arrangements and effects of assessment, statementing and appealing. For example, only 6 per cent published data on parents' rights of appeal and 11 per cent failed to mention their duties with regard to integration (Rogers, 1986).

A follow-up study analysed the published guidance which LEAs distributed to headteachers, teaching staff, educational psychologists and other professionals working in the education service. It showed that this material was equally bereft of relevant information. Only 50 per cent of LEAs, for example, told the staff of their duty to integrate and only 8 per cent gave guidance on how to involve parents in the assessment process (Rogers, 1986a). That there has not been a general outcry among professionals over this situation suggests that their principal loyalties lie with their employers rather than the users of the education service, namely disabled children and their families.

The concept of parents as partners is evidently rhetoric rather than reality. The Government-sponsored disability survey conducted between 1985 and 1988 and published in 1989 showed that only 22 per cent of parents of children with impairments had heard of the assessment and statementing process, and many of these children were being educated in special schools (Meltzer, Smyth and Robus, 1989, p. 51).

The survey found that of the estimated 360,000 children under sixteen with impairments, 60 per cent of whom are males, only 2 per cent lived in residential establishments. This is a lower estimate of the numbers of disabled children in the general population than had been made in previous studies. Thirty-four per cent of disabled children living in private households and 63 per cent living in 'communal establishments' are educated in segregated special provision (see Table 3.1). Moreover, the OPCS survey does not show the numbers of children from ethnic minorities in these schools but it should be remembered that other studies have found that for them the figure is disproportionately high (Barton, 1986; Tomlinson, 1982, 1985).

Disability was classified in terms of severity from 1 to 10. Of disabled children living at home, 63 per cent had not been assessed and 30 per cent had been assessed. Only 14 per cent had a formal statement. It might be argued that only severely impaired children would need statements, yet in the most severe category only 62 per cent had been assessed and 35 per cent had a written statement. More alarming still, 58 per cent of the children who were reported to have been assessed had no formal written statement, and 14 per cent of those who had not been assessed were receiving special educational provision in special schools (Meltzer, Smyth and Robus, 1989, p. 52). Since the 1981 Act makes it illegal to provide special education without a formal statement it is evident that the law is being ignored by many LEAs.

Table 3.1. Where Disabled Children are Educated

Type of Education	Disabled children living in private households %	Disabled children living in communal establishments %
Special school	24	45
Remedial unit of secondary school	5	4
Remedial unit of primary school	4	3
Other special provision	1	0
School/class attached to residential home (local authority, voluntary or hospital)	0	17
Ordinary schools	66	27
Not known	0	4
Total	100	100

Source: Adapted from Table 6.12, p. 57 and Table 12.7, p. 109, in Meltzer, Smyth and Robus, 1989.

Swann has noted that it has been hard to discern anything that could be termed a national integration policy since 1981. No clear steps have been taken by the DES to reduce the numbers of pupils going to special schools. They have not issued guidance to LEAs on how they should interpret the integration clauses of the 1981 Act. This point was taken up by the House of Commons Select Committee Report on the implementation of the 1981 Act. The DES also came under criticism from the same source for failing to monitor the consequences of the Act. Moreover, although the Committee called both for more effective monitoring and guidance from central Government there has been no response (Swann, 1989).

Table 3.2. Numbers of Children in Special Schools in relation to School Population as a Whole

	No. of children in school*	No. of children in special schools†	%
1977	9,278,268	131,151	1.41
1978	9,915,672	132,384	1.44
1979	9,094,150	131,688	1.45
1980	8,933,033	129,724	1.45
1981	8,720,123	128,125	1.47
1982	8,501,527	126,487	1.49
1983	8,276,185	124,811	1.51
1984	8,096,233	120,097	1.48
1985	7,955,879	116,273	1.46
1986	7,832,067	113,554	1.45
1987	7,721,209	100,865	1.41
1988	7,610,240	105,070	1.38
1989	7,553,484	102,064	1.35

* Includes full- and part-time pupils in nursery, primary, secondary and independent schools.
† Includes full- and part-time pupils in maintained independent schools.
Source: Adapted from Table A30.89, pp. 175–6, DES, 1990.

Although Table 3.2 suggests that segregation declined during the 1980s it is important to note that in 1989 it stood at only 0.06 per cent below that of 1977, the year when the Warnock Committee was finalising its report which endorsed the need for integration. It should also be noted that these figures are misleading. Local education authorities vary greatly in their levels of segregation. While many LEAs have reduced their level of segregation, others have increased it. Recent evidence from the Centre for Studies on Integrated Education (CSIE) shows that since 1981 fifteen English LEAs have increased the proportion of children they send to segregated special schools, and three of them, Doncaster, Rotherham and St Helen's, did so by more than 25 per cent (Swann, 1991).

Also, the age structure of pupils in segregated schools is cumulative. More children are directed into special schools as they grow older (Meltzer, Smyth and Robus, 1989). As Swann points out, a more accurate picture of segregated schooling could be seen by looking at the numbers of children transferred each year from mainstream to segregated provision. This is referred to as the inflow rate. It has been shown that there was a fall in the inflow rate in 1983, but it increased in the following two years (Swann, 1988). Later figures for the annual rate of inflow into special schools for each LEA are not yet available (Swann, 1989).

Another important factor which needs to be borne in mind in relation to the rhetoric of integration is that there has been a considerable reduction in the child population during the 1970s and 1980s. This is clearly reflected in the numbers of children attending school. Disabled children are marginal members of school communities. When mainstream school places are in short supply, segregation is the order of the day. When registers are empty, schools are less reluctant to exclude pupils with SEN.

Since the 1981 Act it has often been argued that progress on integration is slow because of the cost involved. According to the latest estimates (the Education Statistics Estimates 1988–9 published by the Chartered Institute of Finance and Accountancy quoted in CSIE, 1989), LEAs in England and Wales spend more than £820 million a year on special education. A vast amount of this money is spent on special education rather than integration. The main problem is not simply a lack of resources but a lack of commitment to transfer resources from segregated provision to the mainstream sector. It is not a lack of funds which is the key to integration but unwillingness to change (Brighouse, 1989). The directive for change must come from Government. It is unlikely, however, that integration will be helped by Government reforms carried out in the late 1980s.

The 1988 Education Reform Act and its Implications.   A threat to the development of the integration of disabled children into mainstream schools is contained in the Education Reform Act of 1988. Briefly, this legislation allows schools to opt out of LEA control and become self-governing. It also introduced the national curriculum and encourages competition among schools through open enrolment (Blaine, 1989).

Up to September 1989 schools in the state sector were able largely to devise their own syllabuses, define their own attainment targets for individual children, set their own tests and choose which external examinations to prepare for. The new Act enables the Government to prescribe compulsory courses of study and to dictate examination arrangements and attainment targets in all state schools, except special schools in hospitals. Why these schools are excluded is not clear. In addition, the new curriculum can be 'modified' for children with SEN. Indeed, pupils may be excluded from all or part of the new system if they are members of defined groups or pupils with a particular kind of special need; pupils with statements; or children whose special needs are likely to be temporary (Blaine, 1989).

It has been noted by several sources (see for example ACE, 1989; Blaine, 1989; Darlington, 1990; Swann, 1988; Simpson, 1990) that the mainstream sector's inevitable preoccupation with meeting the new requirements will make provision for disabled children an even lower priority. In order for mainstream schools to concentrate on the national curriculum it is probable that children with a 'modified' curriculum will increasingly be placed in a separate unit or school. Disabled children will be identified by their inability to cope with a curriculum designed for the majority, namely the non-disabled majority.

Given the increased pressure on mainstream schools to achieve specified attainment targets, schools which are unable to meet these targets will be labelled accordingly. Competition between schools will intensify, and teachers keen to maintain their own and their schools' reputation may see full assessment and statementing as a means to exempt children who are unlikely to do well. Moreover, if special schools are able to offer a 'modified' version of the national curriculum, they might well appear more attractive to parents of children who have been categorised with SEN, particularly if it is evident that their needs are not going to be met elsewhere. The 1988 Act could squeeze disabled children out of the mainstream sector altogether.

Discrimination in Practice

Special Schools. Whether or not disabled children should be educated in segregated schools remains a contentious issue. Some would claim that these schools are a form of positive action as they are better placed to give disabled children the intensive tuition they need, and therefore 'a better start in life' (Simpson, 1990). There is relatively little evidence to support this view. Segregated or special schools are a fundamental part of the discriminatory process, not simply because they create and perpetuate artificial barriers between disabled children and their able-bodied peers, but also because they reinforce traditional individualistic medical perceptions of disability, and generally fail to provide their pupils with either an adequate education or the skills necessary for adulthood.

At the time of writing there are 1,414 special schools in England and Wales. At the time of the Warnock Report there were 1,591. This represents a fall of only 177, and contrasts markedly with the mainstream sector where the numbers of schools have declined to a far greater degree over the same period, with 2,962 having been closed (see Table 3.3). In the broadest sense special schools can be defined as schools which cater specifically for children with SEN. However, definitions are problematic since special schools come in a variety of different forms.

In general special schools tend to be smaller than their mainstream equivalents. Scrutiny of a succession of recent reports by Her Majesty's Inspectors (HMI) which have looked at a collection of special schools shows that their average size is around 50 pupils, although a substantial number are smaller. Most appear to take pupils ranging widely in age and ability. Many accommodate children of from two to nineteen years. There are more boys than girls in special schools. Some specialise in education for children with a particular impairment while others cater for a variety of needs. Some are day schools, some take both day pupils and boarders, and others are solely residential. In general they have a larger catchment area than most mainstream schools (DES, 1986, 1989a, 1989b, 1989c). It is not uncommon for a special school to have a catchment area of 100 square miles or more.

Many pupils who go to special schools every day experience long travelling times, sometimes of up to two hours each way (DES, 1989c). This has obvious negative implications with regard to a child's ability to learn either in the classroom when they arrive at school, or when they return home for homework. Moreover, attending a school well outside the local community does not help disabled children make friends with peers who live near their home. This problem is far worse for children who are boarders. The negative effects of uprooting children from their family, peers and the local community are increasingly well documented (Oliver, 1983; ILEA, 1985; Reiser and Mason, 1990).

Table 3.3. Numbers of Special Schools in relation to Mainstream
Schools

	No. of schools in mainstream sector*	No. of special schools
1978	29,059	1,591
1979	28,960	1,599
1980	28,869	1,597
1981	28,602	1,593
1982	28,195	1,571
1983	27,858	1,562
1984	27,362	1,548
1985	26,990	1,529
1986	26,682	1,493
1987	26,489	1,470
1988	26,305	1,443
1989	26,097	1,414
Total change	− 2,962	− 177

* Includes maintained nursery, primary, secondary and independent schools.
Source: Adapted from Table A30.89, pp. 175-6, DES, 1990.

The recent OPCS disability surveys show that 12 per cent of disabled children who live at home and 44 per cent of those who permanently reside in residential homes and who attend special schools are boarders (Meltzer, Smyth and Robus, 1989). Many LEAs continue to 'export' children with SEN to maintained or independent residential special schools out of their area, usually on the grounds that local schools cannot meet their needs. In 1987 one LEA sent just over 0.5 per cent of its total school population to private sector special schools (Swann, 1989).

This practice cannot be justified on the grounds that the accommodation and resources in special schools are any better than those in the mainstream sector, because this is clearly not so. As will be evident later, access, which does not just mean physical access but also sensory and communications access, is a major problem in all schools.

In each of the HMI reports mentioned, accommodation and resources were considered at best 'satisfactory' and at worst 'downright dangerous'. For example, when describing the buildings used for educating pupils with 'emotional' and 'behavioural' difficulties the HMI inspectors included the following phrases: 'of bleak exterior', 'shabby and unkempt', 'barren and uninviting', 'in serious disrepair', 'an air of sad neglect', 'drab and dingy', 'run-down' and 'poorly heated' (DES, 1989a, p. 3).

In a report titled *Educating Physically Disabled Pupils* another team of inspectors noted:

> Difficulties include inadequate storage space, particularly for wheelchairs and other large equipment; inappropriate safe provision for the charging of batteries for electric wheelchairs; too small hygiene and toileting provision that limits wheelchair access; inappropriate furniture for changing children in privacy; poor disposal facilities for soiled material; and inappropriate and inaccessible facilities . . . (DES, 1989b, p. 11).

In terms of resources the picture is similarly bleak. Although a minority of special schools are well resourced, many are underfinanced and heavily reliant on charity for funding. In many instances private sponsorship is responsible for appropriate furniture, wheelchairs, school visits, the school minibus, and essential teaching equipment, particularly communications devices, information technology and computers (DES, 1989b). For a variety of reasons, not least the frequent underfunding of special provision by LEAs, teachers and parents will intentionally seek to raise money in this way. Open days, sports days and sponsored activities of one kind or another are a regular feature of the special school calendar. The pupils are inevitably involved in these events. Hence they are repeatedly reminded of their dependence on others, their low social status, and the need to perform and conform. In this way they are taught, albeit unintentionally, to adopt the passive dependent posture of the stereotype disabled person.

The lack of resources has an obvious effect on the type of curriculum which can be taught in special schools. Although the importance of core subjects such as science and maths for pupils with SEN was continually re-emphasised by the DES in the late 1980s, there is a general lack of teaching facilities in these areas in many of these establishments. For example, a recent HMI report, *The Effectiveness of Small Special Schools*, pointed out how specialist science facilities were rare. 'Satisfactory' resources were noted in only four of the thirty-six schools studied. The report concluded that the absence of facilities was a 'serious barrier to pupils' access to the subject' (DES, 1989c, p. 14).

It is frequently stated that staff in special schools are better equipped to educate pupils with SEN. There is little evidence to support this view. Although in recent years there has been something of an increase in teachers with advanced qualifications in special schools, the majority of teaching staff are qualified 'only by long experience'

(DES, 1989b, p. 9). The lack of curricula expertise among teachers is a key issue in special education. Each of the reports quoted has commented on the general lack of subject-specific knowledge in core areas. Particular examples include; science, mathematics and craft, design and technology (DES, 1986, 1989a, 1989b, 1989c). In addition, the provision of relevant in-service education and training (INSET) has not been extensive. It is plain that most LEAs do not have formal policies to meet the staffing needs of special schools.

A similar situation is apparent with non-teaching assistants (NTA). The provision of NTAs in special schools varies. A recent study of thirty-five special schools for physically disabled children found ratios ranging from 4.4: 1 to 16: 1 (DES, 1989b, p.9). Most NTAs have National Nursery Examining Board (NNEB) qualifications with only additional informal training in schools. Again there is no general policy in this area.

It has long been noted by disabled people who have been through the special education system that medical considerations take precedence in special schools (see Barnes, 1990; BCODP, 1986; Oliver, 1983, 1985, 1990). This has recently been confirmed in official documents. One study pointed out that doctors often hold clinics in special schools and that there is a growing tendency to introduce elements of 'conductive education' (a controversial method of developing individual physical abilities in accordance with the traditional medical view of disability, see Oliver, 1989) into the curriculum in schools for physically impaired children. It is still common for disabled pupils to be removed from classes regularly for physiotherapy, speech or other therapies (DES, 1986, 1989a, 1989b, 1989c). The learning time lost because of such practices can be considerable.

Given these considerations it is not surprising that academically the learning experience in special schools compares unfavourably with that in the mainstream sector. Indeed the quality of teaching and learning in special schools varies considerably, according to official sources. One survey of thirty-six small special schools considered standards to be generally 'satisfactory' when compared with larger special schools (DES, 1989c). Other studies which have looked at a range of special schools have been less complimentary when comparing standards to those in the mainstream sector. For example, a study of seventy-six segregated units for children with 'emotional/behavioural difficulties' stated:

Although the majority of the schools claimed to be implementing a mainstream curriculum and to have as a major aim the reintegration of pupils into ordinary schools, it was unusual to see a conscious attempt being made to reflect in the special school the work which a pupil of similar age and ability would be undertaking in the local school (DES, 1989a, p. 10).

It is significant to point out here that the DES publish annually information showing the type of courses studied by pupils in all secondary schools in the mainstream sector, along with the results of examinations taken (see for example DES, 1990). No comparable information is available for special schools.

Although nationally recognised examinations and assessments such as the GCSE and A level GCE are open to the same type of criticism as all assessments (see above), they are a major feature of all British schools. While the purpose of these examinations is to provide a 'fair' appraisal of an individual's ability and skills in a particular subject area, the assessment procedures are generally geared to the needs of the able-bodied pupil. For example, examination papers are usually printed and illegible to individuals who experience visual or reading difficulties. People with impairments therefore are at a considerable disadvantage from the outset.

If disabled candidates wish to take these exams they must arrange with the examining body for special arrangements to be made. This is a long-drawn-out and complicated process which demands a great deal of time and effort, often from the disabled candidate. It is an added and unnecessary burden which many disabled people have to face when taking examinations. It is a burden that able-bodied candidates never have to experience.

Briefly, in conjunction with teachers a disabled student must find out which examination body to contact — there are twenty-eight different examining boards in England and Wales (Simmons, 1990) — and what to apply for. S/he must then make sure that the special arrangements being sought are appropriate to her/his needs. For example, candidates who are unable to write manually sometimes use a modified typewriter, extra time can be arranged if students tire easily etc. Special arrangements need to be applied for well in advance and supporting evidence, usually in the form of a doctor's letter, has to be obtained and provided. These arrangements also have to be applied for every time an individual sits an examination, regardless of whether the student's impairment is permanent or not (for a fuller discussion of this procedure see Simmons,1990).

The Mainstream Sector.   Integration is not simply a question of being placed in the same groups or institutions as others. It is a process which requires continued and planned interaction, particularly in mainstream schools. It is evident, however, that the policies

[handwritten: It was stated in 1991 that however 1994 Act changed this as did the DDA.]

and resources needed to facilitate this process are not being provided. Few LEAs have a comprehensive policy statement on integrating children with SEN into the mainstream sector. Consequently, in terms of accommodation, organisation, staffing, attitudes, and the classroom experience, barriers remain.

With regard to accommodation, the suitability of buildings depends largely upon when the school was built. In 1972 legislation was passed to ensure that all new schools should be accessible to disabled people (Reiser and Mason, 1990). Unfortunately, however, building new schools has been a low priority ever since. Since 1977 the numbers of schools in the mainstream sector has fallen dramatically (see Table 3.3).

A series of recent Government documents concerned with provision for SEN in mainstream schools has consistently drawn attention to the unsuitability of the design of school buildings for children with impairments. For example, an HMI report on services for primary-aged pupils with SEN in forty-three mainstream schools in eleven LEAs, pointed out that while many disabled children were not 'seriously disadvantaged' by inaccessible buildings, some were. Most classrooms had insufficient space to accommodate pupils who needed personal aids and equipment, as well as support from NTAs. In most classrooms the quality of acoustics was judged to be 'poor' and in some schools 'suitably adapted toilets and changing facilities for non-ambulant and incontinent pupils had not been provided' (DES, 1989d, p. 7). What was meant by 'seriously disadvantaged' was not discussed.

A report which looked at integration in secondary provision stated that in the majority of schools where individuals with physical impairments were placed, few adaptations had been made. In most cases access to practical subjects such as science for pupils who experienced mobility problems was limited. The inspectors noted how dangerous the situation was in one instance where a disabled pupil had to be carried up and down three flights of stairs between lessons (DES, 1989b, p. 11). In many cases this situation prevented independent study in important subject areas and seriously restricted the choice of options in years 4 and 5 — the years when most pupils select which external examinations they will take.

Health and safety regulations are often presented as a reason for not admitting disabled pupils to mainstream schools. The most commonly voiced concerns are about the means of escape in the case of fire. This is both discriminatory and unnecessary.

The British Standards Institute (BSI) issued a set of guide-lines in 1988 (BSI, 1988, part 8) which recommends appropriate policies for this particular eventuality. For example, one strategy advocated by this document suggests that buildings should have areas on each floor which remain resistant to fire for a period of half an hour so that disabled people can be taken out of the building by trained emergency service staff. Unfortunately these policies are not mandatory. LEAs do not have to implement them, and frequently choose not to on economic grounds. They are free therefore to discriminate at will. Only recently a young wheelchair user who had passed the eleven plus examination and was ranked in terms of marks among the top 25 per cent in his area, was refused entry to all the local grammar schools on the grounds that none of them was adapted for wheelchairs (Collins, 1988).

Frequently in discussions about the difficulties encountered in integrating pupils with SEN into mainstream schools, attention focuses upon the need for peripatetic advisory and support services as an interim solution (ILEA, 1985; Reiser and Mason, 1990; Warnock Report, 1978). A DES survey published in 1989 which looked in detail at these services in England and Wales found that there was a wide variation in what was currently available. In some LEAs provision was judged to be good, in others it was said to be completely inadequate. Indeed policies which direct the work of support services are explicit in only a minority of LEAs. Few appear to have the facilities, resources and clerical back-up appropriate for this work (DES, 1989e).

It is evident that where once support services were mainly concerned with peripatetic teaching and assisting individuals in the classroom, the bulk of the work is now concerned with advising teachers and NTAs through short INSET courses (DES, 1989e). This is necessary because there is widespread ignorance and indeed hostility about integration and SEN among staff within the mainstream sector.

There is a real danger that such a policy might initiate segregation (Fulcher, 1989), but in order to facilitate integration the Warnock Report (1978) suggested that there was a need for all teachers at every level to undergo training in SEN, either in teacher training colleges for those who are new to the profession or via INSET courses for those already qualified. In many instances this has not occurred. Several studies have focused on the lack of training among teachers with regard to SEN, their general ignorance about impairments, and their hostility toward disability in the classroom (Center and Ward 1987, 1989; Clunies Ross, 1984; Danks, 1989).

In general, the teaching profession's attitudes toward integration are positive, as long as the appropriate back-up services are provided, and as long as it does not mean extra work for them.

However, they are less amenable to the idea of including children with intellectual impairments in mainstream schools than they are to children with physical limitations. And they are only willing to teach children with specific physical impairments. They are tolerant toward integrating children with 'mild mobility difficulties' but intolerant of children with impairments which require non-teaching management and/or assistance in the classroom. Examples include blindness, severe physical mobility problems, and incontinence (see for example Center and Ward 1987, 1989; Clunies Ross, 1984; Danks, 1989).

Discriminatory attitudes among teaching staff in the mainstream sector have also been confirmed by recent HMI reports. For example, the survey of provision for primary-aged pupils mentioned above (DES, 1989d) noted that pupils with SEN were not wholly accepted by teachers in a number of mainstream schools. The attitudes of some staff members were said to be 'patronising', while others were reluctant to work with disabled pupils. Where negative staff attitudes were present the inspectors noted how they were quickly picked up by non-impaired pupils. This had an adverse influence on their behaviour toward their disabled peers. Other studies have noted similar findings.

It is also common for some staff to be overprotective. This was mentioned in each of the studies discussed. The survey of provision for children with physical impairments, for example, said that although many schools acknowledge the need for independence they regularly fail to promote the emotional attitudes in students and staff which would support its development (DES, 1989b, p. 8).

Reiser and Mason (1990) pointed out how the widespread tendency for only a minority of staff in mainstream schools to have training in SEN helps to perpetuate these problems. 'Ordinary' teachers often resent being called upon to teach children whom they feel they are not qualified or being paid to teach. Conversely staff with responsibility for SEN are frequently reluctant to give up their privileges and their status.

Teachers who specialise in SEN are rarely subject to the same external pressures as their counterparts in either curriculum planning or content, or with regard to parents' expectations concerning their children's potential academic achievements. In addition, able-bodied teachers who work with disabled children are often held in high esteem by their peers, because teaching SEN is generally perceived as particularly tedious, intellectually unrewarding, and often unpleasant.

The separation of responsibilities among staff within mainstream schools is often reflected in the actual learning process. It is common for pupils with SEN to be removed from their designated class to be given individual tuition or to join a small group of pupils with supposedly similar needs. This frequently happens in mainstream schools which incorporate a segregated special unit or department. In such schools children can be registered in a mainstream class but spend as little as 3 per cent of their time with their able-bodied contemporaries (Swann, 1988).

Frequently the content of lessons taught in 'withdrawal' sessions in special units does not relate to the curriculum in the mainstream sector. The HMI report concerned with provision for primary-aged pupils stated that in several schools pupils with a variety of impairments were taught in special classes solely by the teacher responsible for SEN. These classes were small and covered the entire primary age range. This made it difficult to ensure that each pupil had access to a broad and balanced curriculum. In addition, the teacher was unable to help children with SEN elsewhere in the schools (DES, 1989d). It has also been shown that pupils with a first language other than English are particularly disadvantaged in this type of teaching environment (DES, 1988).

There is also evidence that pupils with SEN are placed in classes with younger children. For example, one fifth-year boy described as having 'severe learning difficulties' was placed in a third-year infant group. Although he was due to transfer to secondary school the following academic year, his experience of junior school would have been limited to one class. The Inspectors concluded that these practices needed careful monitoring (DES, 1989d).

It is also common for children with impairments in mainstream schools to be regularly removed from the classroom to be treated by therapists and doctors. If the local authority provides the appropriate funding these services can be provided within the school by peripatetic staff. If they are not, then children have to travel to clinics or hospitals. Either way valuable learning time is greatly reduced (see DES, 1988, 1989b, 1989d; NAHA,1988).

The problems associated with integrating children with impairments in mainstream schools are exacerbated by the failure of the majority of LEAs and governing bodies to adopt policies which deal with discrimination against disabled people. The race and gender relations laws introduced in the 1970s apply to pupils, students, teachers and others who work in the education system. All schools acknowledge these laws and act accordingly. No such policy exists with regard to disabled people, either nationally or in schools. Few LEAs actively pursue policies to combat discrimination against disabled people in schools. Reiser and Mason (1990) noted that the Inner London Education Authority (ILEA) adopted this policy in principle in 1983, but it was another four years before it produced a leaflet outlining the strategies needed to support it.

The fact that discriminatory attitudes permeate the education system can be partly explained with reference to some of the teaching materials and books used in schools. Children's literature is replete with negative images of people with impairments. Well-known examples include Blind Pew, the disabled person as sinister and evil, in Stevenson's *Treasure Island*, and in *Heidi*, the disabled person as pitiful or sad. It is widely acknowledged by educationalists that children's literature can be a powerful influence on shaping beliefs and attitudes, and that if books are chosen with care they can refute stereotypes and construct positive images of disadvantaged groups. One authority on this subject stated:

> There is enough evidence . . . to justify a teaching intervention which tackles the problem directly, by including a planned element in the curriculum specifically designed to encourage positive attitudes and actions toward peers with special needs, just as there is a case for a curriculum to foster racial tolerance and gender issues (Quicke, 1985 quoted in Reiser and Mason, 1990, p. 107).

There has been a sizeable body of work done to counteract the stereotype representations of women and ethnic minorities in books and other teaching materials used in British schools. But apart from a few notable exceptions little has been achieved on disability. Moreover, further progress seems unlikely unless it is sanctioned by Government, since 70 per cent of the curriculum is now controlled by the DES due to the 1988 ERA reforms.

Negative stereotypes are also evident in some of the newly-produced teaching aids designed to raise disability awareness in mainstream schools. One of the best publicised examples of this is the resource pack titled *Understanding Disability* produced by the Understanding Disability Trust. The information provided by this organisation adheres rigidly to the traditional individualistic medical view of disability (see Chapter 2). It is divisive since it assumes that its audience, both teachers and pupils, will be able-bodied. It presents impairment as the primary cause of disability and ignores social factors such as prejudice, the built environment, and gender and cultural differences between disabled individuals and groups. In short, the pack foments and perpetuates the ignorance and discrimination which it is designed to undermine.

It is often argued that LEAs could combat discrimination by employing more disabled teachers. Disabled role-models in positions of authority within mainstream schools are necessary to combat discrimination not only in education but also in society as a whole. Indeed, the Warnock Report (1978) recommended that disabled entrants should be encouraged to join teacher training schemes and that the medical criteria necessary to become a teacher should be relaxed. However, the Government has yet to implement this recommendation. In the 1989 teacher training regulations the DES still has the power to declare disabled teachers medically unfit to teach (Reiser and Mason, 1990). According to a recent report by the National Union of Teachers, this is one of the most difficult barriers facing disabled people wishing to enter the teaching profession. Other major barriers include inaccessible teacher training colleges and discriminatory attitudes on the part of non-disabled teachers. At present less than one in 100 teachers is a disabled person, and if teaching were barrier-free the figure could be comparable with the number of disabled people in the population as a whole, namely one in ten (NUT, 1991).

The extent of institutional discrimination within the mainstream sector adds weight to those who would argue for the maintenance and development of segregated provision. For example, the general antipathy toward non-oral communication within British schools poses a particular and serious problem for the deaf community, a community which has a history of able-bodied people attempting to wipe out their language and culture through education, the consequences of which have proved educationally, psychologically and socially disastrous for many deaf people, particularly in their formative years. For deaf people, therefore, integration can represent a return to the oppression of the past (BDA, 1984).

The difficulties and animosity frequently experienced by disabled people within the mainstream sector also fuel the fears of parents of children who are 'safely' settled into special schools. For them the rhetoric of integration could represent nothing more than a politically convenient ploy to reduce public expenditure on an already severely disadvantaged section of the community, which by tradition is 'unable to take care of itself'. Without a firm commitment to eradicate discrimination in all its forms within the mainstream sector from those who are responsible for state education, namely the Government and LEAs, these fears might well be justified.

In addition, it is apparent that whether disabled children attend sheltered or mainstream schools they are less likely to attain the same academic qualifications as their able-bodied peers (see for example Walker, 1982). This is particularly important considering the value placed upon recognised educational success in employment. The serious implications for disabled young people without qualifications are clear, and this situation is particularly alarming when considered alongside the poor quality of careers preparation they receive before leaving school.

In a recent review of research into disabled young adults' preparation for work, which covered studies of provision in both special and mainstream schools, Parker concluded:

> Adequate school leavers' programmes for those with special needs still seem to be the exception rather than the rule. The opinions of both young people and their parents indicate a considerable gap in preparation for life beyond school. Young people with disabilities, especially when they are physical, are less likely to be placed in work experience schemes than other pupils (Parker, 1984, p. 71).

There has been no subsequent research published to dispute this view. It is not surprising then that an increasing number of disabled young people continue their education after the age of sixteen.

Further Education. As the statutory school-leaving date approaches, young people with impairments are confronted with a combination of three alternatives, apart from unemployment: open or sheltered employment (the former refers to jobs which are open to all, the latter to work in sheltered or protected workshops where the overwhelming majority of employees are disabled people — see Chapter 4); some form of further or higher education; or placement in a day centre, adult training centre (ATC), or residential home or hospital which frequently incorporates an element of further education (FE) or training.

Finding paid work is the preferred option for all young people; an influential DES survey (1983) of the views of young people found that employment was seen as the principal definition of adulthood and that getting a job was a goal all were striving for. However, successive studies have shown that it is an option frequently denied to disabled school-leavers (see for example Brimblecombe *et al.*, 1985; Hirst, 1984, 1987; Kuh *et al.*, 1988; Walker, 1982). Further education is therefore often presented as an appropriate alternative.

Unfortunately much of what passes for FE for disabled young people is simply a continuation of what is available at the primary and secondary levels, and consequently similar criticisms apply. Most of it is segregative, accommodating only those with SEN. There is a general tendency for courses in this area to concentrate on life and leisure skills rather than academic subjects or employment training. And the majority of mainstream colleges and universities are inaccessible to students with impairments, and many are unable or unwilling to provide the necessary support services to make them accessible.

Although tertiary provision for students with SEN varies according to region, it generally comes in a variety of different forms. There are, for example, school/college link courses, day centre link courses, outreach courses, transition courses, Youth Training programmes (YT), special courses and some provision in the mainstream sector. Funding for FE can come from a number of sources, including DES, the Department of Employment-Training Agency (TA), etc. or voluntary organisations and charities such as the Royal National Institute for the Blind (RNIB) and the Spastics Society. Attendance may be full-time, part-time or residential.

The recent OPCS disability survey estimated that around 78,120 or 3 per cent of disabled people under retirement age were either in FE or in adult training centres (ATCs) (Martin, White and Meltzer, 1989). Being situated in an ATC does not necessarily mean that a person is being educated or trained (see below). The DES collects statistics on FE and higher education (HE), but it does not include data on students with impairments.

However, a national survey of state-sponsored FE and HE colleges conducted by Skill (the National Bureau for Students with Disabilities) suggests that the numbers of people with SEN in post-school education is 43,540. This represents an increase of almost five times since the Warnock Committee reported in 1978 (Stowell, 1987). This stands in marked contrast to the numbers of students in FE generally, where the figure has only risen marginally. In 1978 there were 1,590,779 students in post-school provision while in 1987 there were 1,672,294, an increase of only 81,515 or 4.8 per cent. It is important to note, however, that according to the same source only 3,419 or 7.8 per cent of students termed SEN were being educated in the mainstream sector (see Table 3.4).

Many disabled young people are introduced to the idea of continuing their education after sixteen well before they leave school. Pupils with a statement are subjected to another 'full' assessment by professionals at the age of fourteen (Glendinning, 1989), and the local college of FE as well as the local Social Services Department is informed of their 'special' needs. Moreover, since it is generally agreed by professionals and careers officers that pupils with SEN, particularly those who have only experienced segregated education, are unable to benefit 'immediately' from mainstream courses (Stowell, 1987) these young people are usually directed toward more of the same.

Some pupils are, however, encouraged to stay on at school. While

Table 3.4. Numbers of Students with Special Educational Needs
in Further Education

Type of Course	Under 19 years of age	Over 19 years of age	Total
School/college link	8,030	386	8,416
Adult/centre link	638	3,204	3,842
Other link	177	76	253
YTS special	3,483	105	3,588
Transition	2,549	591	3,140
Other special	1,981	5,533	7,514
Outreach courses	–	13,405	13,405
Mainstream	1,721	1,698	3,419
Total (*estimates*)	18,579	24,998	43,540

Note: The survey did not ask the age of outreach students but it was assumed that the vast majority were over 19 years old. These estimates do not take account of the 3,700 disabled students in colleges supported by the voluntary sector, nor those in universities.
Source: Adapted from Tables 96 and 97, pp. 95–6, Stowell, 1987.

this has obvious advantages if students are attending a mainstream school and preparing for examinations, there are few, if any, if they are situated in a special school, particularly where it is the only school they have ever been to, and where the school accommodates children from two to nineteen. It does not help them gain the experience necessary for adulthood, but simply serves to reinforce the commonly held belief that people with impairments are immature for their years, that they never grow up, and that they should be treated as 'eternal children'.

In some areas pupils with SEN are encouraged to join school/ college link courses where pupils stay at school but attend a local college for one or two days a week. Many of these courses start when pupils are in the fourth or fifth year. They usually involve further assessments by college staff in order to decide which courses would be the most appropriate. It is significant that large colleges which operate link courses provide a wide variety of courses for SEN, often as part of a package in connection with YTS, outreach, transition, and other special courses. It is estimated that one in four pupils in special schools in the relevant age-range are attending one of these school/college courses. Colleges which provide these facilities tend to specialise in 'low-level' work. Colleges and polytechnics which offer over 25 per cent Advanced Further Education (AFE) courses tend not to operate link courses (Stowell, 1987).

In the absence of link courses, pupils in special education are frequently introduced to the idea of going to a day centre or an adult training centre (ATC). The vast majority of these establishments, however, are highly segregative. Most only cater for people with impairments, the vast majority of whom are elderly. In addition, the activities provided usually revolve around 'leisure' and 'craft'-based skills like basket weaving, or boring repetitive work such as packing screws or rubber bands. Most day placements and services are organised around notions of 'care' rather than user participation and control. They are paternalistic and attendance tends to perpetuate dependence rather than encourage self-reliance (see Barnes, 1990; Kent *et al.*, 1984).

Although day placements are generally unpopular among young disabled people, they are often presented as the only alternative to doing nothing. It is often pointed out, for example, that the intense competition for places may mean that a vacancy might not be available later, perhaps when the potential user has completed FE. As an added 'attraction' many day centres and ATCs now run FE classes in conjunction with local colleges. These can be referred to as adult centre link or outreach courses. The former are courses where the student is registered in a day unit but attends a college for a specified period during the week, and with the latter FE teachers hold classes within the centre. Again the colleges which tend to run these courses are those which are the main providers of services for SEN. And the curriculum and course content is generally the same as on other special courses; they specialise in 'social training' and 'education' programmes including 'general life skills', adult literacy, leisure pursuits — art, pottery, dressmaking — and specialist disability skills such as lip-reading and braille (Stowell, 1987).

Youth Training (YT) programmes — referred to as Youth Training Schemes (YTS) until May 1990 (DE, 1990) — are said to offer opportunities for training, vocational education and work experience for 'all' young people, but these opportunities are somewhat limited for disabled school-leavers. Their avowed aim is to help young people acquire and develop specific job skills leading to a qualification recognised by potential employers. They are run by the TA and organised locally by local colleges of FE, LEAs, voluntary organisations and private employers, hence provision is subject to much regional variation. Although all young people aged sixteen or seventeen are eligible for places on YT courses, this does not apply to young people with impairments, who can be denied places on the grounds that they are unlikely to find employment.

Moreover, while able-bodied sixteen- and seventeen-year-olds have two years and one year on YT schemes respectively, disabled young people considered fit for work are allowed to join up to the age of twenty-one. They can also stay on the course for the full two years, 'because of their impairment' (Glendinning, 1989). They may also receive up to six months extra tuition, which can include a period of initial training before the full YT programme begins (Cooper, 1989).

Although these extra facilities are presented as positive or affirmative action, they re-emphasise difference and encourage negative attitudes, because they are available only to disabled young people, not only in the minds of able-bodied tutors and students, but most importantly in those of potential employers. Without the appropriate legislative support to ensure open employment for disabled people, these and similar policies simply endorse the traditional view that they are an employment liability rather than an asset. Indeed, although the Skill survey only collected data on college-based YTS courses, it showed that a mere 278 students with SEN were on mainstream courses (Stowell, 1987).

Since it has not been considered possible or 'desirable' to train students with impairments on mainstream YTS programmes, 'special' YTS schemes have been created. However, the colleges operating these schemes are by and large the same ones that are providing other forms of SEN provision. Special YTS courses therefore form part of a package of other special courses. The large majority of trainees on these courses, 77 per cent, were on college-based courses with little or no work experience other than in college workshops (Stowell, 1987). Such practices are unlikely to provide these young people with the appropriate experience to find work in open employment.

There are a variety of 'special' courses in FE, some part-time, some full-time and others residential. Part-time courses are those on which attendance is less than 21 hours a week. They are popular among students with SEN and their families because they allow the students to attend college without jeopardising their state benefits. If students attend college full-time, i.e. for over 21 hours, then they forfeit their right to certain state welfare payments such as income support. Since many students and their families are wholly dependent upon these payments for their livelihood, this policy acts as a powerful incentive for young people not to take up full-time education, although it might be in their best interest to do so.

Courses specifically for students with SEN come under a variety of headings, for example 'Foundation Course', 'Bridging Course', 'Foundation Workshop', 'Preparation for Work'. Despite this apparent diversity, however, their content is usually the same as that mentioned above, although in most colleges 'computing skills' has recently been added to the list. Although many of these are described as transition courses and claim to prepare students for open employment or mainstream FE, there is no substantial evidence to show that they achieve these goals. After completing these courses many students find themselves in sheltered employment, day centres or adult training centres. Part of the reason for this situation lies in the fact that, on the whole, people with SEN are not welcome within mainstream FE. Students with SEN are often directed into special courses in residential colleges because they are not provided in local colleges.

Despite the recommendations of the Warnock Committee (1978) that all colleges of FE and HE should have and should publish a policy on the admission of students with SEN, fewer than one in five have a formal policy. Those that have tend to be the major providers for SEN (Stowell, 1987). As a result, support — whether it be human, financial or in the form of equipment — tends to be uneven and provided on an *ad hoc* basis. On the whole, colleges do not feel it is their responsibility to provide this support. It has recently been shown that most establishments believe that extra provision should come from government resources or a combination of such funding and the student's own disability allowances (Smith, 1990).

The recent Skill survey reported that less than 25 per cent of the colleges sampled could claim that they were supporting visually impaired students on mainstream courses, less than a third provided assistance to hearing-impaired students, only 21 per cent supported students with learning difficulties, and fewer than one in seven provided help for students with behavioural or emotional difficulties. Whilst a quarter said that they supported students with physical impairments, this support was limited. The same number said that they had only 'part' of their college buildings adapted for students with physical impairments. Less than a third were able to offer physical access in all their teaching blocks, almost half of which were deemed inaccessible. And more than one in five stated that they might have to reject a student 'with a physical handicap' because of poor access or inadequate support (Stowell, 1987). A more recent survey of polytechnics and universities in the whole of Britain drew similar conclusions. Indeed, in these establishments disabled students only constituted 0.3 per cent of the entire student population (Smith, 1990).

Several colleges and universities are clearly opposed to the idea of admitting disabled people, and regularly confront intending students with various objections of a dubious nature. Disabled people are refused admission on the grounds that they are a fire risk, or they are told that attendance is possible only if they agree to be accompanied at all times by a responsible able-bodied adult such as a parent or a personal assistant. It is not uncommon for establishments to discriminate openly on the grounds that they do not provide facilities for disabled people. Only recently a well-established Scottish university refused entry to a potential social science student because she was a wheelchair user; it acknowledged that she had the appropriate entry qualifications, but was unwilling to make facilities accessible for her wheelchair (Macgee, 1990).

Since many colleges and universities do not provide the appropriate support for people with impairments on mainstream courses, disabled students intending to take up this option have to provide that support themselves. Educational support of whatever form is generally expensive, and this alone is enough to deter many disabled people from going to college. However, those on AFE courses are entitled to some financial help through the Disabled Students' Allowance (DSA), and two new allowances introduced in March 1990 specifically for this purpose (see Cooper, 1990). Since a full academic year in which the new benefits were available to disabled students had not elapsed by the time of writing, it is impossible to say whether they have proved adequate. However, the DSA has hitherto proved 'woefully inadequate'.

In common with other student allowances, the DSA is paid by LEAs under guide-lines drawn up by the DES. These leave much to the discretion of individual LEAs, which means that claiming is often a difficult and long-drawn-out process with no guarantee of support at the end of it. Students and their families have difficulties in obtaining the grant because of the necessity to provide evidence of financial need and impairment before even the minimum payment is made. As with all mandatory student awards the size of the grant is dependent upon the size of the family income, and is therefore not available to students whose parents or partner are relatively well off, when they are expected to meet the cost of support (Patton, 1990). Also, because the DSA is only available to people on advanced courses, the vast majority of disabled students do not get financial help for educational support unless they look to the voluntary sector.

In British society to seek help from charities carries with it a considerable stigma. In addition, when applying for assistance in this way disabled people are usually confronted with similar problems to those described above. Eligibility has to be proved, provision is not a foregone conclusion, and getting it usually takes time. Given these considerations, many disabled people choose not to look to the voluntary sector for support. Also, providing disabled individuals with funding for support from whatever source, although vital, does not prevent institutionalised discrimination within FE, or eradicate the ignorance surrounding disability among those who provide it.

There is little understanding of the problems faced by students with SEN among teaching staff in colleges of FE and HE. Indeed, they are less likely to have experience of working with people with impairments than their colleagues in the primary and secondary sectors. Teachers in tertiary education, whatever their level, are not required to have a formal teaching qualification, and many enter the profession straight from industry, commerce or university. Nor is teaching special needs an essential component of teacher training courses geared toward FE. In addition, specialising in SEN at this level is traditionally regarded as a low-status occupation.

This is clearly reflected in the Burnham Regulations on teachers' pay, which until 1987 were used to set the levels at which teachers in FE were paid. Those who concentrated on special needs were paid at Grade V, the lowest grade on the scale. This is in marked contrast to teachers who teach special needs in schools, who are generally paid an additional allowance for this type of work.

There is also a general absence of non-teaching staff with experience of SEN in mainstream further education. Just over a third of the colleges in the Skill survey reported employing non-teaching staff expert in this area. Many of these were medical staff or clerical workers (Stowell, 1987).

In view of this situation there is a growing tendency for colleges to run in-house development courses on SEN, or to send staff on short external courses which deal with this issue. The prime providers of these courses are the DES, HMI and Skill. There is also a City and Guilds course titled 'The Teaching of The Handicapped in FE' (731–4), which some staff are encouraged to take. In the main, however, each of these schemes adheres to the traditional individualistic medical model of disability discussed earlier, and hence is unlikely to change the prejudices and perceptions of those who attend them.

In the final analysis, while it is often said that post-school education enhances social and work skills and improves the probability of employment, this is not generally so for young people with impairments. There is no evidence of any substance to show that the kind of FE that the vast majority of disabled young people receive does anything other than prepare them for a life of under-employment and/or unemployment, and a disproportionate — and unnecessary — dependence on others.

Conclusion

From the outset the mainstream education system was not constructed for disabled people with 'special educational needs'. Indeed, after over a century of largely state-sponsored education, they are still not legally entitled to the same education as their non-disabled peers.

Although education in its present form is socially divisive and highly discriminatory for all pupils and students, it is especially so for those with impairments. Historically they have been marked out for a particular form of 'special' educational provision which in general is both socially and educationally inferior. Clearly, traditional attitudes toward the education of disabled children and young people have hardly been challenged by recent events. Despite much rhetoric to the contrary put forward by those responsible for providing education, the data show that the impetus toward integration has been only slight. Moreover, what little progress has been made is now under serious threat of reversal due to the introduction of the 1988 Education Reform Act.

The evidence shows that the environmental, attitudinal and educational barriers which prevent disabled pupils' and students' successful integration into mainstream provision remain largely intact, hence segregated 'special' education continues to thrive at every level and is likely to do so in the future. This is despite the fact that it is one of

> the main channels for disseminating able-bodied/minded perceptions of the world and ensuring that disabled school leavers are socially immature and isolated. This isolation results in passive acceptance of social discrimination, lack of skills in facing the tasks of adulthood and ignorance about the main social issues of our time. All this reinforces the 'eternal children' myth and ensures at the same time that disabled school leavers lack the skills for overcoming the myth (BCODP, 1986, p. 6).

By producing socially and educationally disabled individuals, the 'special' education system perpetuates and legitimates discriminatory practices in all other areas of social life, particularly employment. Therefore, if institutional discrimination against disabled people throughout British society is to be eliminated, this system must be eliminated also.

4

EMPLOYMENT

It was noted in the last chapter that paid employment is widely recognised as a major signifier of adulthood. Indeed, work is central to our society, not simply because it produces the commodities which are necessary for survival but also because it has a profound influence on human relationships. People are categorised through work in terms of class, status and influence. Apart from income, work provides a sense of identity and self esteem, opportunities for social contacts outside the family home, skill development and creativity, as well as a sense of time, obligation and control (Fagin and Little, 1984). The economic, social and psychological implications for people who are excluded from the workplace are clear. The majority of disabled people have been denied access to the workplace since the industrial revolution.

Prior to industrialisation most disabled people were able to make an economic contribution to the life of the community because of the nature of work and the way it was organised. With the coming of the urban factory-based system, however, the nature of work changed and as a result disabled people were excluded from the workplace. A group who were once economically productive suddenly became economically unproductive and dependent. Disabled people were systematically removed from the community and put into workhouses or other 'residential' settings. While the wholesale incarceration of disabled people has largely disappeared, the attitudes which stimulated it persist, particularly in relation to work. Disabled people are still denied access to meaningful employment because of their supposed inabilities.

This chapter is divided into three main sections. The first provides substantial quantitative evidence of institutional discrimination against disabled people in employment. The second examines the main factors which cause that discrimination. And the third evaluates Government policies concerned with the creation of employment opportunities for disabled people, in particular, strategies of enforcement and persuasion, and employment services for disabled people.

Evidence of Institutional Discrimination in the Labour Market

Unemployment. There is little dispute that disabled people are more likely to be out of work than their able-bodied contemporaries. In the mid-1960s, for example, the general unemployment rate was well below 2 per cent whilst among disabled people it was over 7 per cent. Until the mid-1970s disabled workers were three times more likely to be out of work than their able-bodied counterparts. In the early 1980s the gap narrowed somewhat not because unemployment among disabled people declined but because of the rise in unemployment generally. In 1982 it was estimated that the general unemployment rate was 12 per cent and 16 per cent for disabled workers (Grover and Gladstone, 1982).

The newly-published 'Employment and Training for People with Disabilities' (DE, 1990) suggests that up-to-date comparisons are difficult because current unemployment figures include only people available and looking for work, and the more recent estimates of unemployed disabled people incorporate those who want work, but are not actually looking for it. However, the same source notes:

> It is clear that the chances of someone with a disability being unemployed are significantly higher than someone without a disability. The 1989 EC Labour Force Survey puts the rates at 20.5% and 5.4% respectively (DE, 1990, p. 13).

The most recent official assessments suggest that 3.8 per cent (1,272,000) of the working-age population, 16–65 for men and 16–60 for women, termed 'economically active', that is in work or seeking it, are 'occupationally handicapped', the current term used to describe people who encounter institutional discrimination in the workplace. Of these 22 per cent (285,000) are unemployed and want a job (DE, 1990). However, these estimates do not take into account the 84,400 disabled people of working age living in residential establishments (Martin, White and Meltzer, 1989). Nor do they include those disabled people who would be termed 'discouraged workers'.

As noted earlier the phrase 'economically active' usually means in work or looking for it; it does not include people who choose not to work, or who do not have to work. Disabled people are far more likely than non-disabled people to be in one of these two categories. This is because the majority of individuals with impairments are only too aware of the obstacles facing them in their search for work, as well as the type of low-grade jobs they are likely to find in the modern labour market (see for example Morris, 1989, 1990; Oliver *et al.*, 1988; Thomas, 1982; Walker 1982). Disabled people are also aware of the economic and social pressures placed upon them not to look for work.

Recently researchers have acknowledged the difficulties encountered by disabled people in the search for jobs, and extended the concept 'economically active' to include people who want work but are not 'actually seeking it' (Prescott Clarke, 1990; Martin, White and Meltzer, 1989). This does not account for that group of people referred to immediately above. The OPCS surveys, for example, found that 85 per cent of the men and 65 per cent of the women who were not looking for work and who defined themselves as 'unable to work' had previously taken steps to find work but given up (Martin, White and Meltzer, 1989, p. 68).

There is also evidence that at every age disabled people are likely to experience unemployment for considerably longer periods than others. In 1982 it was reported that three times as many disabled people as able-bodied people were unemployed for more than two years. This trend has persisted throughout the 1980s (Lonsdale, 1986; *Hansard*, 1989; DE, 1990), and people who are born with an impairment are less likely to be in work than those who acquire impairments later in life. A succession of studies since the mid-1970s have found that unemployment among disabled school-leavers is disproportionately high in comparison with their able-bodied equivalents (see for example Walker, 1982; Hirst, 1987; Kuh *et al.*, 1988).

Additionally, the recently-published Government-sponsored Social and Community Planning Research (SCPR) study noted that a higher proportion of disabled people without employment had been born with an impairment (Prescott Clarke, 1990). At the other end of the age range disabled workers are far more likely than their able-bodied counterparts to withdraw early from work (Glendinning, 1990). The OPCS survey found that 31 per cent of disabled men and 16 per cent of disabled women 'retired' early (Martin, White and Meltzer, 1989).

Direct Discrimination.   There is substantial quantitative evidence to show that employers discriminate against applicants with impairments looking for work. For example, a recent survey of the employment policies of Regional and District Health Authorities demonstrated that almost a third of the twenty-six Authorities sampled chose not to employ disabled people. They claimed that disabled workers were not employed because they could not fulfil the employment criteria necessary for work in the health service. These criteria included lifting of patients and general heavy work, the need for a professional qualification or 'a range of physical and intellectual skills', and the need for staff to be medically and/or scientifically trained 'in addition to having all their faculties'. It is notable that many disabled people are capable of lifting and heavy work generally, some have qualifications in nursing, accounting and general administration, and others are in full possession of all their faculties (Dyer, 1990).

Two studies published by the Spastics Society found similar results in the private sector. Using scientifically approved techniques similar to those used to measure racial discrimination; research carried out by Fry (1986) and Graham, Jordan and Lamb (1990) has established conclusively that employers discriminate directly against disabled people at the initial point of applying for a job. Discrimination was measured by examining employers' responses to two fictitious applications, which differed only in that one purported to be from a disabled applicant and the other was not. The applications were sent in response to 152 job applications in the first study and 197 in the second. The second survey was controlled in order to account for changes in the employment market during the period between the two studies, in particular the relative decline in unemployment generally and the increase in job vacancies. It showed that the level of discrimination encountered by disabled people remains virtually unchanged; almost identical results were achieved. Able-bodied applicants were around 1.5 times more likely to receive a positive response to an application than were applicants with an impairment, and a disabled candidate was six times more likely to receive a negative response (Graham *et al.*, 1990, p. 5).

Underemployment. When disabled people do find work the majority find themselves in poorly-paid, low-skilled, low-status jobs which are both unrewarding and undemanding — the type of work which has been termed 'underemployment' (Walker, 1982; Thomas, 1982). Social analysts who have looked at the labour market in relation to other forms of employment disadvantage such as race and gender have developed what is termed the dual labour market theory. This is where the labour force is divided into two sections referred to as the primary and the secondary sectors. Primary sector jobs are those with high wages, high skill levels, good working conditions, job security and ample opportunities for promotion; examples include lawyers, doctors and engineers. Secondary sector jobs are those with low wages, low skill levels, poor working conditions, little job security, and few if any possibilities for promotion and advancement. Routine office work, general

Table 4.1. Comparison of Occupations of Disabled and Non-
             Disabled Workers

Type of Work	Disabled workers			Non-disabled workers		
	Men %	Women %	All %	Men %	Women %	All %
Professional or managerial	15	8	12	30	11	21
Other non-manual	19	44	30	17	53	33
Skilled manual	37	10	26	38	8	25
Semi-skilled or personal service	21	30	25	13	20	16
Unskilled manual	5	7	6	3	7	5

Source: Adapted from Prescott Clarke, 1990, p. 34.

labourers, catering jobs and cleaners would fall into this category (McCrudden, 1982).

In 1982 Walker found that the overwhelming majority of disabled school-leavers 'lucky' enough to find jobs were working in the secondary sector (Walker, 1982). There is substantial evidence that this is so for the vast majority of disabled workers of all ages. For example, the SCPR survey found that considerably greater numbers of disabled workers work in semi-skilled jobs than is the case in the working population as a whole and considerably fewer are in professional or managerial posts. Compared with able-bodied male workers, only half as many disabled men are in professional or managerial jobs. For women the most marked fall is in the number of non-manual jobs, with a correspondingly larger proportion in semi-skilled and personal service jobs. There is a heavy concentration of disabled women in two sorts of occupation, namely routine clerical work and the service sector, notably cleaning and catering. Table 4.1 compares the type of work done by disabled workers with that done by non-disabled workers.

It has been shown that advancement in many organisations is determined by the original entry job (McCrudden, 1982). In the Civil Service, for example, only university graduates occupy the top jobs. Research on the employment of disabled people in the Civil Service by Greville Janner MP (a member of the Select Committee on Employment) has shown that there are no disabled people employed in the highest grade of the service, and none in the top seven grades of the eight Departments (Janner, 1990 quoted in Graham *et al.*, 1990).

Although this unequal division of labour is prevalent through-out industry as a whole it is also true of most of the organisations claiming to specialise in the affairs of disabled people, not only in the public sector (see below) but also in voluntary agencies. For example, Outset is a national charity which was set up in 1970 to 'improve the quality of life of disabled people' (Mainstream, 1990, p. 54). A major part of Outset's work is concerned with employ-ment, yet the majority of its senior staff are able-bodied people (Hurst, 1990).

Table 4.2. Comparison of Gross Weekly Wages of Disabled and Non-Disabled Males in Full-Time Employment

Weekly gross pay	1989 SCPR Survey %	1989 New Earnings Survey %
Under 100	13	2
100–149	25	12
150–199	25	21
200–249	16	21
200–299	10	16
300–399	7	17
400–599	3	9
600 or more	2	3

Source: Adapted from Table 9.3 in Prescott Clarke, 1990, p. 88.

In terms of earnings generally, disabled workers earn much less than their able-bodied counterparts. A comparison of the weekly earnings of disabled men in full-time employment (31 or more hours per week) with those of their non-disabled colleagues, taken from the SCPR study and the 1989 New Earnings Survey, shows that the wages of the former are much lower than those of the latter. On average disabled men in full-time work earn almost a quarter less per week than their able-bodied equivalents. On average disabled men earn £150–£199 per week before deductions for tax and so on, whilst the corresponding figure for non-disabled male workers is £200–£249 (see Table 4.2).

The SCPR study did not collect information on the gross weekly earnings of disabled women workers. There is, however, evidence that in line with the disparity in earnings in the working population as a whole disabled women are paid less than disabled men. The recent OPCS studies, for example, showed that disabled women workers earned almost a third less per week than their male equiv-alents (Martin and White, 1988).

It cannot be argued that the different wage levels paid to disabled and non-disabled workers is due to the former working fewer hours than the latter. The SCPR study found that the majority of employed disabled people worked a full 5-day week and a 7- or 8-hour day. Part-time work accounted for only a quarter of those with jobs, but of a much higher proportion of women (46 per cent) than men (9 per cent). About a quarter worked regular overtime, averaging 45 or more hours a week (Prescott Clarke, 1990).

Table 4.3.   Comparison of Hourly Pay of Disabled and Non-Disabled Workers, 1985

Type of work (full-time)		Disabled workers	Able-bodied workers	Disabled workers' pay as % of able-bodied workers' pay
Men	Non-Manual	4.80	5.70	84
	Manual	3.20	3.60	90
	All	3.80	4.50	84
Women	Non-Manual	3.40	3.60	94
	Manual	2.40	2.50	96
	All	3.40	3.30	91

Source: Adapted from Table 3.1 in Martin and White, 1988, p. 17.

It has been shown that when the hourly rates of pay of workers with impairments are compared with those of workers without impairments the disparity persists, although it is less significant in relation to the difference between disabled and non-disabled women (see Table 4.3). While this might imply that disabled women fare better than disabled men in employment, women generally are at a disadvantage within the British labour market, particularly in terms of pay (Lonsdale, 1986).

Assessment, Rehabilitation and Training.   The Tomlinson Committee laid the foundation for rehabilitation for employment. It was for people whose impairments were physical and recently acquired, and who were just out of a course of medical treatment. This meant the provision of special centres in which facilities to assist 'full recovery to physical fitness' were to be provided. These facilities included fresh air, good food, physical training and exercises 'together with a limited amount of useful occupation' (Tomlinson Committee, 1943, para 43). Little attention was paid to people born with impairments, or those with experience of mental illness. During the early 1980s, however, the idea of employment 'rehabilitation' was extended to all the long-term unemployed, regardless of impairment (Lonsdale, 1986).

Although the early Employment Rehabilitation Centres (ERCs) set about training people for low-skilled manual work, in recent years this appears to have given way to a more medically-based approach, thus reinforcing the traditional assumptions surrounding disability. The first ERC opened in 1943. There are now twenty-six throughout Britain. Originally equipped along factory lines, they obtained low-skilled production work from local firms or Government departments. Users were taught manual work and low-status occupations, hence this service perpetuated the traditional pattern of disabled people's employment. However, the amount of contract work declined during the 1980s (Lonsdale, 1986).

In addition to ERCs there are now five Asset centres. These were set up in 1982 to provide assessment and rehabilitation services in areas where there were no ERCs. Unlike ERCs, Asset centres do not have in-house workshops (DE, 1990). Today, the function of both ERCs and Asset centres is to assess the individual's physical and psychological capacity in relation to the needs of the workplace, and provide her/him with the 'appropriate' skills to find work. To achieve this, both ERCs and Asset centres employ 'specialist' staff such as instructors, social workers and psychiatrists. They also have access to the Health and Safety Executive's employment medical advisers and nurses 'who play a vital role in their operations' (DE, 1990).

Another recent but significant development in the Employment Resettlement Service (ERS) is the greater involvement by the voluntary sector. Government initiatives since 1981 have encouraged the voluntary agencies to provide rehabilitation and support in ERCs and Asset centres. In 1990/1 it is expected that of the 15,250 courses of rehabilitation, about 4,500 will be provided by these organisations. The Government has called for a further shift in the balance of the rehabilitation programme toward these agencies (DE, 1990).

By coincidence, the ERS is now run by the DE's Training Agency rather than the Disablement Resettlement Service (DRS) or the Disability Advisory Service (DAS), despite publicly expressed reservations from the Public Accounts Committee about the lack of a unified service for disabled people. In addition, it has trebled the number of people it attempts to see by reducing the time spent on assessment from 2–8 weeks to an average total of ten hours. It is also claimed that staff shortages have led to non-qualified personnel conducting these assessments (Graham *et al.*, 1990).

Moreover, recent data show that assessment and rehabilitation do not necessarily lead to employment. In 1989/90, for example, about half of the 25,000 people for whom the service provided assessments and 'guidance' did not move on to employment, but proceeded to a 'further period of rehabilitation' (DE, 1990, p. 26).

Although it is intended that the number of ERCs be reduced, the facilities for assessment are to be expanded. The number of ERCs that remain (the number is still unspecified) will focus on developing what are termed 'new techniques of employment rehabilitation and assessment' and will also assist where appropriate in the training of staff. They will provide services to a number of 'clients' and, by doing so, be able to adopt a 'teaching hospital role' (DE, 1990, p. 21). Based on past experience, it is highly unlikely that these developments will improve disabled people's employment prospects.

Adult Training Centres.   Adult Training Centres (ATCs) are another form of employment-training service run by local authorities and voluntary organisations. They cater mostly for people with learning difficulties. In the mid-1980s it was estimated that there were 45,000 people attending 480 centres up and down the country (Lonsdale, 1986). Indeed, the majority of young people with learning difficulties are placed in ATCs by professionals as soon as they leave school (Hirst, 1987).

Originally it was intended that the function of ATCs would be to train disabled people for employment. It is evident, however, that in practice little training takes place in ATCs and there is virtually no movement into other forms of employment. One study estimated that only about 4 per cent of ATC trainees found work elsewhere each year, despite staff estimates that approximately 37 per cent were eligible for open or sheltered employment (Whelan and Speake, 1977).

Although initially concerned with the training of 'craft' skills, ATCs began to take on contract work during the 1960s, work which was considered both repetitious and monotonous. In return workers were paid appallingly low wages. Faced by an acute shortage of work during the 1970s, centre managers began to take on subcontract work at unrealistically low prices. Since there is no statutory requirement on ATCs to pay their employees/trainees, many centres encouraged users to take up social security benefits instead. The limit on disregarded earnings (after which deductions are made on benefits) acts as a disincentive to increase wages beyond this point. One early study noted that only 1 per cent of trainees earned more than the then earnings limit. Fifty per cent earned less than half, and 3 per cent were not paid at all (Whelan and Speake, 1977). Other evidence indicates that ATC workers work an average of 30–39 hours per week (Walker, 1982).

It is clear that training has been superseded by exploitation. This was recognised by the National Development Group for the Mentally Handicapped, who in 1977 recommended a comprehensive programme of reform for ATCs. These recommendations were ignored, the group was disbanded (Lonsdale, 1986) and the exploitation continues. A recent study, for example, noted that although the earnings disregard was raised from £4 to £15 in 1988, most people who work in ATCs received only a small increase in pay, if any at all (*Same Difference*, 1989).

Institutionally Secured Employment. There are two forms of institutionally secured employment; both were provided for under the 1944 legislation. These are designated employment and sheltered workshops. Only two specific occupations were designated for disabled people under the Act, namely car park attendant and lift operator. People in these jobs could not be counted against an employer's quota (see below). This policy has attracted criticism because both occupations are of low status and poorly paid (Lonsdale, 1990).

Sheltered Workshops. Depending upon medically-based functional assessments, disabled people can be registered for employment under one of two categories. Section 1 indicates that individuals are suitable for 'open' or mainstream employment, and Section 2 indicates that they are not. It is a rigid arrangement which takes no account whatsoever of the fluctuating nature of impairment, or the social or environmental consequences of disability. Additionally, it has been shown that the categorisation process is applied arbitrarily. Disablement Resettlement Officers (DROs) are responsible for deciding which category an individual should be listed under. They receive no training for this task, and there is a general consensus that most decisions are based on DROs' personal opinions and experience (Mainstream, 1990).

Originally envisaged as providing a 'bridging experience' to mainstream employment, the foundations of sheltered employment were laid in Section 15 of the 1944 Act. This enabled the setting up of sheltered workshops which would be run as non-profit-making companies subsidised by public funds (Lonsdale, 1986). Sheltered employment schemes were set up to cater for people who had 'severe' impairments (people categorised as Section 2), who were considered unable to obtain or keep mainstream employment.

Under the 1944 Act sheltered employment is provided by local authorities, voluntary organisations and a non-profit-making Government-sponsored company set up in 1945, originally known as the Disabled Persons Employment Corporation Limited but later renamed Remploy. Approximately 14,000 disabled people were working in sheltered workshops in 1989, the majority of whom, around 9,000, worked for Remploy (DE, 1990).

Remploy is a large organisation operating through ninety-three factories. It has a head office in London employing specialists in marketing, finance, personal planning, training and public relations. The Secretary of State for Employment appoints the Chairperson and the Directors of the company, and the DE lays down broad guide-lines on how the company should be run. It is notable that most of the 20 per cent of the Remploy personnel who hold management posts are not disabled people (Dutton *et al.*, 1989).

The average weekly wage of workers on the shop floor at Remploy in 1989 was around £90 per week (*Hansard*, 1989); figures for 1987 show that workers in the local authority workshops earned slightly less than Remploy employees (Dutton *et al.*, 1989). According to the Government's own estimates the average weekly wage for able-bodied workers during the same period stood at between £200 and £249 (Prescott Clarke, 1990). Family Credit, a Government means-tested benefit paid to people with families on low wages who are considered to be living in poverty, starts at £110 per week. People who work in sheltered workshops are some of the poorest wage-earners in the country (*Hansard*, 1989).

Remploy has a diverse range of businesses including furniture-making, bedding, knitwear, packaging and assembly work. Some products are manufactured under the company's own label, but it also completes contract work from Government departments. Remploy's total income from annual sales is not enough to cover its total costs. The DE makes an annual grant to meet the operating deficit and provides loans to finance the purchase of assets (Dutton *et al.*, 1989).

Local authorities were empowered under the Disabled Persons (Employment) Act 1958 to provide sheltered employment for 'severely' disabled people in their area. The cost of local authority workshops is met partly by revenue from the Community Charge and Government grants. The DE pays grants to cover the losses, provides funds for capital expenditure on sheltered employment facilities, and meets the wage costs of trainees in workshops and any other training costs incurred (Dutton *et al.*, 1989).

Sheltered workshops are also provided by voluntary organisations such as Mencap and the Spastics Society. The DE pays grants toward the losses incurred by voluntary agency-run workshops and this covers 100 per cent of the deficit, subject to a *per capita* ceiling. Capital grants and training wages and fees are paid in the same way as they are in the local authority workshops. Some voluntary bodies provide facilities as agents of local authorities, and in these cases the main grant is paid to the local authority concerned, but the DE training and capital grants are paid direct to the voluntary agency (Dutton *et al.*, 1989).

In 1987/8 the average gross cost per person in sheltered workshops was estimated at £6,268 for Remploy employees, £6,446 for local authority workers, and £4,967 for people who worked in workshops run by voluntary agencies. However, the net cost of sheltered workshops is reduced dramatically when the flowback into the Exchequer from taxation, National Insurance payments and savings in social security payments is taken into account. A recent analysis by the DE Research Division which compares the net expenditure and flowback from the sheltered employment programme for 1987/8 suggests that the net costs are considerably less, standing at £2,600 for Remploy workers, £3,300 for local authority employees, and £390 for people who work in workshops run by voluntary bodies (Dutton *et al.*, 1989).

Until the late 1970s the role of sheltered workshops was widely regarded as humanitarian rather than economic. The 1944 and 1958 legislation, the phrase 'sheltered workshops', and their administrative position — local authority and voluntary body workshops are run by the Social Services Committees of the local authority in association with the DE — all endorse the notion that sheltered workshops are a charitable concern rather than a commercial enterprise. This was officially reaffirmed in 1973 when a major review of sheltered employment stated that their primary function was social rather economic (Lonsdale, 1986).

Since the mid-1970s, however, concern has been expressed over the amount of money spent on sheltered workshops, and there have been increasing demands for them to become more cost-effective. In 1983 Remploy was asked by the DE to produce a business plan with a view to eliminating their trading deficit, so that the Government grant did not exceed the wages bill for the disabled workforce. This they achieved in 1986/7. This effectively signalled the end of any pretence that sheltered workshops were to provide a gateway to mainstream employment. Economic pressure encourages management to discourage competent disabled workers from moving elsewhere. In the following year the Public Accounts Committee expressed concern over the company's lack of accountability (Mainstream, 1990).

Considering the constraints under which sheltered workshops operate, it is highly doubtful whether these objectives can be achieved. The distribution of provision has developed haphazardly, and largely in response to paternalistic rather than commercial considerations. Remploy factories, for example, were established in response to political rather than economic criteria, with the result that workshops were set up in unsuitable premises and locations. Consequently their profitability varies considerably. There are also wide differences in the way in which workshops are managed. Although the DE has a degree of influence over how Remploy is run, this is not necessarily so with regard to workshops operated by local authorities and voluntary agencies (DE, 1990).

Moreover, it has long been argued that the economic viability of sheltered workshops could be greatly improved by harnessing the enormous purchasing power of local and central Government. For example, the National Advisory Council for the Employment of Disabled People (NACEDP), set up in 1944 to advise Government on disabled people's employment, suggested that Government purchasers should give preference to sheltered workshops when placing contracts. Their report to the DE in 1977 pointed out that the amount of public sector business received by sheltered workshops was extremely low. It seems, however, that subsequent administrations have chosen to ignore this advice. In the mid-1980s Lonsdale reported that Government purchases amounted to only about 1–2 per cent of the products made in sheltered workshops (Lonsdale, 1986). The advent of widespread privatisation throughout the public sector since then makes it even less likely that this figure will rise in the future (DE, 1990).

Using mainly economic arguments, the DE has recently argued for the systematic run-down of sheltered factories and workshops for disabled people in favour of 'additional sheltered placements' (DE, 1990). While this is to be welcomed if only because the very existence of sheltered workshops might be seen as segregative and discriminatory, it also represents a significant retreat from the idea that disabled people have a legal right to employment, as the following section will show.

The Sheltered Placement Scheme. The Sheltered Placement Scheme (SPS), until April 1985 known as Sheltered Employment Groups, was introduced to provide integrated employment opportunities for disabled people categorised as Section 2 within mainstream employment. The number of people on SPS has grown dramatically since the scheme's introduction; in 1989 there were around 6,500 (DE, 1990). The scheme is presented by the DE as an acceptable and positive alternative to designated and sheltered employment (DE, 1990). Unlike designated employment or sheltered workshops, however, there is no statutory requirement for employers to employ disabled people; it is an entirely voluntary system. The SPS is nothing more than a Subsidised Placement Scheme. The emergence of SPS, therefore, signals a significant retreat from the idea of employment as a right, and a return to the begging bowl.

Under the scheme a sponsor, which may be a local authority or a voluntary agency, employs a disabled person and subcontracts her/him out to a host-company. The host-company provides the work, tools, workplace, training etc., and pays the sponsor. The amount paid by the host-firm is based on the disabled person's output. So, if the disabled worker is assessed as able to produce 50 per cent of an able-bodied worker, the host-firm pays only 50 per cent of her/his wages. The DE will only support disabled workers who are estimated to have between 30–80 per cent of the productive abilities of an able-bodied worker. The sponsor, either the local authority or a voluntary agency, is responsible for paying the disabled person's wages and making deductions for tax and so on. The costs to the sponsor are offset by payment from the host-firm and contributions from the DE (Dutton *et al.*, 1989).

While there are some limited advantages for disabled people from the psychological benefits of work in an integrated setting, there are several major drawbacks to the scheme. First, as noted above, the criteria for registration under Section 1 or 2 is dependent upon the DRO's judgement. The guide-lines for assessment can be interpreted in such a way as to enable less severely disabled applicants, who might be more acceptable to employers and therefore more easily accommodated within the scheme, to become registered. As SPS places are scarce, this can exclude disabled people with less 'acceptable' impairments (*Same Difference*, 1989b).

Secondly, because the disabled person is employed by the sponsor rather than by the host-firm, sponsored workers do not receive the same benefits as their workmates, although they work in the same firm, and might even be doing the same job. They will not, for example, be entitled to the same redundancy packages, sick pay schemes and so on. While there is nothing to stop employers offering sponsored workers the same facilities as other workers, they rarely do (Mainstream, 1990).

Thirdly, there is a limit on the DE's contribution to each SPS place. In 1989 this was set at £2,600 for local authority sponsors and £3,280 for voluntary agencies. This has to cover both wages and national insurance contributions. Hence, SPS is a cheaper alternative to other forms of sheltered employment. It is designed for low-skilled, low-status jobs. Placements are in less well-paid jobs. Since most workers on the SPS are assessed as being able to produce only 50 per cent of an able-bodied worker's output, their average wage cannot go above £6,000 a year (*Same Difference*, 1989b). Employers are able to pay more as workers become more skilled, but this is extremely rare. In general workers on SPS earn less than their peers in Remploy (Dutton *et al.*, 1989).

Fourthly, the official guide-lines suggest that once a worker achieves 80 per cent output they should move out of SPS; in other words the subsidy to the employer stops. Since most employers are unlikely to want to lose this regular source of income, the chances of people moving from SPS to mainstream employment are slim. Indeed, a recent study stated that although SPS is presented as a helpful transition to mainstream employment, few within the DRS expect it to happen. There is no training programme to help people move on from SPS. Instead this is seen as the employer's responsibility (Mainstream, 1990).

The Welfare System.   The long-term consequences of unemployment and/or underemployment are not only economically and socially stigmatising, but also psychologically and physically debilitating. Disabled people frequently face additional cost of living expenses which able-bodied people never encounter. These are for, among other things, extra heating, special foods, special clothing, medication and transport (see Chapter 5). These expenses do not diminish when disabled people find work. This additional financial burden must be seen in relation to income. The combination of disproportionately low wages and the added costs of disability forces a great many disabled people out of the labour market altogether.

A recent Government Report noted that there are many instances where disabled people have found employment and then realised that the money they will earn in wages does not match what they get from state benefits (IFF Research, 1990). Indeed, the welfare system is a major factor in the discriminatory process, but as we shall see in the following chapter, state benefits do not cover the financial cost of impairment. The link between poverty and disability remains unbroken. Moreover, the association between occupational status, psychological disorders and illness generally is well established (Fagin and Little, 1984; Lonsdale, 1986). Significantly, the SCPR study found that there was a much higher incidence of mental illness and health-related problems among disabled people without jobs than there was among those in work (Prescott Clarke, 1990). It is evident that the extent of institutional discrimination within the labour market ensures that the economic and social dependence of disabled people is perpetuated.

Institutional Discrimination in the Labour Market

Employers' Attitudes. There is a substantial amount of data recording the extent of negative and discriminatory attitudes among the general public with regard to disabled people and employment. A recent DE report on Jobclubs for people with impairments, for example, stated:

> Attitudes within the community toward people with disabilities are often such that the disability tends to overshadow the ability of the person. As a result some people find it difficult to obtain jobs which are genuinely suited to their capacities (IFF Research, 1990, p. 45).

There is also evidence from Government sources that these attitudes are particularly prevalent among employers.

Current Government research into the policies and practices of firms on the employment of disabled people (Morrell, 1990) shows that out of a representative sample of 1,160 employers in both the public and private sectors, only 75 per cent of respondents interviewed said that they would not discriminate against disabled people. The most common response recorded was that applications from people with impairments would be 'considered on merit'. The Report also noted that generally interviewees fell into neither the extremely positive nor negative categories, but 'the balance was toward the latter'. Thirteen per cent said that they would only take on disabled workers for certain types of jobs, and 6 per cent said that they would not employ disabled people 'under any circumstances'. Significantly, only 4 per cent said that they would positively encourage applications from disabled people (Morrell, 1990, p. 13).

But we have to remember that there is a world of difference between what people say and what they actually do. Public attitude surveys on sensitive and emotive issues such as discrimination against minority groups are notorious for producing misleading results. Most people, particularly those in positions of authority, are unlikely to admit to a complete stranger that they hold prejudiced and discriminatory attitudes, especially if that stranger is a Government researcher. A recent study of discrimination against disabled people within the workplace has rightly pointed out that surveys of employers' views tend to show a much more positive attitude toward the employment of disabled workers than the true one (Graham *et al.*, 1990).

Considering the high level of disadvantage experienced by disabled people in relation to employment, outlined above, a more realistic impression of employers' perceptions might be gleaned from the following extract from an interview with the senior personnel director of a major national company.

Society is embarrassed and frightened of those people who are 'different', those who have physical disabilities. It's this unease which makes the employment of a disabled person undesirable as their disruptive influence on a team at work can endanger the smooth running and the productivity of the organization as a whole. . . . People work closely in groups and those who are perceived as being different from the norm – in its broadest sense – are a potentially disruptive force on the group. And as any job is critical to the future of the company, a person who disturbs the working environment jeopardises the business (Graham *et al.*, 1990, p. 10).

Although this statement refers specifically to 'physical disabilities', other studies have noted that employers hold similar attitudes toward the employment of people with non-visible impairments such as mental illness (Dyer, 1990) and epilepsy (IFF Research, 1990). The Government-sponsored SCPR study found that at least one disabled worker in ten with a job encountered prejudice and ignorance from the employer (Prescott Clarke, 1990, p. 55).

Other Factors Contributing to the Discriminatory Process.   In general employers legitimise discrimination in a number of ways. DE research has identified several 'problems' which employers claim they face when employing people with impairments. Of 1,160 employers interviewed in the study referred to above, 68 per cent said that the jobs in their firms were unsuitable for disabled people, 61 per cent that there was a lack of disabled applicants, and 52 per cent that their premises were unsuitable. A further 14 per cent mentioned access problems and transport difficulties, 8 per cent spoke of shift work as a problem, and 5 per cent cited 'other' difficulties which were not discussed in detail. Significantly only 9 per cent of the employers sampled felt that employing disabled people would not be a problem (see Table 4.4).

Although 'lack of disabled applicants' can largely be explained by the notion of 'discouraged workers', the other items on this list provide a useful introduction to the barriers facing disabled people in the labour market.

The fact that the majority of employers described most of the work in their establishments as unsuitable for disabled workers, especially in view of what they described as 'vital abilities to do the job', can be seen as a further illustration of the extent of

Table 4.4. Employers' Perceptions of Problems
Faced in Employing Disabled People
(*Sample total: 1,160*)

	%
Unsuitable job types	68
Lack of disabled applicants	61
Unsuitable premises	52
Difficult access/journey to work	14
Shiftworking	8
Other	5
No problem	9

Source: Adapted from Table 20 in Morrell, 1990, p. 14.

employers' biased and discriminatory assumptions. This view was implicitly endorsed by the report's conclusion that 'many of these so-called vital abilities would not stand objective analysis' (Morrell, 1990, p. 23). Since about the beginning of the 1980s, there has been a wealth of published information, much of which has been produced by Government-sponsored agencies and aimed specifically at employers, which shows that the majority of disabled workers are as productive as their able-bodied colleagues (see for example DE, 1988, 1990; Kettle, 1979; Massie and Kettle, 1986; Prescott Clarke, 1990).

Attitudes of Working Colleagues. One of the major factors influencing employers' decisions on disabled people and their suitability for employment is the attitudes and assumptions of able-bodied workers and colleagues. The ability to fit into a team is considered crucial in modern industry and commerce. Department of Employment (DE) research shows that workers without impairments hold broadly similar views to those of employers (Morrell, 1990). It has also been reported that able-bodied workers regularly engage in discriminatory behaviour against disabled workmates. This can range from largely unintentional and unconscious activities which devalue and denigrate people with impairments (Chinnery, 1990) to intimidation and open hostility (Morris, 1990a).

Whilst employers' and able-bodied workers' negative assumptions regarding disabled people and employment can be partly explained by past discrimination and prejudice, they are constantly being reinforced by several factors associated with the labour market which are not directly linked to the work process. Apart from Government policy and employment agencies generally (see below), one of the most important is the medical profession. Doctors are often involved in the employment selection process and in the assessment of abilities after workers have contracted an impairment.

Medical Screening. Although some occupational health experts have expressed scepticism about the value of medical tests in relation to work, a recent survey of nearly 500 employers found that 63 per cent had some form of pre-employment health screening. These tests are normally justified on the grounds that they allow employers to assess an applicant's 'fitness' for the task for which s/he is to be employed (Labour Research, 1990). In other words they allow employers to discriminate, to select workers for a particular work situation. This has significant implications for disabled people.

First, the historical connections between doctors and disabled people have helped to perpetuate the widespread belief that impairment is the same as ill-health. This has particular importance in relation to work, since employers often associate illness with poor performance and excessive absenteeism. As a result they are likely to be wary of employing anyone with a history of illness, and by association anyone with an impairment (DE, 1988). Secondly, since industry and commerce developed largely without disabled workers it follows that the workplace is often not accessible to them. Hence, to employ a disabled person might involve some investment of resources in order to adapt the workplace accordingly. In such situations an able-bodied worker is a more attractive proposition.

A recent study by Labour Research examined the health questions included in fifty job application forms and found a huge variation in the information required. Only fourteen did not ask questions specifically about health. This does not, however, exclude the requirement of a health check at a later stage of the selection process. Four applications studied included comprehensive health questionnaires that were available to the employers' medical officer only. All of these asked for permission to contact the applicant's doctor. Most important, only one of the fifty forms examined stated that a 'health problem or disability would not preclude full consideration for the job' (Labour Research, 1990, p. 16).

Repeatedly, research documenting disabled people's work experiences have shown that medically-based assumptions have been used as a basis for discrimination, both to deny people with impairments access to meaningful employment (Fry 1986; Graham *et al.*, 1990; IFF Research, 1990) and as a reason for dismissal (Martin, White and Meltzer, 1989; Prescott Clarke, 1990).

Education. The idea that disabled people do not have the 'vital' qualities needed for work is also endorsed by the education system. Application forms, aptitude tests, formal and informal interviews and other similar recruitment procedures now used by many employers are all, to varying degrees, dependent upon skills learnt through education. The importance of 'paper qualifications' in relation to finding employment is becoming increasingly important, particularly for young people (Roberts *et al.*, 1986). Significantly, even disabled people with recognised educational qualifications are more likely to have a job than those without (Prescott Clarke, 1990).

As we have seen in the last chapter, the type of education that the majority of disabled children and young people receive does not provide them with the confidence, skills or qualifications necessary to find meaningful employment. Several studies have noted the appalling lack of self-confidence, basic literacy skills and recognised educational achievement among disabled school-leavers looking for work (see for example Barnes, 1990; Walker, 1982).

Although it is known from other sources that a substantial proportion of the workforce also has no qualifications, that proportion is higher among disabled workers. For example, according to the SCPR analysis, the 1986 Labour Force Survey showed that 27 per cent of economically active able-bodied men aged 16–64 and women aged 16–59 had no qualifications. The proportion of disabled workers without qualifications is appreciably higher: 46 per cent (Prescott Clarke, 1990).

Age. Unsuitability for employment can often be determined by age. This can be a major problem for some disabled people looking for work since many are in the older age-groups; the likelihood of impairment increases with age (Martin, Meltzer and Elliot 1988). Many employers refuse to employ workers above or below a specific age. Although 'ageism', i.e. discrimination on the grounds of age, is a problem for mature able-bodied workers looking for work, it has a disproportionate effect on many disabled workers in the same age-group. These workers have to confront employers' negative attitudes regarding not only age, but also disability. Although the DE has sought to persuade employers not to impose age-limits on jobs (*Hansard*, 1989), a national survey of vacancies registered at Job Centres showed that age restrictions were placed on 39 per cent of all vacancies examined (Jones and Longstone, 1990).

Experience. Another factor which employers often view as 'vitally' important is experience. Workers who can show ability to adjust to the work situation with the minimum of training are far more attractive to employers than those who cannot. Loss of the work habit and lack of experience are a particular problem for all the long-term unemployed, but particularly for those with impairments. Employers' doubts about employability increase the longer people are out of work. It has been shown that while only 10 per cent of employers would screen out the newly-unemployed, 50 per cent would screen out those who have been unemployed for a year or more (Crowley-Bainton, 1987). As noted above, successive research has shown that unemployed disabled people are without jobs for far longer than unemployed able-bodied people.

Moreover, many young people born with an impairment have no work experience whatsoever (Barnes, 1990; Clarke and Hirst, 1989; Kuh *et al.*, 1988; Prescott Clarke, 1990). The following statement illustrates the position of many such young disabled people: 'I cannot get work without work experience. Because I'm disabled, employers won't take a chance' (Graham *et al.*, 1990, p. 5). Twenty-seven per cent of all the vacancies advertised in Job Centres were for applicants with previous experience (Jones and Longstone, 1990).

Appearance.   Ten per cent of all vacancies displayed in Job Centres require that applicants should be 'clean and tidy' or of 'generally good appearance' (Jones and Longstone, 1990). Here employers' personal preferences and prejudices will play a crucial role. What is perceived as 'clean and tidy' often depends upon the type of clothes an applicant wears at the interview. Many disabled people are significantly disadvantaged in this, not only because they cannot afford a 'smart' suit of clothes appropriate for interviews because state benefits do not accommodate such luxuries (see Chapter 5), but also because some disabled people do not have 'conventional' body shapes. Most clothing manufacturers cater exclusively for the mass market, namely the able-bodied population (Melville, 1986). Moreover, what constitutes a 'good appearance' is a particular problem for disabled women (Campling, 1981; Morris, 1989). In modern Britain as in most western societies great emphasis is placed by many male employers upon physical desirability and attractiveness. There is evidence that some employers in the service sector feel that the sight of a disabled woman disturbs clients (Morris, 1989).

Environmental Factors.   Environmental factors are central in the discriminatory process. 'Unsuitable premises' and 'difficult access' can relate to either the built environment or access to the work or production process, or both. The built environment in the workplace and elsewhere presents a major problem for many disabled people. At present only new shops, restaurants and hotels have to be made accessible and with hotels this need only affect the main entrance level (see Chapter 7). Although modern technology has meant that very few jobs cannot be done by people with impairments, there is no legislation requiring employers to use it.

Evidence shows that employers consistently use these criteria as an excuse for not employing disabled people (Fry, 1986; Graham *et al.*, 1990; Morris, 1989). Additionally, the recent OPCS surveys noted that amongst disabled people with jobs, only 30 per cent of males and 23 per cent of females felt that their employers had done anything to make it easier for them to work. Fifty-seven per cent of the men and 61 per cent of the women said that their employer had done nothing to help their employment needs (Martin, White and Meltzer, 1989, p. 84). Unmet employment needs were also recorded by the influential SCPR study (Prescott Clarke, 1990).

Transport. With the journey to work we come to the issue of transport. Like the built environment generally, public transport systems are not constructed for disabled people. They are virtually inaccessible to many, and for others using them is physically and mentally exhausting beyond what is unavoidable (see Chapter 7). They form a major barrier to the successful integration of disabled people into the economic and social life of the community. As a result simply travelling to and from work, which is little more than an unpleasant inconvenience for the able-bodied workforce, can be particularly daunting for people with impairments. The SCPR study found that 38 per cent of all disabled workers with jobs found travelling to work extremely tiring. Additionally, because of transport problems 9 per cent said that they had to pay more than non-disabled people to travel to and from work (Prescott Clarke, 1990, p. 8).

It also seems that there is an increasing number of jobs which are dependent upon workers' ability to drive. Large numbers of disabled people are not able to acquire these skills because of the nature of their impairment or because they do not have the money to learn. This criterion, however, is sometimes used by employers to reject job requests from disabled people. For example, a negative response to an application by a disabled candidate for a clerical post stated 'it is frequently necessary for all staff to travel between the subsidiary companies using a company vehicle' (quoted in Graham *et al.*, 1990, p. 5). The point here is that the candidate was rejected without any evidence of her inability to drive, but was based on the sweeping assumption that no disabled people are mobile.

Geographical Mobility.   During the last fifteen years geographical mobility has become especially important in the search for work. Unemployed workers have increasingly been encouraged 'to get on their bikes' to look for jobs. The OPCS surveys showed that there were more disabled people living in the north of England, Yorkshire and Humberside, and Wales (Martin, Meltzer and Elliot, 1988), which are traditional areas of higher unemployment (Lonsdale, 1986) than the south. In addition, it is now common for people already in work to move to other parts of the country to gain advancement. In present circumstances, however, geographical mobility is difficult if not impossible for many disabled people. Apart from the difficulties associated with Britain's transport system mentioned above, they face the additional problem of finding somewhere to live. Although there is a shortage of available housing generally, houses accessible to disabled people are in particularly short supply (see Chapter 7). Also, many disabled people use personal and domestic services provided by local authorities or voluntary agencies. The provision of these services is extremely limited and varies dramatically throughout the country (see Chapter 6).

Shiftworking.   In the main 'shiftworking', another problem employers cite as a barrier to disabled people's employment, is not a problem for the majority of workers with impairments who, as we have seen, work the same number of hours as able-bodied workers. There is, however, a minority of disabled people who are only able to work at particular times of the day, such as those who require some form of personal assistance in the mornings and evenings. The Department of Social Security (DSS) estimates that approximately 140,000 people fall into this category (DSS, 1990). Their employability is severely hampered by the lack of flexibility on the part of service providers.

Government Policy relating to the Employment of Disabled People

Although there had been isolated attempts to provide employment services for disabled people during the nineteenth century, mainly within the voluntary sector, they were not developed nationally until after the 1914–18 and 1939–45 wars. The political and moral appeal of making provision available for war casualties led to the setting up of Government Training Centres in 1919.

These initiatives were given a further boost during the 1939–45 conflict by politicians concerned over Britain's potential for post-war economic recovery, largely because of the acute labour shortage due to the war effort. A Government-sponsored Committee on the Rehabilitation and Resettlement of Disabled People (the Tomlinson Committee) was set up in 1943, and its recommendations were embodied in the Disabled Persons (Employment) Act 1944 which is still in operation.

The 1944 Act made provision for the setting-up of a disabled persons' employment register, assessment rehabilitation and training facilities, a specialised employment placement service, a quota scheme which compelled employers to employ disabled workers, designated employment for disabled people, and a National Advisory Council and Local Advisory Committees to advise Government on the employment needs of disabled people (DE, 1990).

This was the first legislation to treat disabled people as one group. It was also the first to address seriously the question of their employment. Not only did it provide a range of specialist services designed to find disabled people jobs, but with the quota scheme, and to a limited degree designated employment, it acknowledged and established their legal rights to employment.

Government policy since 1944 is said to have focused on the creation of job opportunities for disabled people. To achieve this, policy-makers have adopted strategies which focus both on the demand and on the supply side of labour. Policies focusing primarily on the demand side of labour are those which centre on the social organisation of the workplace. They include the quota scheme and institutionally-secured employment. Policies which focus on the supply side of labour are those which centre mainly on the workforce. They are designed to persuade employers through a combination of financial inducements and education programmes to take on individual disabled workers. Since the 1960s Government policy appears to have shifted away from demand-side policies in favour of financial inducements and educational programmes.

The Quota Scheme. Special employment services for disabled people, namely the Disablement Resettlement Service (DRS) and, to a lesser extent, the Disability Advisory Service (DAS), can be seen as a compromise between policies of enforcement and those of persuasion. Central to these services is the quota scheme. Under the 1944 Act all employers with twenty or more employees are required to employ 3 per cent of registered disabled people on their workforce.

This means that a register of people with impairments must be kept. Employers are also required to keep records of their operation of the quota. Employers who fail to fulfil their quota requirements are liable to a fine or imprisonment. The employer is, however, only breaking the law if s/he is below quota and does not hire a registered disabled person when taking on new staff. It is also an offence to dismiss a registered disabled person if this means that the employer falls below the quota, but no penalty is fixed here.

The maximum fine for not complying with the quota scheme, £100, was set in 1944 and has never been updated. Since the introduction of the quota scheme only ten employers have been prosecuted for non-compliance. The last one was in 1975. One case was dismissed, two received the maximum fine, and the rest received fines of £5, £25 or £50. Fines from the seven prosecutions totalled £434 (*Hansard*, 1989).

The number of employers abiding by the law and meeting the quota has dropped steadily since the 1960s, falling from 53.2 per cent in 1965 to 26.8 per cent in 1986. Although it is not an offence for employers to be below their quota, an exemption permit is needed before any vacancies can be filled with non-disabled workers. From 1972 onwards the number of employers given exemption permits by the DE has exceeded those complying with the scheme. This has continued to be the case ever since. Block permits are issued and the process of applying for exemption has become routine. In the past five years 18,000 have been distributed. Indeed, it is estimated that in 1986 no less than 17.2 per cent of those not meeting the quota had no permit and were thus breaking the law (*Hansard*, 1989).

It is not only employers in the private sector who avoid fulfilling their obligations. Although the quota requirement is not binding on the public sector, state-run agencies are also expected to accept the same responsibilities as other employers. Currently no government departments meet the quota requirements in Britain; nor do nationalised industries and public authorities, regional water authorities, electricity boards, regional and district health authorities, and other bodies within the National Health Service. Only a handful of local authorities do meet it (*Employment Gazette*, 1990).

The relevance of the quota scheme has been increasingly questioned by the policies of successive Governments in the 1970s and 1980s. The DE suggested that the scheme should be scrapped and replaced with a voluntary system in 1973. This led to the transfer of responsibility for the scheme's operation to the Manpower Services Commission (MSC) (DE, 1990). A second attempt to end the scheme was made during 1979–81 which was decidedly more thorough. The MSC issued a discussion document which posed the question 'Is special employment protection for disabled people by statutory means still necessary and justifiable for the future?' (MSC, 1981, quoted in Lonsdale, 1986, p. 136).

Although this document contained a number of recommendations, including both statutory and non-statutory policies, it was clear that its authors were highly critical of the quota scheme and wanted it abolished in favour of a voluntary or educative approach. On each occasion the attempt was unsuccessful due to strong protests from disabled people and their organisations. Yet despite this the issue was reopened in 1985 with another review from the MSC which called for further research. The recently published *Employment and Training for Disabled People* reiterates Government 'doubts' as to whether the quota scheme can be made to work (DE, 1990).

Two main arguments have been put forward for the quota scheme's abolition or 'modification', namely the problems encountered enforcing the scheme and the fall in registration (see below). However, although the tension inherent in a policy which requires the use of force as well as persuasion can partly explain the problems of enforcement, they are also clearly due to the lack of commitment of successive administrations.

The DRS was created both to police the quota scheme and to find individual disabled people jobs. These tasks are performed by DROs, which are required to ensure that firms meet their quota obligations, assess applications for exemption, and find individuals work. These tasks are completely contradictory. On the one hand DROs must monitor the activities of employers, and threaten prosecution if they fail to obey the law. On the other hand they are expected to build up a relationship with local employers in order to persuade them to take on disabled workers. The stress which arises from this contradiction may help to explain why most DROs are in favour of abolition of the scheme (Stubbins, 1983; Mainstream, 1990). Moreover, recent research clearly shows that they are constantly coming up against prejudice and negative attitudes from employers (Mainstream, 1990).

Enforcing the quota scheme has also been made more complex by the splitting up of the DRS during the 1980s and the severe staff cuts which followed. After publication of the *Review of Assistance for Disabled People* in 1982 by the MSC, the service was split into two, the DRS and the DAS. Subsequently, the number of DROs was drastically reduced and the size of their caseloads became 'totally unrealistic' (Mainstream, 1990, p. 117).

The introduction of the DAS marks an important shift away from policies of enforcement, since its main function is marketing and education specifically aimed at employers. Seventy DAS teams have been created throughout Britain to provide specialised help to businesses, 'encouraging them to develop good employment practices relating to the recruitment, training, and career retention of disabled workers'. It has also been noted that, along with the DRS, the DAS is seriously under-resourced and understaffed, and that staff morale is 'rather' low (Mainstream, 1990).

Much of the explanation for this can be found in a leaked internal Government report titled *Review of the Organization and Staffing of the Employment Service* (July 1989) which stated that 'Work with disabled people is given little status, and even less priority by the Employment Service.' The leaked report went on to note that there is little senior management commitment to work with disabled people and resources are being taken away for activity not related to disabled people's employment, and considered of 'greater importance' (Graham *et al.*, 1990, p. 14).

The lack of commitment by central Government to employment services for disabled people might also explain the lack of disability awareness training among DROs. Training is haphazard and not mandatory. What training there is consists of four courses spread over four weeks. It includes information about specific employment schemes and common medical conditions. Instruction is provided by psychiatrists, doctors and representatives from voluntary organisations such as the Royal National Institute for the Blind (RNIB) and the Royal National Institute for the Deaf (RNID) (Mainstream, 1990). Repeatedly, studies documenting the experiences of disabled people have shown that in the main DROs have little understanding of the problems faced by disabled people when looking for work. A common criticism is that they invariably undervalue disabled people's potential, and try to direct them into menial low-skilled, low-status jobs with little financial reward (see for example Graham *et al.*, 1990; Morris, 1989).

Mainstream Employment Services.   The likelihood of the quota scheme remaining unenforced is strengthened further by the recent emphasis by Government on the need for disabled job-seekers to use mainstream employment services such as Job Centres, Jobclubs and Restart (DE, 1990). Both the latter are organised programmes sponsored by the DE to help the long-term unemployed. The normal six months' unemployment qualifying period for both schemes has been waived for disabled people (DE, 1990). In addition, many of these facilities are now being run by private agencies, which signals an alarming shift away from statutory responsibility and regulation. However, if Job Centres, Jobclubs and other mainstream employment-finding services were accessible to disabled people, then this would be welcomed greatly by disabled people and their organisations, but unfortunately in many cases they are not.

In terms of physical accessibility, for example, a recent survey of fourteen Job Centres found that there was a lack of access for people who used wheelchairs 'or for the seriously unfit' (Mainstream, 1990, p. 99). Similar findings have been reported by the DE's own research division. Access to Job Centres generally was judged only 'fairly good' by a recent Government report. There were some instances where Job Centres were located on the first or second floor of a building and the only way up was by the stairs. At one Job Centre 'people who were unable to manage to walk up the stairs would either have to drag themselves up by their hands or were aided by more able-bodied members' (IFF Research, 1990, p. 16).

In general, accessible toilets were not widely found. The researchers noted that they only came across a 'handful of cases' where they were available, and in one of these 'the toilets themselves were on a different floor' (IFF Research, 1990, p. 16). There is also a lack of special aids and equipment, such as interpreters for people with hearing impairments and reading aids for visually impaired people, in many Job Centres, especially in centres run by private agencies. It has been found that some agency-run Job Centres are not aware of the needs of disabled people at all. This was attributed to a lack of communication between these organisations and DROs and the DAS (IFF Research, 1990).

There are also official data showing widespread ignorance about disability among Job Centre staff outside the DRS (Tozer and Parsons, 1989). Some Job Centre staff felt ill at ease when dealing with people with impairments and consequently referred everyone to the DRO (Leah *et al.*, 1990). This was confirmed by the Mainstream study which found that the bulk of referrals received by DROs were from 'in house' sources; frontline Job Centre staff, Restart officers and benefit claimant advisers (Mainstream, 1990). There is also evidence of direct discrimination among Job Centre personnel, particularly against people who have had a mental illness. One Jobclub leader said, 'I wouldn't allow potentially disruptive members to join. For example, anyone with mental illness or who was very manic' (IFF Research, 1990, p. 36).

The IFF study noted that there was some difficulty in finding 'general Jobclubs with members with disabilities to interview'. One explanation for this is that in general Jobclub leaders prefer not to take on too many 'people with disabilities' for fear of upsetting their 'throughput targets'. Jobclub users are given a course of instruction on how to look for jobs, and staff are required to reach a 'throughput quota', i.e. get a specified number of users through the course in a given time. It is widely believed among able-bodied Jobclub staff that it takes twice as long to get disabled users through the course. 'Throughput pressure' can lead to recruitment biased against disabled people in mainstream Jobclubs (IFF Research, 1990).

Another Government-sponsored report found that Job Centre staff were concerned that due to staff changes and the use of casual workers on the 'frontline' in Job Centres, disabled people were not getting an acceptable level of service. People who required 'extra but not necessarily special' help were not being catered for. The report went on to say that there was a need for staff in Job Centre offices to receive training in the 'wider aspects of services for people with disabilities' (Leah *et al.*, 1990).

There is also a general lack of training for work with people with impairments in Job Centres, even in Jobclubs specifically for disabled people. Most Jobclub leaders, for example, have been on a training course run by the DE which can last 2–5 days, or have studied the Jobclub manual. Neither the training course nor the manual deals specifically with the problems faced by disabled people in the labour market. There is also a general tendency for Job Centre personnel to underestimate disabled people's intelligence (IFF Research, 1990).

Inducement Policies.   The relevance of the quota scheme has also been undermined by the DE's obvious preference for policies of persuasion. These are financial inducements or bribes to employers to take on individual disabled workers, and education and marketing campaigns designed to 'sell' individual disabled people to businesses.

As for financial inducements or subsidies, there are a number of schemes currently available. The Job Introduction Scheme, for example, is designed to enable disabled people to prove their worth to an employer. Under the scheme employers are encouraged, usually by the DRO, to take on disabled workers for six weeks and the employer is paid a grant toward their wages, currently £45 per week (DE, 1990).

There is, however, no obligation on employers either to continue to employ the new recruits after the subsidy has been paid, or even to employ them for the full six weeks. Subsidised disabled workers are not entitled to the normal forms of job protection available to non-subsidised able-bodied workers. Other inducements to employers include the Adaptations to Premises and Equipment Scheme, and the Special Aids To Employment Scheme. The former provides funds for employers who wish to make their businesses accessible to disabled workers, and the latter makes money avail-

able to employers with disabled employees or workers with impairments who need special equipment at work (DE, 1990).

Historically, however, there has been a very poor take-up rate for
these schemes. For example, although the Job Introduction Scheme
is widely available and has been for some time, it is only rarely used
(Mainstream, 1990). As for the Adaptations to Premises and Equipment Scheme, sometimes referred to as the Capital Grants Scheme,
Lonsdale has reported that originally £500,000 was allocated, but
that only £5,000 or 2 per cent was distributed to twenty-six projects.
Within five years the allocation was reduced to less than one-third
of its original amount (Lonsdale, 1986). Graham, Jordan and Lamb
have pointed out that the applications for funds from the scheme
remained virtually static in the late 1980s at 253 for 1986/7, 252 for
1987/8 and 247 for 1988/9 (Graham *et al.*, 1990).

Using subsidies as a policy to reduce unemployment has a number
of advantages. It has been used traditionally by the DE to encourage
employers to set up firms in areas of high unemployment, and more
recently to find work for other disadvantaged groups, e.g. young
people during the early 1980s. Subsidies reduce the cost of labour
and thus stimulate employment without reducing wages or increasing manufacturing costs. They also offer policy-makers a cheap
alternative to welfare payments and lost tax revenues.

For disabled people, however, there is a number of major disad-
vantages with such a policy. First, the very act of giving employers
a financial reward for employing disabled workers, within the context of the long history of discrimination and exclusion from the
workforce, simply reaffirms the institutionalised belief that they
have less to offer than non-disabled workers. A second problem
occurs where people are hired for as long as they qualify for the subsidy and are then replaced by other target workers. A third difficulty
arises if employers take on subsidised workers in place of non-
subsidised workers. This might stimulate negative attitudes toward
disabled people among able-bodied workers, which in turn would
fuel direct discrimination. Fourthly, the extra administrative cost of
filling in forms, claiming subsidies etc. for employers who take on
subsidised workers can act as a major barrier to disabled people's
employment. Fifthly, the heightened involvement of Government
officials and specialist agencies in businesses which employ disabled
people because of the subsidy-claiming process can have the same
effect.

Finally, schemes which only aim to make specific buildings or
particular production processes accessible to disabled people are
only a partial solution to the problem. While a minority of disabled workers might receive some psychological benefit from their

implementation, if only because they are able to work, that benefit is extremely limited and indeed may in the long term be detrimental. Their occupational mobility is still limited in comparison to the non-disabled workforce. They are tied to a particular workplace or work situation, and cannot leave their job in the knowledge that there is another factory or office around the corner which is also accessible to their needs. In addition, their promotion prospects will also be harmed. Promotion may mean moving to a part of the building which has not been made accessible, or the acquisition of new equipment — considerations which are bound to influence employers' decisions when they are looking for promotion candidates.

Marketing and Education.   During the 1970s the DE put its full weight behind two Government campaigns known as 'Positive Policies' and 'Fit for Work'. Both hinged on the assumption that voluntary action would do more to get disabled people jobs than compulsory measures. In 1977 the campaign known as 'Positive Action' was launched. It aimed to persuade employers through extensive publicity and visits by DROs to develop enlightened internal policies which would improve the employment prospects of disabled people. Publicity material was sent out to 55,000 firms encouraging them to adopt recruitment policies which would give equal consideration to disabled people for all vacancies, retain newly disabled workers, improve the training and promotion prospects for disabled employees, make the work process and premises accessible to workers with impairments, and liaise closely with DROs (Lonsdale, 1986).

The 'Fit for Work' campaign followed two years later. One hundred awards were to be made annually to businesses which made 'outstanding achievements in the employment of disabled people'. The award lasts three years and includes a presentation plaque, citation, desk ornament and the right to use the award emblem in publicity. To receive the award an employer must show that s/he has adopted similar policies to those advocated in the 'Positive Policies' programme. Even more than its predecessor, the 'Fit for Work' scheme emphasised the shift away from policies of enforcement and equal rights to one of charitable benevolence and official approval (Lonsdale, 1986).

Persuasion rather than enforcement was further endorsed in 1980. Under the Companies (Director's Report) Employment of Disabled People Regulations 1980, the annual reports of firms employing more than 250 workers must contain a statement of the company's policy toward the employment of disabled people. This should cover recruitment, training and career development

(Lonsdale, 1986). This obligation was reiterated statutorily in the Company's Act 1985 (DE, 1990).

In 1982 the MSC recommended that the quota scheme be abandoned in favour of a largely voluntary scheme supplemented by a weaker form of statutory protection. The voluntary component of the scheme was a general obligation to promote equal opportunity policies, and the statutory part was the disclosure of company policy, which had already taken effect. It was suggested that the general duty be linked to a code of good practice. The MSC then produced a draft code of good practice which was also published in 1982. This document represented little more than an educational approach, offering guidance and suggestions rather than establishing a legal framework for the protection of disabled people's rights (Lonsdale, 1986).

In 1984 the Government followed this up with a major publicity campaign to launch its 'Code of Good Practice on the Employment of Disabled People'. A video was produced one year later. Another major marketing campaign was forthcoming in 1986, with yet another in 1988 when the Code was updated. In October 1990 the DE spent £400,000 on a publicity drive to launch a new 'good practice' logo which is supposed to denote that an employer 'is committed to good policies and practices in the employment of people with disabilities' (*Disability Now*, 1990c, p. 3). The most remarkable point about this new campaign is that employers do not have to prove anything in order to adopt the logo. Its use is completely voluntary.

Hitherto none of these initiatives has had much success. The 'Positive Policies' campaign was judged to have had 'very little effect' (Lonsdale, 1986, p. 134). The 'Fit for Work' scheme, which is still in operation, has been described as little more than a 'cosmetic public relations exercise' designed to give the impression that disabled people get a fair deal in employment. It can be seen as rewarding employers, but ignoring completely the achievements of disabled people (Mainstream, 1990, p. 142). Moreover, recent Government research suggests that only 21 per cent of all employers have a formal written policy regarding the employment of disabled people (Morrell, 1990, p. 12).

As for the Code of Good Practice, although over 120,000 copies have been distributed (Graham *et al.*, 1990), Government estimates suggest that it has been received by less than a fifth of all employers (Morrell, 1990); according to the same source, the accompanying video has only been seen by 2 per cent (Morrell, 1990). Indeed, the evidence shows that this campaign has been as unsuccessful as its predecessors in influencing employers' attitudes towards disabled people and employment, with regard both to employers' compliance with the quota scheme, and to the promotion of better employment practices generally.

Additionally, Government data show that of the few employers who have received the document only a third felt that it had high-lighted the 'employability of people with disabilities' (Morrell, 1990, p. 21). There is also evidence that even some employers who claim to be operating an equal opportunities policy still discriminate against disabled employees (Morris, 1990; Mason, 1990). A recent independent analysis of employment opportunities for disabled people generally concluded that 'persuasion through voluntary means has simply not worked. And there is no evidence that it is likely to in the future' (Mainstream, 1990, p. 153).

Registration.   One of the main arguments continually put forward by a succession of Government officials to justify the scrapping of the quota scheme is that the declining register makes it impossible for employers to meet the quota requirement. In the 1950s there were 936,196 disabled people registered with the DRS, but in 1989 there were only 366,768 (*Same Difference*, 1990e). The Minister of Employment recently stated: 'Only 1 per cent of the workforce have registered as disabled. So by definition it is not possible to meet the 3 per cent quota' (*Hansard*, 1990b).

This is particularly alarming when current Government estimates suggest that 3.8 per cent of the working population are 'occupa-tionally handicapped', or eligible for registration (Prescott Clarke, 1990), and when other DE research shows clearly that disabled people would register if they felt that to do so would lead to a positive outcome, such as access to a worthwhile training scheme or a job (Foster, 1990). Also, while there are still thousands of firms illegally below quota and thousands of unemployed disabled people, it is 'inappropriate' to use the declining register as an argument to explain non-compliance by employers (Lonsdale, 1986, p. 135).

This argument ignores the reasons why disabled people do not register. There are no incentives to do so other than to find work, and while the quota scheme is not enforced employers will not comply with the law. The DE has acknowledged that the increase in the distribution of exemption permits is a response to the decline in registration (DE, 1990). Consequently a vicious circle has been created whereby disabled people do not register because they believe registration is a waste of time and DE policy simply confirms that belief.

Policies used by Other Governments.   Government policy also ignores the evidence from abroad. Several western societies accept that compulsory powers are necessary to ensure that employers employ disabled workers. The United States, for example, has a system of 'affirmative action' rather than a quota scheme, and it has been noted that the machinery adopted to ensure compliance is in sharp contrast to the British experience (Lonsdale, 1986). The new U.S. anti-discrimination legislation which passed through Congress on 22 May 1990, with 403 senators voting for the Bill and only 20 against, states that by 1992 businesses with more than twenty-five employees will be required by law to make their 'physical plants' accessible to disabled workers. By 1994 this is to be extended to businesses with more than fifteen employees (*New York Times*, 1990).

In addition, a number of European states have adopted compulsory measures to secure disabled people's rights in the workplace. In the Netherlands, for example, a quota is set at between 3 and 7 per cent, depending on the type of industry, in both the public and private sectors. Fines are imposed on employers who are below quota. Portugal is introducing a 5 per cent quota for private industry and 10 per cent for the public sector. France has had an employment quota for some time. It was considerably strengthened in 1988. The existing quota is set at 3 per cent, and is set to rise 1 per cent a year until it reaches 6 per cent in 1993. Employers who cannot or will not comply with the scheme will have to pay into a fund to improve the employment prospects of disabled people along similar lines to the German model (*Same Difference*, 1990e).

The German quota scheme was introduced in 1974. It is set at 6 per cent and operates for firms employing more than fifteen people. Registration has increased steadily since the scheme's introduction and the system is said to be 'thriving'. Germany has a central disability fund raised from fines levied on firms that do not obey the law, currently bringing in the equivalent of £100 million per annum, which is used to support disabled people's employment. Commenting on the scheme's progress Herbert Neseker, Director General of Westfalen-Lippe, stated: 'Since we've had this system we've been able to give many people work, and to ensure that others keep their jobs' (quoted in Graham *et al.*, 1990, p. 13).

Conclusion

This chapter has demonstrated that the discriminatory attitudes and institutionalised practices which disproportionately disadvantage disabled people in employment are entrenched within the British labour market. They are evident in the policies and practices of employers and employment agencies, both public and private, and, most important, Government efforts to influence the work system. As a result unemployment and/or underemployment are common among disabled people.

The data show that disabled people are more likely to be out of work than the rest of the community, they are out of work longer than other unemployed workers, and when they do find it, it is usually low-paid, low-status work with poor working conditions. It is evident that assessment and rehabilitation services, ATCs and institutionally-secured work schemes under the 1944 Act have done little to change the traditional pattern of disabled people's employment. Assessment, rehabilitation and training rarely lead to mainstream employment, and the overwhelming majority of disabled workers in Government-sponsored workshops are in low-status occupations working for below subsistence wages.

Institutional discrimination against disabled people is prevalent throughout the British labour market. Clearly, widespread prejudice and ignorance regarding disabled people's work potential persist among employers and able-bodied workers. Moreover they are constantly being reinforced by a range of factors, both social and environmental, outside the context of the workplace which have a great effect in excluding disabled workers when they apply for work or seek promotion.

Official policy during and immediately after the 1939–45 war went some way to address these problems by introducing policies which focused on both the supply and demand sides of labour. Besides establishing a system of specialist employment services designed to find disabled people jobs, the 1944 Act gave them legal rights to paid work with the introduction of the quota scheme and sheltered workshops. It is clear, however, that almost from the outset these rights have been seriously undermined by ensuing Government policies.

With regard to the quota scheme it is evident that there is widespread evasion of the law by employers in both the public and the private sectors. We examined the Government's lack of commitment to the scheme, notably during the 1970s and 1980s, and its obvious preference for voluntary policies of persuasion which focus mainly on labour supply, namely individual disabled workers. This was manifested in DE policy statements, subsequent developments in employment services for disabled people, and the introduction of a succession of inducement policies and marketing campaigns designed to 'sell' disabled people to employers as a subsidised commodity.

The only possible conclusion is that for disabled people policies which centre solely upon the supply side of labour simply do not work. Because individual disabled people are packaged and sold as different from other members of the labour force the traditional divisions between them and non-disabled workers are underlined and, indeed, deepened. Moreover, giving individuals with impairments specific aids for particular forms of work in a specified work environment does not provide them with the same employment opportunities as their able-bodied contemporaries.

Such policies can only achieve a limited success in specific cases, but at the general level they are certain to fail. The only policies which might succeed are ones focusing primarily on the demand side of labour, namely on the workplace. These are policies creating a barrier-free work environment and requiring employers to use production processes accessible to the entire workforce, policies aimed at the 'social organization of work' (Oliver, 1990, p. 124).

5

THE DISABILITY BENEFITS SYSTEM

> Benefits which are not carefully related to the struggle for integrated employment and active social participation will constantly be used to justify our dependence and exclusion from the mainstream of life — the very opposite of what is needed (UPIAS, 1976, p. 15).

Since at least the seventeenth century poverty has been an inevitable consequence of living with an impairment. This form of poverty is the direct result of the systematic exclusion of disabled people from the social processes which make employment possible. As a consequence disabled people are perceived as objects of pity dependent upon the charity of others. Since 1945 the overwhelming majority of disabled people have been supported by a state-sponsored charity or welfare benefits system which maintains that dependence.

This Chapter will show how the modern welfare benefits system is a major factor in the disabling process because it fails to provide disabled people with an adequate income, compounds their dependence upon professionals and professional organisations and, most important, does not facilitate their integration into mainstream employment. It is divided into two main sections. The first examines economic deprivation in relation to impairment-related expenditure, and the second focuses on the benefit system with particular emphasis on changes during the 1980s.

Economic Deprivation and the Additional Costs of Impairment

Economic Deprivation and Disabled People. Since at least the 1960s there has been growing concern over the financial circumstances of disabled people. A succession of studies has documented the extra financial costs incurred by impairment and the very low levels of income upon which the overwhelming majority of disabled people and their families have to rely (Baldwin, 1985; Buckle, 1984; Hyman, 1977; Stowell and Day, 1983; Townsend, 1979). This has been accompanied by repeated calls for a complete reappraisal of social security benefits for disabled people (DA, 1975, 1987; DIG, 1987).

Official Estimates of Economic Deprivation among Disabled People. In response to this long-standing concern the Government promised a comprehensive review of the benefits system. This was to be preceded by a national survey of disabled people to provide an up-to-date basis for future planning. The previous Government-sponsored survey of disability (Harris, 1971), which had been conducted during the 1960s to provide data for the expansion of services for disabled people, was considered inaccurate and out of date. Although this research showed that impairment results in extra expenditure, no attempt was made to quantify that cost.

The Office of Population, Censuses and Surveys (OPCS) looked at disabled people's incomes in the report *The Financial Circumstances of Disabled Adults Living in Private Households* (Martin and White, 1988). This found that the majority of disabled adults, 78 per cent (54 per cent of those below retirement age), lived in households containing no wage-earners whatsoever. The significance of welfare benefits was correspondingly great. Although half of all disabled people interviewed had another source of income besides earnings or benefits, the most common of these were pension or redundancy payments from previous employers or income from savings or investments, and were thus more likely to be received by older disabled people.

Comparisons with the equivalent incomes of the general population showed that families with a disabled member below retirement age had significantly lower incomes than those without a disabled member — 72 per cent lower. Although this can be attributed to the high levels of unemployment among disabled adults, families with one or more wage-earners still had lower than average incomes than similar households with no disabled members. The incomes of disabled people over retirement age were not much different from those of their able-bodied peers (Martin and White, 1988). This is because most people's incomes are reduced radically after retirement. For example, in 1983 64 per cent of people above retirement age were living in poverty or on its margins, compared with only 24 per cent of those under retirement age (Abberley, 1990, p. 13).

Impairment-Related Expenditure. The OPCS researchers, who only asked questions about items bought in the twelve months prior to the survey, found that impairment involved some additional financial cost regardless of the degree of severity. This was divided into three types, capital expenditure on lump-sum purchases, regular expenditure on items related specifically to impairment, and expenditure on items required by most people, but on which disabled people need to spend more. Lump-sum purchases were of items such as wheelchairs, special aids and equipment, special furniture and car adaptations, which are only bought occasionally. Expenses of this nature were only incurred by 16 per cent of the sample, and amounted to an average of £78, although there was considerable variation among individuals. The average for all disabled adults worked out at £12.50 per year. Because of the limited timespan the OPCS researchers admit that this is likely to be a low estimate of this type of outlay.

Regular expenditure on impairment-related items such as hospital visits, personal and domestic assistance and prescriptions was incurred by 60 per cent of all disabled adults. This increased along with the degree of impairment. The average weekly cost for those who incurred these expenses was £2.20, or £1.20 for all disabled adults.

A higher level of expenditure than that incurred by able-bodied people on 'normal' items such as fuel, clothing, food, travel and home maintenance was reported by 71 per cent of those interviewed. This amounted to £6.70 per week for those incurring it, or £4.80 for all disabled adults. The estimated extra impairment-related expenses for all disabled adults amounted to £6.10 per week or £329 per annum.

Overall, however, there was considerable variation in actual expenditure according to the degree of impairment. As well as rising with severity, average extra costs also rose with income within categories of severity. This indicates that respondents would probably have spent more money had it been available. In all 24 per cent of all disabled adults thought they needed to spend more on impairment-related items but could not afford to do so (Martin and White, 1988, Chapter 4).

Having to spend a proportion of one's income on items associated with impairment reduces disposable income, which is normally the amount available for everyday living after tax, National Insurance contributions and housing costs have been met. The OPCS report examined this in terms of 'equivalent resources'. This was arrived at by calculating disposable income remaining after disability-related expenditure had been subtracted, and using equivalence scales to adjust the remaining income for differences in family composition. Disabled adults had, on average, lower equivalent incomes than families in the general population, so that when the extra financial costs of impairment were taken into account, disabled adults had lower equivalent resources available to spend on other things.

In general, impairment-related expenses amounted to 8 per cent of all disabled adults' disposable income. Although the average amount of such expenditure was lower for those on lower incomes, they spent a higher proportion of their resources on disability-related expenses. The proportion rose with severity of impairment; those considered the most severely impaired were spending an average of 15 per cent, compared with 4 per cent for those with the least impairment. Eight per cent of disabled householders said that they were getting into financial difficulties, and objective tests based on experience of debt and arrears confirmed this (Martin and White, 1988).

The standard of living of disabled people was judged to be generally lower than that of non-disabled people. Assessments of living standards are usually constructed in terms of the lack of named items or activities considered basic, such as a warm winter coat and consumer durables such as a refrigerator and a telephone. In terms of 'relative deprivation' some consumer items such as video recorders would be considered a luxury whilst others are deemed 'normal' at a given point in time. A washing machine, for example, is now considered an essential, whereas in the 1950s it was thought of as a luxury.

The significance of these items is central to the ongoing debate about what is considered 'absolute' and 'relative' deprivation. A criticism often levelled at studies of poverty is that they fail to distinguish whether or not a lack of resources or consumer choice explains the absence of basic items owned by a given population. The former would be an indicator of economic deprivation whilst the latter would not. The OPCS study took account of this problem and found a proportion of both luxuries and basic items absent from choice. There was, however, a definite relationship between impairment and the inability to afford desired items. This was most evident among unmarried disabled people below retirement age. These people generally lacked the greatest number of consumer durables and the most basic items (Martin and White, 1988).

Some Criticisms of Government Assessments from Disabled People and their Organisations. As Abberley (1990) has noted, it is evidence of the growing strength of disabled people and their organisations that a number of detailed responses to this report were quickly forthcoming. In particular, the Disablement Income Group (DIG) and the Disability Alliance (DA) produced reports which welcomed this official recognition of the connection between impairment and economic deprivation, but criticised the methods used by the OPCS researchers, which had yielded data that seriously underestimated the true financial cost of impairment (DA, 1988; Thompson *et al.*, 1989, 1990). Each of these documents takes the individualistic approach of the OPCS for granted but argues that its methods produce the wrong answers to what are 'tacitly assumed to be the right questions' (Abberley, 1990, p. 17).

The inaccuracy of the findings of the OPCS survey is explained by a number of factors. First, the study was carried out before the major benefit changes of April 1988, which resulted in a reduction of income for over a million disabled people (see below). Secondly, major capital expenditure on single items such as a car, house adaptations and electric wheelchairs were generally excluded from the OPCS survey because of the decision to ask questions only about items bought in the year prior to the interview. Thirdly, the sampling technique was biased in such a way as to exclude people with more severe impairments, i.e. those most likely to incur the highest additional expenditure. The OPCS researchers designated ten categories of impairment of which categories 1–3 were people whose daily lives were not seriously restricted. Almost half the sample were defined thus; on this basis they estimated that 2,742,000 people were in these three categories. This left 3,038,000 disabled people in the remaining categories, a figure very close to the estimate of 3,071,000 made by the first OPCS survey (Harris, 1971), which excluded people with learning difficulties and non-visible impairments.

Fourthly, the form of questioning, interview technique and the time taken for the interviews limited the amount of data which could be collected. The OPCS survey was a large-scale study in which 10,000 people were interviewed. Each interview lasted approximately 90 minutes and only a portion of that time was devoted to questions of finance. As is common in this type of research, no prompting or clarification of the interviewees' responses was permitted. Inevitably there were a significant number of 'don't know' answers, particularly in relation to regular expenditure such as heating costs. Forty per cent of interviewees failed to answer all the questions asked (Martin and White, 1988, p. 35).

Finally, it is likely that the OPCS findings seriously underestimated the real level of need. Although the survey showed that 71 per cent of respondents had impairment-related expenses, only 24 per cent said that they needed to spend more but could not afford to. The items cited most were basics such as fuel, food and clothing. Abberley (1990) has rightly noted that accurate responses in this area are notoriously difficult to achieve, particularly from people over retirement age. Sixty-five per cent of the OPCS sample fell into this category (Martin and White, 1988).

In a society which places such a high premium upon individual self-sufficiency, need is frequently associated with financial incompetence, and because financial incompetence is a source of shame, need is often concealed. This casts serious doubt on the value of the OPCS study's conclusion that around 70 per cent of all disabled adults expressed 'satisfaction' with their standard of living (Abberley, 1990; DA, 1988; Thompson *et al.*, 1990).

There is a wealth of evidence to show that the OPCS findings concerning the financial costs of impairment are grossly inaccurate. For example, in the 1970s Hyman found that impairment expenditure for wheelchair-users amounted to £14.50 per week (Hyman, 1977). A study in the early 1980s showed that shopping cost disabled people an extra £3.36 per week (Stowell and Day, 1983). Apart from the costs of special diets, clothes etc., many shops are simply not accessible to disabled people. A study of people with learning difficulties found that their impairment-related expenses were £19.50 per week (Buckle, 1984). Of course, the amounts quoted would be considerably higher today on account of inflation.

In response to the publication of the OPCS survey, the DIG has conducted research showing that among 'severely' disabled people impairment-related expenditure is much higher than Government estimates. To demonstrate the gross inaccuracy of the OPCS findings the DIG researchers used a questionnaire similar to that used for the OPCS study. They then compared the results with data from research which employed a semi-formal interview technique widely used in small-scale in-depth studies which dealt with the same subject, but allowed respondents to think about and clarify their answers. The sample used in the study, however, differed from that of the OPCS survey in size, severity of impairment and age. Thirteen people were interviewed, all described as 'significantly' impaired and only two over retirement age.

Using only the OPCS-type questions, an average extra weekly expenditure of £41.84 was recorded whereas the response of the same subjects to the DIG questionnaire yielded an average of £65.94, a difference of 58 per cent between the two methods (Thompson *et al.*, 1988). To verify these findings a second, larger study was undertaken using the same approach. It reported remarkably similar results. Eighty-seven people were interviewed, 74 per cent of working age. Although a number of the sample was less severely impaired than in the earlier study no one was considered below OPCS category 3. Their average weekly impairment-related expenses totalled £69.92 per week (see Table 5.1).

The DIG study made it clear that the financial cost of impairment increases dramatically with severity, is determined by available income, and is related to receipt of impairment-related benefits. It was also evident that spending on certain important items, such as food, is constrained by limited financial resources (Thompson *et al.*, 1990, Chapter 4).

Table 5.1. Average Weekly Impairment-related
Expenditure on Selected Items

Item	Amount
Home treatment	0.49
Home services	27.55
Informal assistance	6.89
Prescriptions	0.22
Chemist items	3.14
Laundry	2.23
Clothing	2.51
Wear and tear depreciation	3.14
Food	6.93
Heating	3.95
Travel	8.22
Telephone	3.41
Helper's presents	0.54
Insurance	0.70
Total	**£69.92**

Source: Adapted from Table 4.6, Thompson *et al.*, 1990,
p. 33.

The Government's Response. The Government's review of benefits for people with impairments, titled *The Way Ahead*, was published in January 1990 (DSS, 1990). In conjunction with a number
of measures announced four months earlier, this review proposed
a number of small extensions to existing benefits. These included
the introduction of additional financial support for people who
acquired impairments early in life. Three new measures were also
introduced: the administration of the two main disability benefits
was rationalised; a new lower-rate payment was introduced for less
severely disabled people, and non-elderly people who require inter-
mittent assistance; and a new social security benefit was to be paid
to encourage disabled people into employment by supplementing
earnings from low-paid or part-time work (Disability Benefits Consortium, 1990).

Despite repeated Government commitments to the contrary,
the review which formulated these proposals did not consult with
disabled people and their organisations. It has been described as
a 'grubby public relations exercise' which will only help a small
number of disabled people in a limited and piecemeal way. The new
proposals will not eradicate the 'inadequacies and discrimination'
which characterise the disability benefits system, or eliminate the

economic deprivation faced by disabled people and their families every day of their lives (DA, 1990).

It is unlikely, therefore, that the economic circumstances of the overwhelming majority of disabled people will improve in the foreseeable future. This is a key feature of the discriminatory process, since access to adequate financial resources is crucial in a society in which conspicuous consumption is increasingly assumed to denote status and prestige. However, poverty alone does not separate disabled people from the rest of the community. It is the disability benefits system itself which does that.

The Benefit System

The Organisation of the Benefit System for Disabled People.   The organisation of the present benefit system for disabled people has developed in a largely unplanned and *ad hoc* manner since before the 1914–18 war. Until the 1970s, state-funded welfare payments were focused mainly on people who had acquired impairments due to war or industrial accident, and who had a qualifying record of National Insurance contributions (DSS, 1990).

War and industrial disablement schemes were set up to provide compensation benefits based on a percentage assessment of functional limitations arising from a war or industrial injury. As a result, people who acquire impairments in the armed forces or at work can sometimes receive a substantial war or industrial pension. In addition, specific payments are provided for attendance services, and for limited mobility in the case of the war pension scheme, as well as other special additions including payments for reduced earnings. Those eligible for these schemes are also entitled to claim other impairment-related benefits such as Invalidity Benefit (IVB) and Mobility Allowance (MA), provided that they qualify (see below).

People who acquire impairments because of an accident may also be eligible for large sums of money in compensation, if it can be proved that an individual's impairment is the result of someone else's negligence, as in a road traffic accident. Compensation of any sort, however, is only attainable for a minority. In a recent study of the experience of spinal cord injury, only 39 per cent of a representative sample of seventy-seven felt that there was any possibility of legal compensation for their injury. Of these only 63 per cent had their claim settled at the time of the accident, although this does not mean that they did not experience delays in payment. The remainder encountered major delays. The length of time waiting for settlement, or until the completion of the settlement, varied between less than one year and seven years (Oliver *et al.*, 1988).

These delays can have serious negative financial and psychological implications for disabled individuals and their families. While some people receive interim payments to alleviate financial hardship before the final settlement, many are kept in ignorance of the amount due or, indeed, of whether they will get anything at all. This financial uncertainty, coupled with the additional worry of protracted and complicated legal battles, can cause debilitating psychological distress. Further, since the size of the compensation is normally determined by the degree of impairment there is little incentive for claimants to overcome any impairment-related problems which might ensue during the litigation process (Oliver *et al.*, 1988).

It has been suggested that some of these problems might be overcome with the introduction of a no-fault compensation system similar to that advocated by the Pearson Commission (1978) for motor vehicle injuries (Oliver *et al.*, 1988). Until fairly recently this idea has received little support from the insurance industry (see *CII Journal*, 1978) and indeed from successive governments. But the idea of no-fault compensation for 'small motor vehicle accidents' is being debated by the Lord Chancellor's Department and a statement was due to be produced in late 1991. Also the notion of no-fault compensation for injuries through treatment by the National Health Service is now supported by a variety of agencies, including the British Medical Association (BMA, 1990), and some politicians.

One of the factors which precipitated this interest is the public concern over the protracted legal battles for compensation paid to people with haemophilia who contracted human immunodeficiency virus (HIV) through blood products provided by the NHS. On 25 October 1990 the Labour MP Harriet Harman introduced under the ten-minute ruling a no-fault compensation for medical injuries bill (House of Commons Bill 208) (*Hansard*, 1990d). Although it was defeated, it has since been adopted by the Independent Social Democrat MP Rosie Barnes, who has extended it to include injuries through drugs and appliances prescribed through the NHS. Ms Barnes put the National Health Service (Compensation) Bill before the House on 1 February 1991. It was defeated on its second reading by 193–81, a majority of 112 against (*Hansard*, 1991).

Until the general expansion of benefits during the 1970s, disabled people who were not eligible for any form of compensatory benefit had to rely entirely upon means-tested assistance. In 1971 a long-term benefit to replace earnings was introduced, the Invalidity Benefit (IVB). This was followed in 1975 by its counterpart for people who had not paid enough National Insurance contributions to qualify for IVB. Originally known as the Non Contributory Invalidity Pension (NCIP) it is now referred to as the Severe Disablement Allowance (SDA) (DA, 1990).

In 1970, 1973 and 1976 respectively, higher and lower rate Attendance Allowance (AA) and Mobility Allowance (MA) were introduced. These last two benefits were specifically designed to cover some of the impairment-related expenses discussed above. Whilst the aim of the MA is to assist disabled people with the additional costs of transport, replacing the provision of the invalid vehicle service, the purpose of the AA is less clear. It was generally intended to provide funds to cover impairment-related expenses with the need for 'attendance' serving as a means of identifying the most 'severely' disabled people, those considered most in need. However, although 'self-care' ability is used as a means of measuring need, AA was not introduced to pay for personal assistance (Large, 1990). In December 1990 the higher rate of AA was £37.55 per week, the lower rate £25.05 and MA £26.25 (Large, 1990).

In 1975 the Invalid Care Allowance (ICA), a benefit paid to people of working age who act as personal assistants (PAs) to disabled people in receipt of AA, was introduced. It was not, however, available to the vast majority of personal assistants, namely married women, until 1986 and it is not available to those people who act as PAs to disabled people not in receipt of AA. Invalid Care Allowance can be worth up to £45.05, but £28.20 of this is deducted from the benefits, in particular the severe disability premium, paid to the disabled person receiving the PA service (DA, 1990, p. 117). It is important to note how low this allowance is compared to the wages of other full-time workers. (One of the consequences of this exploitation of PAs is discussed in the following chapter.)

It will be evident that, in common with state benefits generally, allowances for impairment-related expenditure are allocated for a specified purpose and named accordingly. This bureaucratic regulation carries with it unmistakable assumptions of social incompetence which might prove unacceptable to other sections of the community. How many wage-earners, for example, would tolerate their wages being divided up in this way? These assumptions are especially marked in the case of impairment-related benefits because of the use of explicitly disablist language which emphasises and reinforces difference and dependence. Of particular note is the term 'invalidity', the etymology of which is quite clear, namely in-valid. Moreover, assumptions of social incompetence are also clear in that the state is willing to pay PAs an ICA rather than giving the allowance to recipients of the service so that they can pay the PAs themselves.

The traditional divisions between disabled and non-disabled people are also enhanced by the number of allowances 'targeted' specifically at people with impairments. This perpetuates the wide-spread view that disabled people have their needs adequately catered for by the disability benefits system (Thomas, 1982) and are consequently better off financially than other sections of the poor. This is particularly important since financial hardship is increasingly common among non-disabled British citizens. A recent analysis, for example, found that between 1979 and 1987 the number of people with incomes below the 'benefit line', which is widely regarded as the 'official poverty line', rose by 18 per cent (IFS, 1990). Large sections of the community now find themselves wholly or partly reliant on state benefits as a major source of income. However, as was demonstrated clearly above, disproportionate economic deprivation is particularly acute among disabled people. The DIG study found severely disabled people (category 10 in the OPCS scale) were spending £146.47 per week on impairment-related expenditure (Thompson *et al.*, 1990).

Besides emphasising differences between disabled people and non-disabled people, the organisation of the disability benefits system also creates significant economic and social divisions within the disabled population as a whole. Each of the benefit systems mentioned above has a different set of criteria for eligibility. Age at the onset of impairment, the cause of impairment, its severity, an individual's work record, National Insurance contributions, and even country of residence for the previous twenty years all have an important bearing on the amount which can be received. As a result people with similar impairments can be entitled to vastly differing sums of money. For example, someone considered to have 'severe' impairments on the war disablement scheme can receive up to £287 per week, whilst a similarly impaired individual who has not paid National Insurance contributions, and who has not lived in Britain for ten of the previous twenty years would only be eligible for AA and MA, which in 1990 amounted to a meagre £63.80 per week. People who have not been in Britain for ten out of the past twenty years cannot claim SDA (DA, 1990, p. 2).

Recent Changes in the Benefit System.   Contrary to official rhetoric throughout the 1980s, the value of impairment-related benefits has been reduced by successive Government attempts to cut public expenditure generally. Although the demand for benefits among the population as a whole has increased, social security expenditure has been singled out for particular attention in these cuts. As a result, between 1979 and 1989 around £11 million has been cut from the social security budget (Lister, 1989).

For example, before 1980 increases in long-term benefits such as IVB were linked to the rise of either wages or prices, whichever was the greater. Under the first 1980 Social Security Act, these benefits were pegged to prices only. The second 1980 Social Security Act reduced Invalidity Benefit by 5 per cent and abolished the earnings-related supplement to short-term benefits payable during the first six months of injury or sickness. This resulted in a loss of over £330 a year at 1983 prices for a family with a disabled member (Franey, 1983, p. 8).

Major changes to the social security system were introduced in 1988 following a series of Government policy reviews. The old Supplementary Benefit system was abolished and with it a range of additional payments hitherto available to large numbers of disabled people on the basis of individual need. These were replaced by a system of fixed premiums which provided extra benefit to people who fitted into particular categories, namely 'disabled' or 'severely disabled'. One of the ways in which claimants were slotted into one of these categories was by being in receipt of AA or MA. Consequently, these benefits have become far more important, not only in themselves but also because they act as a passport to additional financial support (NACABx, 1990a, p. 5).

Changes were also announced in 1988 to the State Earnings-Related Pension Scheme (SERPS). Incentives were introduced to encourage workers into employers' or private personal pension schemes. Disabled workers are often at a disadvantage in occupational and private pension schemes and therefore rely heavily on SERPS. Hence, their future disability and retirement pensions will be adversely affected. Government figures suggest that some 80,000 sick or disabled people, along with 30,000 dependants, will be worse off as a result of these changes (*Hansard*, 1988), while independent estimates put the figure at well over 1 million (DA, 1987).

As well as the cuts in the SERPS and the incentives to join occupational and private pension schemes, responsibility for paying sick benefit during the first twenty-eight weeks of sickness has also been transferred from the state to employers. It is reported that 'early monitoring' of the new system has shown high error rates in Statutory Sick Pay (SSP) payments, widespread ignorance on the part of employees and employers regarding the new scheme, a lack of official supervision and enforcement, and that employees are being sacked or forced to become self-employed by employers who refuse to operate it. Shifting the responsibility for payment of SSP on to employers in this way can only add to the discriminatory practices within the workplace and make employees with real or imagined poor health records more vulnerable to discrimination (Baloo *et al.*, 1986; Glendinning 1990).

In order to achieve cost effectiveness within the social security system the Government used two main strategies: the targeting of impairment-related benefits at those people considered most in need through the use of economic means testing, and the replacement of statutory provision with discretionary grants from Government and quasi-charitable agencies (Glendinning, 1990). Both of these approaches signify a dramatic strengthening of bureaucratic regulation and control, which can only emphasise difference and reinforce dependence — the first because it makes the claiming process even more difficult than it already is and the second because it marks a significant retreat from the idea of disabled people's rights and legal entitlement.

The Disability Benefits Claiming Process. Economic means-testing is a process by which individuals have to provide information about their income and resources to state or other officials in order to receive welfare payments. Economic means-tests were developed during the nineteenth century to separate the 'deserving' from the 'undeserving' poor. They are widely regarded as a humiliating and degrading process, which compounds the difficulties of living on welfare. Successive studies show that the stigma, ignorance and misunderstanding which surround economic means-testing prevents many people from claiming the benefits to which they are entitled (Glendinning, 1990; Young, 1987). To claim their welfare rights, however, disabled people are subjected to at least two means-tests — an economic one and a functional or medical one.

To some extent all impairment-related benefits are dependent upon medical evidence. Sometimes this may be provided by a claimant's own doctor, as with IVB. Department of Social Security (DSS) officials normally base decisions as to whether or not an individual is to be described as incapable of work upon evidence from the claimant's own doctor. However, if the DSS doubts the validity of the doctor's report, it can insist on a second opinion. This means that the individual claiming benefit will be referred to a doctor in the Regional Medical Service of the Department of Health (DoH) (DA, 1990).

To become eligible for either of the two main impairment-related benefits, namely AA or MA, an individual must be examined by a doctor or doctors other than their own. A recent report from the National Association of Citizens Advice Bureaux (NACABx) concluded that these medical assessments cause unnecessary 'humiliation and distress' (NACABx, 1990a, p. 3). Most of the doctors used by the DSS are men. In December 1988 there were 4,863 examining medical practitioners undertaking examinations for AA, of whom only 816 were women. Similarly, there is an absence of doctors of both sexes from ethnic minority backgrounds (NACABx, 1990a, p. 11). Consequently, if a disabled woman or someone from an ethnic minority wishes to be examined by a doctor of the same sex or cultural background then s/he must contact the DSS in advance. This can mean a delay in being examined and hence a delay in receipt of the benefit, or additional travel (DA, 1990, p. 3).

A major problem in the assessment process arises from what doctors are attempting to measure. To qualify for AA an individual must prove that s/he requires from another person 'frequent attention throughout the day', or night, in connection with her/his bodily functions, or 'continued supervision' throughout the day or night to avoid substantial danger to her/himself or others. In other words, people have to demonstrate that they cannot look after themselves. They are expected to go into detailed explanations about the difficulties they experience when doing such intimate things as washing, dressing, eating and using the toilet. Such interrogations are undoubtedly 'degrading and demeaning' (NACABx, 1990a, p. 11).

To qualify for MA, claimants must prove that they are unable or 'virtually' unable to walk due to a physical cause which is likely to last for at least one year. They are asked to demonstrate in a short interview the difficulties they encounter in walking. The claimant's walking ability out of doors is considered with any aids that are used. Other factors taken into account are the distance which can be walked, the length of time that can be spent walking, the manner of walking, and any pain that may result from walking. Environmental or social circumstances, such as living at the top of a hill or on the fifteenth floor of a high-rise block of flats, are not considered (NACABx, 1990a, p. 6).

Although claimants for both AA and MA are examined by doctors appointed by the DSS, claims are dealt with by two quite different adjudication processes. With AA, decisions on whether or not an applicant is eligible are taken by an AA Board which consists of a Chair and between four and nine other members. All but two of the Board's members must be medically qualified. In the majority of cases medical decisions are made by Delegated Medical Practitioners, who are themselves doctors employed by the DSS. They rarely examine the claimant in person but their decision is determined by the report of the examining doctor, who in most cases will only meet the claimant once for the examination. The decision on this aspect of the claim is then passed on to the Adjudicating Officer, who decides the non-medical aspects of the claim.

There is no right of appeal against the AA Board's decision on medical grounds, only a right of review within three months of the decision or in certain other circumstances. Applications for review are dealt with by a further medical examination and reconsiderations by the Delegated Medical Practitioner. If the decision to withhold the allowance is upheld, then the claimant has a right of appeal to the Social Security Commission, but only on a point of law (NACABx, 1990a, p. 7).

In MA claims the process is quite different. The Adjudicating Officer must first obtain a medical report; this is usually provided by Examining Medical Practitioners who will be asked for their 'opinion' as to whether the claimant fulfils the medical criteria for the allowance. The Adjudicating Officer then makes a decision on the claim.

The Adjudicating Officer can refer a claim to a Medical Board, consisting of two or more doctors, for decisions on medical questions. A claimant who is refused on medical grounds may appeal within three months of the medical decision, and then be examined by a Medical Board if this has not already happened. An appeal against a negative decision would go to a Medical Appeals Tribunal consisting of a legally qualified Chair and two medically qualified members. They are independent of the DSS (NACABx, 1990a, p. 8).

Medical criteria are often used to deny access to both AA and MA. Claimants may have to apply several times before allowances are awarded. With the AA, 300 appeals to the Social Security Appeal Tribunal on non-medical questions were cleared in 1988, whereas there were 56,000 requests for the AA Board to review its decisions. Over 30 per cent of initial claims were refused, but the percentage of the reviews decided in the claimant's favour when the reason for the review was dissatisfaction with the original medical decision was 62 per cent. Figures published by the DSS for 1989 are not directly comparable, but as there were 318,380 initial claims, and 56,087 applications for review decided in 1988, questions arise over the proportion of claimants who are dissatisfied with the decision initially given on their claims, and over the decision-making process generally (NACABx, 1990a, p. 10).

With the MA, 29 per cent of the decisions against the claimant were overturned by Medical Boards and a further 42 per cent at Medical Appeals Tribunals. The vast majority of queries arise over the medical conditions, with only 1,812 appeals on non-medical grounds cleared in 1988, compared to 6,547 decisions by Medical Appeal Tribunals and 20,980 by Medical Boards (NACABx, 1990a). Claimants who decide to ask for a review of a refusal or appeal against a negative decision are likely to have to undergo a further medical examination, either by a second doctor, or in the case of the MA by a Medical Board, or members of a Medical Appeals Tribunal (NACABx, 1990a, p. 10).

In line with the proposed merging of the AA and MA into a 'new' Disability Living Allowance (DLA) in 1992, it has been announced that the requirement for successive medical tests for access to benefits is to be abolished. They are to be replaced by 'a single claim' and 'a single medical examination' which has to be submitted to a new decision-making structure (DSS, 1990a). Under the new system decisions will be made by 'non-medical Adjudicating Officers' but medical staff will 'continue to assist and inform the adjudication process' (DSS, 1990a, p. 7).

With the new proposals claimants can opt for a medical assessment or complete a new 'rather more detailed claim form' designed to identify the level of 'disability in relation to both self-care and mobility'. This is because the DLA bundles together AA and MA, and does not acknowledge other impairment-related expenditure (Large, 1990). There are no plans to include environmental and social factors in the new assessments. Claimants can, however, bolster their written claims by supplying supplementary evidence 'about their condition and the effect it has on their ability to perform normal functions' from 'whichever agency is in the best position to make that judgement'. This can include a general medical practitioner, hospital consultant, health visitor or a special school (DSS, 1990a, p. 7). In addition, medical assessments will be carried out on a small number of claimants to act as an audit 'to check on the accuracy of the written statements received' (DSS, 1990a, p. 90).

Dissatisfied claimants will be able to have their claim reviewed by a different Adjudication Officer, who will also have access to 'expert medical advice'. But the Government expects a medical examination to be necessary where the first-tier assessment has been made on the basis of written evidence alone Claimants still not satisfied with the outcome of the appeal will be able to apply to an 'independent appeals tribunal' comprising a 'a legally qualified chairperson; a medically qualified member; and a third member who ideally will have practical experience of people with disabilities' (DSS, 1990a, p. 9).

Clearly, apart from the reduced number of medical tests disabled people will have to endure, little has changed. First, for a variety of reasons, not least the inadequacy of the special education system, many disabled people have difficulties with communication and literacy skills, and consequently the new detailed claim form will present them with a major problem. Secondly, in order to claim their rights disabled people will still have to answer detailed sensitive and intimate questions about their impairments and their functional abilities and be asked about their ability to 'perform key daily tasks' such as 'cooking a main meal' (Brindle, 1990) — a feat which a sizeable proportion of the adult British population may not be able to accomplish. Moreover, if claimants are unable to fill in the form themselves they will have to discuss these delicate subjects with someone else before that person can complete it on their behalf.

Thirdly, since both components of the new DLA are to be paid at very different rates, the AA is to be extended to include a third lower rate of £10 per week and the MA is set to include a second lower rate of a similar amount, claimants will therefore want their claim to carry as much weight as possible to avoid being awarded the lower rate. Additionally, by lowering the payout rates the new allowances will attract many new claimants and the introduction of 'self-assessments' gives Adjudicating Officers far more scope to 'short-change' new beneficiaries (Large, 1990, p. 19). Hence, many disabled people will feel compelled to support their claim with medical evidence.

While a clearly-defined review procedure is to be established, the increasing importance of medical criteria becomes apparent at each stage of the appeals process. Indeed, one of the appeal tribunal members is to be a doctor, one a lawyer and the other an 'expert' on 'people with disabilities'. Who that 'expert' will be, however, remains unclear. Based on past experience, it is unlikely to be a representative of an organisation of disabled people or someone who will be in a strong enough position seriously to challenge traditional wisdom in these matters. Hitherto most official bureaucracies have been particularly reluctant to support organisations of disabled people or their representatives (see Chapter 6).

Overall, disabled people still have to supply sensitive and intimate information to professional 'experts' in order to receive benefits, and it is those experts who will decide on the basis of that information whether benefits should be granted. In short, functional or medical means-testing will not disappear and the welfare bureaucracy will remain intact.

This process brings into full view one of the major problems of the disability benefit system as a whole, namely that it encourages rather than discourages dependence. To receive financial support, applicants are compelled to emphasise impairments and functional limitations as opposed to personal autonomy and skills. Indeed, to secure the maximum economic advantage from the benefit system disabled people are forced to present themselves in the worst possible light (Oliver *et al.*, 1988). This has become even more important in recent years because of the shift away from statutory entitlements to discretionary grants.

The Shift from Statutory to Discretionary Entitlement. Since 1988 the claiming process has become even more complex with the withdrawal of some of the hitherto available statutory payments to cover impairment related expenditure in favour of discretionary grants. Prior to 1988, a number of additional weekly payments were available to recipients of Supplementary Benefit. Ten of the fourteen allowances provided were specifically concerned with impairment or health-related expenditure. A significant number of these allowances had no maximum amounts fixed and therefore, taken together, they could 'virtually' cover the full financial cost of a disabled claimant's needs, including the cost of employing a full-time living-in PA for those who needed one. Claimants were also legally entitled to lump-sum awards to cover major items such as furnishing, clothing and household equipment. As noted above, these are particularly important to disabled people. Following the social security review of 1988 this support was removed (Glendinning, 1990).

It was replaced by two discretionary, cash-limited funds; the Social Fund and the Independent Living Fund. The Social Fund, which is administered by the DSS, is designed to provide single-payment grants for specific items needed by the poorest disabled people, especially if they are at risk of being admitted to a residential home (Glendinning, 1990). The Independent Living Fund (ILF) is run by the DSS with the full cooperation of the DIG. The funding, headquarters and staff are supplied by the DSS and the trustees are chosen in equal numbers by the DSS and the DIG. The ILF was set up to compensate for some of the financial losses incurred by people with severe impairments following the abolition of the Domestic Assistance Addition (DAA) to Supplementary Benefit in April 1988 (*Same Difference*, 1990a).

These developments signify a major shift in the allocation of resources for disabled people away from statutory provision with its commitment to 'demand-led expenditure', in favour of a discretionary-based system with a limited budget controlled by 'quasi-independent organisations' which are publicly accountable only in part. In short, disabled people's rights and legal entitlements have been substantially eroded by Government efforts to control public spending and reduce the power of the welfare state. Under the new system there are no guarantees that even the most urgent needs will be met, no assurances that applicants in similar circumstances or with similar needs will be treated equally, and only very limited rights of appeal (Glendinning, 1990).

These criticisms certainly apply to the Social Fund. A recent report by the NACABx found that in a sample of 550 Social Fund applicants only 20 per cent had their claims met in full. A staggering 55 per cent had been refused support altogether. Of those described as 'sick or disabled', 23 per cent had been refused a grant. Thus, as pressure on the annual budget increases, the major inadequacies of the system in meeting even the most basic needs become apparent. Applicants considered high-priority are refused simply because the local office budget is exhausted. It is, therefore, impossible for an applicant to predict whether s/he will receive a grant, a loan or a refusal. Applicants in the same circumstances will receive very different decisions, and there is no formal appeals procedure outside the DSS (NACABx 1990).

The report showed that people were very reluctant to apply to the Social Fund because in certain instances they were offered loans instead of grants and felt they would not be unable to meet the repayments. People were also put off by the complexity of the claiming process. Moreover, because there are no clear criteria for payment, the onus is on the applicant to provide the appropriate information. This means that applicants with limited communication or literacy skills are at a 'particular disadvantage' (NACABx, 1990, p. 3). At present, the only way this problem can be overcome is by reliance on others. A recent study showed that Social Fund applicants who enlisted the help of a social worker were far more likely to receive payment than those who did not (Community Care and the Benefit Research Unit, 1990).

The Independent Living Fund came about as a result of the DIG's collaboration with the Government after the publication of the 1986 Social Security Act and the social security changes discussed above. The DIG's action was severely criticised by many disabled people because it effectively stifled the possibility of wider public debate on the purpose and practice of funding personal assistance. Moreover, when the ILF was set up there were a number of disabled people with considerable expertise in the process of gaining and using money to buy personal assistance. These experts were ignored when the trustees came to draw up their guide-lines, although some — notably the Hampshire Coalition of Disabled People — did offer their services (Mason, 1990). The ILF currently employs fifty-five staff, the majority of whom are on secondment from the DSS. Their wages are paid out of ILF funding (House of Commons Social Services Select Committee, 1990).

The ILF is a state-sponsored charity whose sole purpose is to keep disabled people out of institutions. While this is a worthy goal in itself, the ILF does not see disabled people as 'whole' people, but merely as 'eaters and sleepers' (Mason, 1990). It provides weekly payments to cover the cost of personal and domestic services as well as one-off payments for special equipment. In the assessment process the only tasks considered eligible for awards are those to do with personal and domestic needs; employment needs are not taken into account. The ILF is not intended to enable disabled people to achieve equal opportunities, and it therefore contributes to the discriminatory process, Moreover, as with all discretionary systems, ILF applicants have to submit to an economic means-test. Hence, any income above the DSS income support level is considered available to pay for essential services. Although the application process for ILF awards is fairly simple and straightforward, claimants are subjected to the indignity of assessment by a visiting social worker (VSW) who will require proof of income and expenditure (*Same Difference*, 1990a).

Originally the Government expected that the ILF would only be used by about 300 people, reflecting the small number receiving the DAA. But the availability of DAA was not widely publicised and like many DSS impairment-related benefits it was difficult to claim. The setting-up of the ILF, on the other hand, received a great deal of publicity and, largely through the efforts of the DIG, was providing financial support to 3,000 disabled people within its first year. In the event, the ILF's budget has risen from £5 million in 1988/9 to £62 million for 1991/92 (Large, 1990).

Many people experience problems with the ILF. Long delays before decisions on claims are common. This causes great anxiety and cash flow problems to anyone involved. There are huge gaps between the VSW's assessment visit, confirmation of the award and when people actually start to receive the money — at present around three months (Mason, 1990).

The cash amounts and the way they are calculated are inadequate for what they are intented to pay for. They do not accommodate basic variables such as staff holidays, weekend pay, night attention and staff change-over, nor do they allow for any sudden irregularities or emergencies — though some of these sums can be recouped at a later date by reapplication. Independent Living Fund support does not allow for administrative and management costs which are regarded as normal by commercial and statutory agencies doing the same sort of work. It does not cover, among other things, insuring staff, advertising, interviewing and training. Disabled people must meet these costs from their other over-stretched resources, which can cause severe cash problems. In addition, the grants paid to fund PAs' salaries are based on the lowest pay rates (Mason, 1990). The reliance upon cheap labour for personal and domestic assistance should not be a basis upon which to structure disabled people's lives.

The conditions under which awards are made do not allow people to employ family or friends as PAs, and the criteria for eligibility can rule out some people who require assistance. The ILF receives 1,800 applications every month, but only one in three is successful. Claimants are, however, entitled to a review if the award is turned down or considered too low. Again, claimants are urged to seek the assistance of a welfare rights worker to help with their claim (*Same Difference*, 1990a).

In 1990, a lack of resources forced the ILF to restrict awards still further. In its response to calls for extra funds by the ILF's trustees, the Government argued that the organisation was making awards to people for whom it was not intended; also, that it was set up as a temporary measure to fill the gap created by the 1988 social security review until the implementation of the social service reforms of 1991/3 (see Chapter 6), when local authorities will take over its responsibilities. This prospect is viewed with alarm by some disabled people because, despite its shortcomings, the ILF has given them direct control over their own personal and domestic support services. To relinquish that control to local authorities' social services departments signals a further denial of disabled people's right to autonomy. 'To replace charity by parish relief does nothing to further the rights of disabled people' (Witcher quoted in *Same Difference*, 1990a, p. 2).

The Benefit System and Employment.   As was shown in the previous Chapter, work is central to our society and disabled people are at a particular disadvantage within the British labour market. Current and proposed social security arrangements act as a major disincentive to their employment, despite Government declarations of intent to remedy the situation.

At present, income maintenance levels draw a sharp distinction between capacity and incapacity for work. Benefits awarded on grounds of incapacity for work, such as IVB or SDA, may be lost in full when an individual actively seeks work or receives employment training. Current social security arrangements — particularly the complexity of the system, the humiliation of the claiming process, and the uncertainty of its outcome — make it particularly difficult for disabled people to move between employment and unemployment. Those who take a job run the risk of losing their right to benefit should they become unemployed within a remarkably short period of time. The risks are greatest for those under twenty, who, following a spell of paid employment, may never be able to re-establish entitlement to SDA. The period under which benefit entitlement is safeguarded is currently eight weeks (Hirst, 1990). Disabled people are forced to choose between competing for mainly low-paid, low-status jobs on unfavourable terms with non-disabled people, and thereby losing some of the impairment-related benefits, or resigning themselves to long-term unemployment.

People on IVB or SDA are allowed to obtain employment, but only if they can prove that this work is medically certifiable as 'beneficial', or if it has 'therapeutic value'. This in itself is remarkable in a society where work is crucial to an individual's self-esteem and the debilitating physical and psychological consequences of unemployment are well known. Moreover, the amount which can be earned is subject to a 'Therapeutic Earnings Limit' of £35 per week. If an individual is able to earn more than this amount, then s/he is no longer considered incapable of work (DSS, 1990, p. 32), regardless of the severity of impairment, and the type of work involved.

As shown in Chapter 4, those people who choose employment are invariably penalised financially. Apart from MA and AA, the granting of which is put at some risk when an individual starts work (given the prevailing assumptions surrounding disabled people and employment, it is likely to be far more difficult to 'prove' functional incapacity if one is in work), the present benefit system does not accommodate impairment-related expenses for disabled people who are actually in employment. For example, there is no state-sponsored system for enabling disabled people to employ a PA for work. Some local authorities (a minority) will pay the full cost of employing PAs, while others will pay less, the ILF providing finance to cover the balance, but this is extremely limited in relation to the work likely to be required and is not consistent throughout the country. Moreover, in both cases the recipients of these services are subject to means-testing, and consequently any income above the level of income support is regarded as available to cover the cost of PAs.

In a minority of cases the employment of PAs can be funded by charities. For example, the Royal National Institute for the Blind (RNIB) can provide a personal reader service, but the readers are mainly paid for either by the employer or by the disabled worker. Since most employers have hitherto proved reluctant to provide any facilities whatsoever to enable disabled people to work (see Chapter 4), most workers who require a PA have to pay for one them- selves. Hence, the disabled worker has to earn the equivalent of two people's wages or there is no financial incentive for her/him to work at all. Indeed, even where a disabled person has sufficient income to employ a PA s/he is not allowed to offset that cost against tax liability. According to the Inland Revenue, 'a PA is a perk, a luxury, not a necessity and therefore its tax liability is increased, not decreased' (Mason, 1990, p. 2).

The Government has acknowledged these problems in its recent review of social security benefits for disabled people, *The Way Ahead* (DSS, 1990). In consequence, a new benefit called the 'Dis- ability Employment Credit', recently renamed 'Disability Working Allowance' (DWA), will be introduced in 1992. It will be paid to dis- abled people in receipt of the new DLA or to those assessed by a doc- tor as only partly capable of work who are getting IVB, SDA, or the Income Support or Housing Benefit premiums. It will also be avail- able to some disabled people in work who were receiving specific benefits before they started work and who are on very low incomes. The new benefit is designed to top up low earnings and result in a higher income for some disabled people. Also, those receiving the new benefit who were receiving either IVB or SDA before starting work will, if they lose their jobs, be eligible for long-term 'incapacity benefits' without having to re-qualify (DSS, 1990). It is officially estimated that only about 50,000 disabled people will be eligible for the new scheme (Glendinning, 1990, p. 14).

There is a number of problems with these proposals. First, there are many disabled workers on extremely low wages who will not qualify for DLA because they have neither 'self-care needs' or mobility problems; only 8 per cent of all disabled adults receive AA and 7 per cent MA (Martin and White, 1988). The rest will not, therefore, benefit from these measures. Secondly, it is not clear how 'partial incapacity' for work will be assessed as there is no precedent for this within the existing benefit system. Originally the Govern- ment proposed that claimants must 'satisfy a doctor that they were only partially capable of work' and that since the new benefit is to be paid for six-month periods only, claims will be subject to 'periodic medical evidence of partial incapacity'. However, a recent House of Commons Social Services Select Committee which looked at these new proposals warned ministers about subjecting disabled workers on low pay to 'inappropriate medical assessments' (House of Com- mons Social Services Select Committee, 1990, p. 29). It has subsequently been announced that self-assessment will be acceptable in order to claim DWA (Brindle, 1990). Claimants are likely, therefore, to have similar problems to those discussed above. Additionally, the question of periodic assessments of part-incapacity has yet to be resolved. Thirdly, the position of those termed 'partially capable' of work is not clear. At the moment they would not qualify for IVB but would be assessed as unemployed and so suffer a loss of income (Graham *et al.*, 1990).

Fourthly, it is not evident whether disabled people working part-time will be eligible for the new scheme or, if they are, at what point the Government will draw the line about the number of hours worked. Fifthly, the new benefit does not accommodate disabled people who lose their jobs for other reasons than incapacity for work, such as discrimination.

Finally, the new benefit, because it involves an economic means-test, does not address the major problem of low-take up. The House of Commons Social Services Select Committee mentioned above expressed fears that the new benefit would, like Family Credit, suffer from low take-up problems as well as a poverty-trap effect. The MPs stated:

> We believe that fears that a claim for the new benefit combined with the existing barriers faced by disabled people seeking entry to the labour market are likely to form a very strong disincentive for disabled people who are keen to work but who are understandably concerned not to jeopardise income in cash or in kind (House of Commons Social Services Select Committee, 1990, p. 29).

Conclusion

This chapter has demonstrated that the overwhelming majority of disabled people and their families are disproportionately reliant upon social security arrangements for their livelihood and experience extreme economic deprivation as a result. The evidence shows that for disabled people the price of living on welfare is a systematic erosion of personal autonomy and excessive bureaucratic regulation and control. It is also evident that this process intensified markedly in the 1980s.

There has been widespread concern over the financial circumstances of disabled people and their families since the 1960s, and repeated calls have been made for a comprehensive disability income. Government research shows that families with a disabled member have significantly lower incomes than those without. This was attributed to the high unemployment rate among disabled people (due to institutional discrimination within the labour market) and the extra financial costs of impairment. Using a more appropriate research methodology, data from the DIG show that although accurate in its conclusions, the Government study has seriously underestimated the true financial cost of impairment and the degree of economic deprivation suffered by most disabled people. The Government has largely ignored this evidence.

This is important because the lack of financial resources in an overtly materialist society such as that in Britain is a major factor in the discriminatory process. Economic deprivation alone, however, does not separate disabled people from the rest of the community. Like other benefit claimants they have the indignity of living on state welfare, which is then enhanced by the disability benefit system, reinforced by the degrading claiming procedures and compounded by its failure to integrate them into mainstream employment.

The disability benefits system in force at the time of writing is clearly an *ad hoc* hotchpotch of grossly inadequate measures which maintain the historical divisions between disabled and non-disabled people. It uses explicitly 'disablist' terminology that perpetuates the illusion of dependence and is characterised by a complexity which encourages the notion that disabled people's economic needs are well provided for. This complexity also creates significant economic and social differences within the disabled community as a whole.

The recent changes to the social security arrangements have made this situation far worse. The policy of targeting benefits at those considered 'most in need' through the use of economic means-tests and the shift away from statutory entitlement in favour of discretionary awards distributed by semi-independent organisations with limited budgets, signifies both an erosion of disabled people's rights and an intensification of bureaucratic regulation and control. The claiming process has become even more tortuous than before and disabled people are now subject to the indignity and humiliation of at least two means-tests, a functional or medical one and an economic one, the outcomes of which are never certain.

The present disability benefits system demands and rewards complete dependence and penalises individual autonomy. Disabled people are forced to elicit the aid of professionals in order to help them emphasise their individual impairments and beg for the allowances to which they are entitled. In addition, because the existing and proposed social security arrangements fail to compensate for the problems faced by disabled people within the context of the labour market, they will continue to be a major disincentive to employment in the foreseeable future. The overwhelming majority of disabled people will therefore remain dependent upon welfare, and their social inefficiency will be preserved. While the introduction of a national disability income might go some way towards making this disadvantaged position a little more palatable, it will certainly not change it.

6

THE HEALTH AND SOCIAL SUPPORT SERVICES

Earlier chapters have shown that since the 1939–45 war Government policies on health and support systems for disabled people have been increasingly geared toward provision within the community. This has led to both an expansion of services at the local level and a proliferation of professional helpers who exercise considerable power over those they profess to be helping. It has also been demonstrated that disabled people's ability to participate in the economic and social life of the community is frequently adversely affected by this provision. This chapter looks in detail at health and social support systems and raises a number of major issues which must be addressed if institutional discrimination against disabled people is to be eliminated.

The Organisation and Funding of Health and Social Support Services for Disabled People

Organisation. Throughout the post-1945 period the expansion of the health and social support services for disabled people has been constructed upon the erroneous belief that disabled people are not competent to make basic decisions about their own individual service needs (Wood, 1990). This has far-reaching negative implications for disabled people, since logic dictates that if they cannot assume responsibility for organising their own lives then they cannot assume the responsibilities of citizenship. Recent developments within these services will do little to change this perception.

Since the rhetoric of 'community care' has intensified markedly throughout the 1980s (Barclay Report, 1982; Audit Commission, 1986; Griffifths, 1988; HMSO, 1989b), it is important to remember the discriminatory implications of the phrase itself. The concept 'community' is a hazy one, but within the context of community care it suggests life outside an institution within a bounded locality characterised by close social networks between neighbours. Broadly, the verb 'to care' means to look after and protect, with a definite implication of dependence in the person cared for (Rae, 1990). Consequently, what is really meant by the term 'community care' is community dependence or, to be more precise, dependence upon the community.

During the 1970s and 1980s community-based services for disabled people remained confused and extremely variable with no clear national guide-lines (Griffiths, 1988; HMSO, 1989b). For example, the Audit Commission in 1986 pointed out that there was an urgent need for wide-ranging organisational changes and new approaches from service providers if effective community-based provision was to become a reality (Audit Commission, 1986). In 1988 a report by Sir Roy Griffiths, then Vice Chairman of the National Health Service (NHS) management board, recommended that there should be sufficient 'ring-fenced' funding made available for the expansion and development of a wide range of community-based services by both statutory and private agencies, and that the responsibility for coordinating this provision should rest with local authorities (Griffiths, 1988).

One year later the White Paper *Caring For People* announced Government plans for the development of community-based services. Briefly, its stated aim was to end the confusion and fragmentation of responsibilities for the provision of services between social security, health, local authorities, private and voluntary agencies; to extend consumer choice; to encourage private and voluntary provision; and to make services more accountable. From April 1991 primary responsibility for planning, coordinating and paying for support services was to be assigned to local authority social services departments, along with instructions to look to the private sector to achieve cost-effectiveness (HMSO, 1989b).

Although the White Paper proposed widespread changes to the administration and funding of community-based services, it did not propose the ring-fencing of funding or recommend any overall increase in resources as Griffiths had recommended. Moreover, recent ministerial concern over the cost of implementation has meant that it has been postponed. Latest estimates suggest that the Government plans will not be implemented until well into 1993 (Langan, 1990).

Viewed in conjunction with the recent changes to the benefit system (discussed in the last chapter), these proposals are unlikely to lead to an increase in choice, control, accountability and autonomy for the overwhelming majority of disabled people. On the whole, disabled people do not have the financial resources to purchase services on the open market, and the only ones available under the new system will be those which have contracts with local authorities (Glendinning, 1990). Most important, the traditional view that disabled people are not able to take control of their own lives has been reiterated and indeed strengthened with the assertion that local authorities should appoint 'case' managers to organise and manage 'care packages' for individual disabled people (HMSO, 1989b).

This clearly ignores the views of disabled people and their organisations, who have consistently called for a more holistic and realistic view of disabled people's needs. Commenting on the new proposals, Richard Wood, Director of the British Council of Organizations of Disabled People (BCODP), has stated that they

> ignored the call from disabled people for self management and concentrated instead on the rehashing of existing inappropriate services and devising new roles for yet another new breed of professionals who will have more control over our lives than we have (Wood, 1990, unpaged).

By ignoring the views of disabled people in this way and by emphasising and expanding the role of professionals, the new proposals add significant weight to the growing belief among disabled people that the British welfare system is organised around the needs of service providers rather than those of the users of those services.

Funding. Notwithstanding that Government spending on community-based provision increased steadily in the 1980s (in 1979/80 it stood at £1,169 million, rising to £3.444 million in 1987/8 [HMSO, 1989b]), it has always been accorded a low priority within the health and social support services. In the NHS it has taken second place to hospital-based facilities for acute patients and in local authorities to child care and the elderly (Beardshaw, 1988).

Recent evidence suggests that this situation is unlikely to change within the foreseeable future. At a time when demand for services will almost certainly increase due to an ageing population, Government spending on the health and social support services is expected to fall (Langan, 1990). Additionally, a Department of Health report recently noted that service developments for disabled people are often 'given a lower priority then service developments for other groups of service users and other local authority service committees' (Warburton, 1990, p. 2).

It should be remembered here that the lion's share of any money allocated to services for disabled people will go to service providers. The biggest consumers of welfare services are the producers of those services (Oliver, 1990a, Wolfensberger, 1980). By far the largest proportion of the health and social services budget, for example, up to 70 per cent in some cases, is spent on staff wages (Oliver, 1990a).

Present arrangements allow state officials considerable discretion as to how funds allocated for services for disabled people are spent at the local level. Information concerning funding for community services is difficult to obtain, and there is little data on expenditure on disabled people. However, a recent report by the Health Economics Consortium at the University of York, commissioned to provide evidence for the Griffiths review, provides some comparative data in this area.

The report examines health and local authority spending on a variety of health and support services for elderly and disabled people. The data are taken from six district health authorities in England and their associate local authorities. The areas were chosen for their diversity. They are not a representative sample and the numbers are too small for the information to be indicative of the national picture, but the report does demonstrate the extreme variation in funding and gives some insight into local priorities.

The report shows that funding for community services comes from a variety of sources, including district health authorities (DHAs), local authorities, social security payments and voluntary agencies. As the focus of the report was public expenditure, no attempt was made to quantify the finances independently raised through fund-raising activities and bequests (Gray *et al.*, 1988).

Table 6.1. Percentage of Total Expenditure on Community-Based Services for Disabled and Elderly People

Source of funding	%
District health authorities	52
Local authorities	34
Benefits (board and lodging payments)	11
Private/voluntary sector	3

Source: Adapted from Fig. 1 in Gray *et al.*, 1988.

There were important differences between localities in who provided what services and the amounts provided. For example, in two of the districts over 70 per cent of funding came from the health authority while in two others the local authority spent more. In general, however, district health authorities were the largest providers, giving 52 per cent; local authorities provided 34 per cent, 11 per cent came from welfare benefits in board and lodging payments, and the private/voluntary sector funded 3 per cent (see Table 6.1).

Table 6.2.   Per Capita Expenditure from all Sources on all Types of Provision for Disabled and Elderly People in Six District Health Authorities, 1985–6

Area	Elderly people	People + mental illness	People + learning diff'ties	People + physical impairments	All
1	72	14	10	5	100
2	71	41	21	7	140
3	72	10	17	6	106
4	49	61	54	8	172
5	63	30	64	4	162
6	60	25	23	5	112
Average	66	24	27	5	123

Source: Adapted from Table 3.4 in Gray *et al.*, 1988.

There was also some variation in the allocation of resources to the different user-groups. The average expenditure per head of the total local population was £123, but two areas spent over £160 while two others spent less than £110. In addition, spending on disabled people was divided three ways, namely for people with mental illness, people with learning difficulties and people with physical impairments (see Table 6.2).

Overall, spending was weighted heavily toward institutional provision of one form or another. Seventy-three per cent of all finance went on residential or hospital-based services, with only 18 per cent toward community provision; 7 per cent went on day care and 1 per cent each on respite care and group homes (see Table 6.3). This is particularly alarming considering that the debilitating psychological effects of institutional life are now well known.

Table 6.3.   Allocation of Expenditure on Community-Based Services for Disabled and Elderly People

Service	% of expenditure
Residential and hospital-based care	73
Community service	18
Day centres	7
Group homes	1
Respite care	1

Source: Adapted from Fig. 5 in Gray *et al.*, 1988.

Clearly, spending on services for disabled people is accorded a low priority within official circles. While this might be construed as evidence of institutional discrimination against disabled people, it is important to remember that underfunding is unfortunately a common feature of the British welfare system as a whole. It is not perculiar to provision for this particular user-group. Institutional discrimination is evident, however, in the way in which most of the money allocated to services for disabled people is currently being spent, namely on professionals' salaries and on outdated and outmoded forms of service provision. Hitherto, professional interventions and traditional facilities have achieved little in terms of giving disabled people the same level of autonomy and independence as their able-bodied peers. Indeed, they have tended to achieve the reverse.

Residential Care

It is evident that despite the rhetoric of community care there remains a strong emphasis upon segregated residential care for disabled people. Traditional prejudices maintain that disabled people are dependent and unable to look after themselves (Wood, 1990). In many cases they are confined to a residential institution and kept from making the most basic of decisions and deprived of the opportunities which able-bodied people take for granted (Brisenden, 1985). Disabled people in such places 'suffer loss of social skills and self-confidence'. The Independent Living Movement (ILM) has repeatedly demonstrated that nobody, regardless of type and extent of impairment, 'need waste her or his life in an institution if provided with appropriate services within the community' (Ratzka, 1988, p. 5).

Here, the term 'independent' does not refer to someone who can do everything themselves, a feat that no human being can achieve, whether they have an impairment or not, but indicates someone who is able to take control of their own life and to choose how that life should be led. It is a thought process not contingent upon physical abilities:

> It cannot be applied to someone living in an institutional setting . . . , because the routine of their life will be predetermined, to a greater or lesser extent, by the needs of the professionals in charge of the institution (Brisenden, 1985, p. 2).

Life in an institution, therefore, is central to the discriminatory process because it denies inmates the right to control their lives as those do who live outside it. Independent living, on the other hand, is primarily about giving disabled people access to and control of a range of community-based services which enable them to identify and pursue their own lifestyles (Evans, 1984).

It is apparent that for many those services are not available within the community. The OPCS surveys showed that 422,000 disabled people, 20 per cent of whom are below retirement age, still live in 'communal establishments' or institutions (Martin, Meltzer and Elliot, 1988). Moreover, it is sometimes suggested that a substantial number of these people are well over retirement age and 'choose' residential living because of the security it brings (Canter and Barnitt, 1982; Harrison, 1987). It is highly questionable, however, whether this would be their choice if adequate community-based support were available, and since it is not (see below) such arguments cannot be seen as a justification for the disproportionate level of funding that residential institutions continue to receive from official sources.

It is ironic that as the criticisms of residential care during the post-1945 period intensified (see Chapter 2), there was something of an expansion of segregated residential facilities for disabled people (Harrison, 1987). At its inception in 1948 the National Health Service (NHS) had some 55,000 beds for the 'chronic sick' in England and Wales. These were left over from Poor Law infirmaries and workhouses which had been administered by local authorities since 1930. They housed a mixed population of disabled and elderly people, many of whom had no need of medical care. Additionally, the 1948 National Assistance Act gave local authorities a responsibility to provide residential facilities for people 'handicapped' by illness, injury or congenital impairment (Royal College of Physicians, 1986).

Throughout the 1950s and 1960s concern over the mix of elderly and disabled people in long-stay hospitals prompted the development of separate facilities for elderly and younger (below retirement age) disabled people. In 1968 the Secretary of State for Health and Social Services instructed Regional Hospital Boards to set up special units for the 'younger chronic sick' within the grounds of general hospitals. In 1971 the NHS Young Disabled Unit (YDU) building programme began with an initial budget of 3 million pounds. By the mid-1980s some fifty-eight YDUs had been built. They presently house around 10 per cent of all younger physically disabled people in residential care (Fielder, 1988).

During the same period there was a significant growth of voluntary sector residential provision. The Leonard Cheshire Foundation, the Shaftesbury Society, John Grooms, the Spastics Society and others began to provide residential accommodation for younger disabled people. Much of the funding for this expansion came from local authorities, which were allowed under Part 3 of the 1948 National Assistance Act to finance support for disabled people in privately-sponsored residential homes (Harrison, 1987). Current estimates suggest that the voluntary and private sectors are responsible for just under half of all the residential accommodation for people with 'physical' impairments who are below retirement age (Royal College of Physicians, 1986). Few local authorities run residential homes for disabled people, of which there were sixty-eight in 1986 (Leat, 1988).

The YDU building programme, local authority and voluntary and private sector residential provision have all developed independently of each other with little collaboration at the local level (Harrison, 1987). The YDUs have been established in isolation from community-based services for disabled people. They are a considerable drain on the limited economic and human resources available to the NHS and their continued support tends to inhibit the development of community-based alternatives.

Despite the growth in institutional provision in the mid-1980s, less than half of all disabled people of working age living in institutions were in places designed specifically for them. The majority were in old people's homes, psychiatric and geriatric hospitals, or ordinary hospital wards. Also, private residential provision for disabled people has increased, fuelled by social security board and lodging payments. Public expenditure on private sector residential care, as a result of these entitlements, rose from £12 million in 1979 to £489 million in 1987 (Land, 1988). Government plans to transfer these resources to local authorities with explicit encouragement to purchase non-residential services have been postponed. Moreover, because there are only a very few private establishments which cater exclusively for younger disabled people, this usually means accommodation in a nursing home for elderly people (Harrison, 1987).

Rehabilitation and Integration

The rehabilitation services which are currently available are highly discriminatory and do a major disservice to disabled people. This is not to deny that some people have benefited from this provision, and that more could do so if more and better services were provided, but we are concerned here with what is actually being offered.

At present rehabilitation is not only a product of institutional discrimination against disabled people; it is also a central component in the discriminatory process. It refers to 'a piecemeal welfare system of professionals and services' specifically designed to 'help' disabled people learn how to cope with 'impossible social, financial, housing and environmental difficulties', which would be totally unacceptable to any other section of the community. In most cases the only part a disabled person is expected to play in the rehabilitation process 'is an inherently dependent one' (Brechin and Liddiard, 1985, pp. 2–3). Indeed, if the economic and social barriers which confront disabled people were removed the need for rehabilitation in its present form would be greatly reduced, if not eliminated altogether (Finkelstein, 1980).

Historically, rehabilitation has been dominated by the medical and remedial professions associated with orthopaedics and rheumatology, and until fairly recently was limited to the restoration of lost abilities after illness or injury (Beardshaw, 1988). Today, however, many disabled people have to endure rehabilitation regardless of the cause of their impairment, whether it is newly acquired or present from birth. One is therefore talking of both 'rehabilitation' and 'habilitation'.

Over the years definitions have shifted away from overtly medical concerns toward a preoccupation with the 'whole individual', or the balance between the medical and the social. The Scottish Health Services Council, for example, concluded that

> rehabilitation must . . . take cognizance of the individual and his environment, in order to restore him to his former status or balance' (Scottish Health Services Council [1972] quoted in Beardshaw, 1988, p. 20).

Brechin and Liddiard (1985) have suggested that what is actually being described here is the 'promotion of a state of health or well being such as we all might strive for, disabled or not' (Brechin and Liddiard, 1985, p. 2).

Within this broader framework several writers have argued that health and well-being depend only minimally on medical intervention and more substantially on the broad social and cultural context (Brisenden, 1985; Ilsley, 1981; Oliver, 1983, 1990). But in this area medical and therapeutic approaches still dominate professional thinking (Royal College of Physicians, 1986) at the expense of other approaches which promote independent living (Brechin and Liddiard, 1985; SIA, 1987). As a result, current provision is patchy, in both quality and geographical spread, hospital-based services have been retained at the expense of community-based ones (Beardshaw, 1988; Harrison, 1987; Royal College of Physicians, 1986), and functional assessments remain crucial to the process of resource allocation (Glendinning, 1990).

Central to the traditional view of rehabilitation is the notion that individual disabled people should be subject to functional assessments by professionals in order to determine need. The importance of this process has been strongly re-emphasised in several recent Government statements on community-based provision. For example, the White Paper *Caring for People* states that the allocation of community services is to be based upon professional assessments

> of what the individual can and cannot do, and could be expected to achieve, taking account of his or her personal and social relationships. All agencies and professions involved with the individual and his or her problems should be brought into the assessment process when necessary (HMSO, 1989b, pp. 18–19).

This has a number of important discriminatory implications for disabled people. Those who need community-based support will be subject to more scrutiny and control by state officials. Comprehensive assessments by social workers and other professionals will have to be made into the individual and family circumstances of disabled people seeking support before access to services is granted. These assessments might include 'mobility, personal care, financial affairs, leisure' and 'employment'. Moreover, since social services departments are to establish and publish 'criteria of eligibility for assessment and the way in which their assessment processes will work' (HMSO, 1989b, p. 20), those receiving services will inadvertently have their economic and social circumstances made public.

In addition, recent changes to the welfare system mean that there is little scope for disabled people to challenge professional wisdom in the assessment process or service allocation. As Glendinning (1990) notes, this represents a significant loss of rights for disabled people. Under the old social security scheme (see Chapter 5), those applying for means-tested social security payments in order to buy essential services had an automatic right of appeal to an independent tribunal if they were dissatisfied with the outcome of their application. There is no right of appeal and no mechanisms for questioning the decisions of social services staff under the new system (Glendinning, 1990). This is important because historically professionals' perceptions of need are frequently at odds with those defined by disabled people and their organisations (Davis, 1990a; Oliver, 1983; GMCDP, 1989; Sutherland, 1981), and disputes between disabled people and professionals over the form and levels of service considered appropriate are not uncommon (Glendinning, 1990).

It may be argued that there is little or no need for appeals procedures and mechanisms which challenge professional wisdom within health and social support systems because disabled people and their organisations are to be involved in the planning and delivery of services at every level. To date, however, this has proved extremely difficult to achieve and recent events would suggest that it is unlikely to happen in the immediate future. The idea that disabled people and their organisations should collaborate meaningfully in the planning and running of services for disabled people was first proposed in the early 1970s by a number of disabled writers (see for example UPIAS, 1976). Over the following decade this idea became more influential and was enshrined in statute in the Disabled Persons (Services Consultation and Representation) Act 1986 (Warburton, 1990).

It is evident, however, that with only one or two notable exceptions this has not taken place. A recent Department of Health and Social Services Inspectorate report which examined the extent to which the Act had been implemented in a one-in-three sample of social services departments, found that while some authorities had made some improvements, 'for many there is much to do'. Many local authorities attributed the lack of progress to a lack of resources, although local authority support grants have recognised the need for spending in this area (Warburton, 1990, p. 1).

As for Section 10 of the 1986 Act, which requires local authorities to co-opt people with specialist knowledge of disability to council committees, there was evidence of widespread discrimination. The report noted that there was 'a gap between intent and practice'. Although Section 10 specifically requires local authorities to consult with organisations of disabled people when making co-options, some authorities 'thought' they were operating according to the law by consulting with voluntary organisations concerned with disability. Only one London borough indicated a positive stance toward organisations of or for disabled people; other respondents did not distinguish between the two. Two authorities, one of which was a London borough, reported that it was not council policy to make co-options on to representative committees. Another said that it had individual disabled people on various committees, but added that such representation is 'cosmetic' (Warburton, 1990, p. 30).

This should not be surprising, since organisations of disabled people have received little support from central Government. The British Council of Organizations of Disabled People (BCODP), the national umbrella organisation of eighty organisations of disabled people with a total membership of over 200,000, received a paltry £30,000 from the Department of Health in 1989/90. By contrast, the Royal Association for Disability and Rehabilitation

(RADAR), the national equivalent for the more traditional organisations *for* disabled people, received £233,000 (*Hansard*, 1990a).
Historically, organisations *for* disabled people have represented
the interests of disabled people to Government and are 'used and
supported by Government for this purpose'. They often 'lack direct
contact with disabled people and are very inadequately accountable
to them' (Large, 1981, unpaged).

Moreover, organisations of disabled people have not been formally involved in the recent social services review, despite the
response to an earlier report on 'community care' by BCODP
(BCODP, 1987), and their repeated calls for more accountability in
service provision, which have been ignored. Although social service
departments are encouraged to 'consult' with disabled people when
preparing their plans for community-based services under the new
proposals, they are not obliged to demonstrate that disabled people
have actually been involved in the planning process (HMSO, 1989b,
pp. 42–3). Complaints procedures are to be established, but as
Glendinning (1990) notes, this is not the same as ensuring that users
and potential users are fully involved in specifying and monitoring
standards of quality.

If services are to move away from welfare paternalism, it is essential that they adopt and are seen to adopt a collaborative approach
between users and providers. Disabled people must also have easy
access to a wide range of interlinked provision. These should include
specialist facilities such as spinal injury units, occupational and physiotherapy services in hospital settings to aid recovery, and a variety
of facilities specifically concerned with independent living (Beardshaw, 1988). As for the latter, these can be summarised within the
framework of 'the seven needs' identified by the Derbyshire Coalition of Disabled People (DCDP): information, counselling, housing, technical aids and adaptations, personal assistance, transport,
and physical access (DCC, 1986; Davis, 1990, 1990a).

Housing, transport and physical access are examined in the
following chapter; here we look at information and counselling,
technical aids and adaptations and personal assistance.

Information, Counselling and Advice

Information is fundamental to any decision, and indeed has been
described as 'the fourth right of citizenship'. In addition to the
general information that all people need, in an able-bodied society
disabled people need specialist information. The lack of this information is as discriminatory 'as a narrow door or a flight of stairs'

(DCC, 1986). Moreover, in view of the extreme economic and social difficulties faced by the majority of disabled people, information on its own may not be used to its full effect without counselling help (Davis, 1990). Hence there is an urgent need for a national network of information and counselling agencies.

It is evident, however, that many disabled people do not have access to this type of service. Previous chapters have shown that disabled people and their families have only a limited knowledge of education systems, employment opportunities and social security benefits. With medical data, research shows that a large proportion of disabled young adults know very little about their impairments (Anderson and Clarke, 1982; Barnes, 1990; Brimblecombe *et al.*, 1985). People with newly-acquired impairments often receive insufficient information and counselling to understand their changed circumstances (Morris, 1989; Oliver *et al.*, 1988). There is also substantial evidence that disabled people and their families have only limited knowledge of community-based health and support services and technical aids and equipment (Martin, White and Meltzer, 1989; Morris, 1989; Oliver and Hasler, 1987; Oliver *et al.*, 1988). Indeed, this general lack of information 'seems to be as common in the 1980s as it was during the 1950s, 1960s and 1970s' (Morris, 1989, p. 33).

Whilst this might be partly explained by the cumulative debilitating psychological effects of institutional discrimination on disabled individuals in other areas, in education and the labour markets for example, it is also due to the 'professionalisation' of disability. As noted earlier, within the context of the welfare system disabled people are confronted by a bewildering array of professionals, those whom Davis has termed the 'denizens of the disability industry' (Davis, 1990b). This not only presents problems stemming from inter-disciplinary communication, and to some degree rivalry, but it also contributes to the process of 'mystification' (Wilding, 1982).

It has been well documented elsewhere that each profession or specialisation tends to assume a language, a set of policies and a code of practice which give professional respectability and status to its work and its practitioners. Preservation of status would appear to depend upon the maintenance of a 'decent gulf between professionals and clients' (Wilding, 1982). This is an inevitable consequence of the traditional paternalistic model of professional work and is an important element in the discriminatory process. All too often professionals confront disabled people who seek their services with their own definition of the problem which substantially ignores the views of those seeking help (Morris, 1989; Oliver *et al.*, 1988; Sutherland, 1981; UPIAS, 1976). Consequently, disabled people find getting appropriate information not only unnecessarily intimidating but also problematic. Moreover, without this information they face great difficulty in gaining any measure of control over how their needs should be met, or even whether their needs will be met at all (BCODP, 1987; Oliver, 1983; Oliver *et al.*, 1988; Wilding, 1982).

There is no uniform approach to advice and counselling services for disabled people within health authorities or in local authorities' social services departments. This task is usually performed by a variety of professionals, such as GPs, social workers, health visitors and hospital doctors, according to their individual interpretation of their professional role. The Seebohm Report (1968) suggested that it should be undertaken by social workers, but this has not materialised. Few social workers are trained for this type of work (Oliver, 1983), and early evidence suggests that they are reluctant to work with disabled or elderly people (Rees, 1978).

Under Section 9 of the 1986 Disabled Person's Act local authorities' social service departments are obliged to give disabled people information relevant to their needs. But this seems to have had little impact on social services personnel. Many appear to think that producing and distributing handbooks or funding information services run by voluntary agencies is all that is required. There is a need for more supervision in this area within social service departments, since it is evident that staff do not take this role seriously and are not fully informed of the wide range of equipment and services currently available (Parratt, 1989). A Department of Health Social Services Inspectorate report published in 1990 concluded that 'it was discouraging that so little had been done by social services departments to provide relevant information in suitable formats for disabled people' (Warburton, 1990, p. 3).

Self-help groups have attempted to fill this gap both locally and nationally. Their emergence over the last couple of decades has been partly in response to the perceived shortcomings of the health and social support services. There are three main differences between self-help groups and other service agencies. First, a common problem or predicament is shared by all or most of the members, and for disabled people this is the experience of discrimination. Secondly, there is reciprocity of helping amongst most of these members and, thirdly, the group is self-managing (Robinson and Henry, 1977). A wide range of advice, information and peer counselling is offered to disabled people and their families by self-help groups (Oliver and Hasler, 1987).

Yet the overwhelming majority of these 'organisations of disabled people' receive little or no financial support from local authorities, and those which do are under the constant threat of having it withdrawn. Cuts in local authority spending that resulted from the introduction of the Community Charge or Poll Tax meant that many self-help groups had their funding drastically reduced (*Disability Now*, 1990a).

For example, the Derbyshire Coalition of Disabled People, one of the best known and most successful self-help organisations in Britain, had £24,000 cut from its annual budget of £48,000 half way through the financial year. Since the funds are allocated periodically over twelve months and used up almost immediately, this amounted to a 100 per cent cut in revenue. As a result, four of the seven part-time staff employed specifically to give peer counselling and advice were made redundant. The Derbyshire Centre for Integrated Living had £100,000 deducted from its annual grant of £420,000. The only way redundancies were avoided was by staff working shorter hours. Remarkably, the other two groups supported by funds from Derbyshire County Council's Equal Opportunities Department, namely women and ethnic minorities, did not have their budgets reduced at all (Davis, 1990c).

Technical Aids and Equipment

Functional impairment can be overcome by the provision of suitable technical aids and equipment (DCDP, 1986). The inability of the British welfare system to provide appropriate aids and equipment for people who experience functional impairment is an important part of institutional discrimination. It not only limits their ability to participate in the mainstream economic and social life of the community but heightens their dependence on others.

The latest estimates suggest that 69 per cent of disabled adults use some form of special equipment. This includes wheelchairs and walking aids, surgical aids and appliances (such as surgical braces and artificial limbs), aids to help vision, hearing and incontinence, small equipment and gadgets, and special furniture and other equipment to help with personal needs. Not surprisingly the use of special equipment increases with severity of impairment (Martin, White and Meltzer, 1989). It should be noted that the OPCS researchers did not count spectacles as special equipment because most disabled adults, 89 per cent, used glasses 'whether they had a seeing disability or not' (Martin, White and Meltzer, 1989 p. 51).

The OPCS survey recorded a significant level of unmet need in this particular area. For example, 7 per cent of people with mobility problems thought that they needed equipment which they did not have, 13 per cent of those with visual impairments said that they needed vision aids, 29 per cent of those with hearing impairments needed hearing equipment, and 17 per cent of the people with continence impairments thought that their current arrangements were inadequate. Also, about a quarter of those with impairments affecting physical dexterity in reaching or stretching felt they needed small aids and gadgets that they did not have (Martin, White and Meltzer, 1989, Chapter 5).

In addition, given the methodological limitations of the OPCS survey, discussed in detail in Chapters 2 and 4, these findings have to be treated with the utmost caution. The real level of unmet need is likely to be far higher than these estimates. To establish whether disabled people needed any equipment which they did not have, individuals with only 'relevant' impairments were shown a card with a list of special aids on it. They were then asked:

> Are there any aids such as those listed on this card which you think would help you but that you don't have at the moment? (Martin, White and Meltzer, 1989, p. 46).

There was no room for discussion or clarification of what the items listed on the card actually were. Indeed, the OPCS researchers themselves appeared somewhat sensitive about their methods on this issue. When explaining their findings, they said that the low proportions of unmet need 'could' indicate that people were 'relatively satisfied' with their present situation, 'but is probably, at least in part, a reflection of the lack of knowledge people have about what sort of equipment is available' (Martin, White and Meltzer, 1989, p. 49).

Beardshaw (1988) has shown that technical aids and equipment supply make up the single most confused area of service provision for disabled people. District health authorities, local authority social service departments, Artificial Limb and Appliance Centres (ALACs) — which till 1991 were controlled by a special health authority, namely the Disability Services Authority (DSA) — regional health authorities and the voluntary sector are all responsible for different aspects of the service. The result is 'chaos' (Beardshaw, 1988).

The supply of special equipment has evolved in an *ad hoc* fashion over a long period. The result is a hotchpotch of provision delivered by a variety of sources, with important service overlaps and omissions. Theoretically, health authorities provide medical aids, while social services departments are responsible for 'aids for daily living'. In reality, however, this distinction is difficult to sustain, particularly since many people use both these things for personal and domestic support. Hence, some equipment is available from social services, while alternatives are provided by health authorities. Moreover, some essential special aids are generally unavailable from any statutory authority (Beardshaw, 1988).

It can easily be seen, therefore, that getting equipment is complex, time-consuming and often frustrating, and that multiple sources of supply for some items, coupled with the absence of provision of others, causes confusion for disabled people and their families. Poor assessment procedures and the prescriptive professional practices mentioned above undoubtedly contribute to this. Because professionals control access to different items of equipment, there are frequently significant local variations due to 'provider discretion' (Cantley and Hunter, 1985).

In general, the quality of provision is not good. Often disabled people feel compelled to accept what is offered from a particular agency instead of choosing an item that would best suit their needs (Beardshaw, 1988). For example, the Association of Spina Bifida and Hydrocephalus (ASABH) has reported that nine out of ten young people with spina bifida arc given wheelchairs that are unsuitable or unsafe (McColl 1986). Many people suffer long delays before getting the equipment they need (Oliver *et al.*, 1988), and maintenance and upgrading are a constant problem (McColl, 1986). A recent review of clinics for disabled young adults found that 27 per cent of users examined had unsatisfactory or worn out equipment (Thomas *et al.*, 1989).

Voluntary sector involvement in this area also varies greatly. Local charities sometimes play a key role in disseminating information about special aids and equipment, and provide funds for items which are difficult to obtain through public agencies. In some areas they help coordinate services by running stores or showrooms from which aids can be selected. In others voluntary bodies have joined with health authorities and local authority social service departments to coordinate a joint supply service for disabled people (Fielder, 1988).

However, in addition to questions about the organisation of technical aids supply, the crucial issue of what is actually being provided also needs to be addressed. Much of the equipment provided by the state sector is simply not good enough. The provision of wheelchairs is an important example. Although wheelchair and artificial limb supply services were censured by an independent working party in 1986 for failing to provide an adequate service (McColl, 1986), and a quasi-independent body, the DSA, was set up a year later to coordinate provision, little changed.

A recent report by the Institute of Health and Economic Affairs concluded that the provision of wheelchairs and other special aids has become stuck in a '40-year time warp' due to the state's mono-poly of services for disabled people. Drawing attention to the tech-nological advances which have transformed the lives of disabled people in other countries, the report states that the wheelchairs pro-vided by the British welfare system are of such low quality that they would not be offered on the open market (Galasko and Lipskin, 1989).

The standard-issue NHS wheelchair was designed in the 1930s. It is heavy and difficult to manoeuvre. Lightweight wheelchairs are generally unavailable through the NHS. Although some people engaged in sporting activities manage to obtain them through the DSA, the majority who want this type of machine have to buy it themselves or get financial help from charities. Lightweight chairs can be obtained through the Department of Employment as long as they are considered necessary for employment. To obtain one in this way the disabled person has to 'prove' that s/he needs it for work.

However, even the provision of lightweight wheelchairs does not give wheelchair-users optimum mobility or independence. To travel any distance they are still dependent upon an ambulant companion. Research shows that at best about 25 per cent of wheelchair-users can push themselves no more than 200 yards in an average urban environment (Segal, 1986). To achieve meaningful independence, therefore, a range of powered wheelchairs capable of indoor and outdoor use should be available by right to all those who need them. Although in 1990 the DSA was given a £1 million grant toward providing powered wheelchairs on the NHS (Massie, 1990), this proved inadequate. Moreover, a recent report by the National Con-sumer Council warned that there is a danger that the situation will get much worse because of the abolition of the DSA. From April 1991 overall responsibility for the supply of wheelchairs and other equipment was returned to local authorities, along with two years' funding to meet disabled people's equipment needs. Once this money is spent, and the amount available is generally regarded as insufficient, wheelchair providers will have to compete with other areas of the NHS for funding (NCC, 1991). Hence, the majority of wheelchair-users will remain dependent upon others.

Personal Assistance

Many disabled people need a comprehensive and flexible system of personal assistance with things they cannot do independently. If independent living is to become a reality then the scope of this assistance needs to go beyond supporting disabled people in their home and 'extend into the community to facilitate social integration' (DCC, 1986, p. 2).

Discrimination occurs when disabled people are unable to secure the appropriate assistance to achieve social integration. As we have seen in previous chapters, only rarely are disabled people able to obtain the necessary support within the context of the workplace. In this section we demonstrate that these facilities are unavailable to the majority of disabled people within the community as a whole.

At present there is no national comprehensive and flexible support system for disabled people. For the last couple of decades the principal function of the health and social support services has been to provide assistance for the families, friends and neighbours of disabled people who provide unpaid informal support, rather than providing services directly for disabled people themselves (Parker, 1990). Government estimates suggest that there are around 4 million people, the majority of whom are women, providing informal assistance of one kind or another specifically to disabled people (Martin, White and Meltzer, 1989).

The main personal support services are organised around supplementary help with 'self-care', 'household management' and the 'relief of carers'. Most disabled people are therefore forced to be dependent on family members, friends and relatives 'at great personal, physical and fiscal cost to all concerned' (HCIL, 1990, p. 12). A comprehensive service is only provided if informal support is lacking or overstretched. Also, this service is usually a combination of statutory and voluntary provision and is never guaranteed. It is no substitute for disabled people's right to a personal support system. Moreover, the organisation of these services is one of the most complex areas of community provision, with considerable fragmentation between agencies as well as a number of important service overlaps and omissions. This causes major difficulties for disabled people and their families when trying to gain access to them (Beardshaw, 1988).

As a consequence, the overwhelming majority of families with a disabled member or members manage with minimal assistance from statutory and voluntary agencies. Government estimates suggest that overall 60 per cent of disabled adults need some form of personal and/or domestic assistance. Twenty-two per cent need some form of personal assistance with self-care: washing, dressing, using the toilet etc.; 58 per cent need help with household management, e.g. cooking, washing up, shopping and book-keeping. Of those who require a 'lot of help both day and night', only 28 per cent receive it from formal sources, namely statutory, voluntary or private agencies. Of the remainder only 20 per cent get this type of support (Martin, White and Meltzer, 1989).

The type of help given takes many forms and is delivered by a variety of professionals from a range of organisations in both the public and the private sectors. These include district health authorities, local authority social service departments and voluntary agencies, both national and local. With specialist services, the OPCS survey found that of the disabled adults living in the community, only 7 per cent had access to a health visitor, 11 per cent to a chiropodist, 10 per cent to a physiotherapist and 1 per cent to a social worker. The OPCS study only reported on whether disabled people had been visited in their own homes by these professionals within a 12-month period; the frequency of the visits was not recorded, nor was the level of user satisfaction with the services given. Additionally, researchers recorded a significant amount of unmet need in each of these areas from people who were not receiving them (Martin, White and Meltzer, 1989).

For self-care, as well as medical care such as in changing dressings and giving injections, NHS district nursing services sometimes provide help (Beardshaw, 1988). Although in a given year 16 per cent of disabled adults living in the community were visited by a district or community nurse at least once (Martin, White and Meltzer, 1989), the amount of personal assistance given is not known.

Most help with housework is provided by families and friends. Although some 'care attendant' schemes (see below) provide assistance with domestic duties, the local authority home help service is the chief source of statutory provision. Indeed, in some areas local authority home helps now provide personal assistance as a supplement to their traditional domestic role. This can be augmented by supplementary services like local authority and voluntary sector meals on wheels. According to the OPCS survey, only 14 per cent of disabled adults living at home had a home help and 4 per cent received meals on wheels (Martin, White and Meltzer, 1989). Support for these services varies greatly between local authorities. With meals on wheels, for example, rates vary by a factor of more than ten (Borsay, 1986). In addition, they are usually only provided to people who live alone and to those in the older age-groups. Almost no one under the age of fifty receives meals on wheels (Martin, White and Meltzer, 1989).

Many services are organised around the needs of the provider rather than those of the user. Statutory provision is usually restricted to 'office hours', with coverage limited or non-existent in the early mornings, evenings, at weekends and during holidays.

Service delivery tends to be structured around predetermined tasks instead of user preferences and is often unpredictably timed (Begum, 1990; Morris, 1989). Service providers are professionally trained, and provision usually reflects professional boundaries and interests. A visit by a social worker, for example, does not mean that a disabled person's personal or domestic needs are being met. Those receiving services are often subject to a succession of interventions from a variety of people. The result is that disabled people are denied the right to organise their daily lives in the same way as the rest of the population. They have little or no control over who enters their homes or what professional helpers do once they get inside (Wood, 1990).

Additionally, if disabled people are to integrate into the community then they need services which are able to respond quickly to changing need. The inflexibility and poor coordination of existing provision makes this almost impossible. A related problem is that people or families with changing needs often find it difficult to 'reactivate' contacts with services when they require help after a period of managing on their own (Oliver *et al.*, 1988).

In some areas voluntary sector 'care attendant' schemes supplement assistance provided by family members and statutory authorities. There are only a handful of schemes catering for all the personal assistance needs of disabled people. With one or two exceptions (see Owens, 1987; Fielder, 1988), these are mostly organised by the voluntary sector. Funding for voluntary sector provision is provided from statutory and charitable sources, with the lion's share coming from the former. Users themselves are also asked to contribute if they can afford to (Beardshaw, 1988).

The Association of Crossroads Care Attendants, the Leonard Cheshire Foundation's Family Support Services (FSS) and the Community Service Volunteers' Independent Living Scheme (ILS) are the three major voluntary sector care-attendant scheme providers. The first two are mainly concerned with providing assistance for families with a disabled member, but in a minority of cases they do provide services to disabled individuals living alone. There is wide variation in the level of assistance given. It can take the form of volunteers occasionally sitting with the disabled person while other family members go out, or regular help with a range of daily tasks. While some areas of the country are well covered by these schemes there are many which are not (Beardshaw, 1988).

The ILS is slightly different in that it places volunteers into disabled people's own homes for a six-month period. Over half of the users work, and others are in further education. Volunteers also help in families where there is a risk of children being taken into care. Although there are schemes throughout Britain, facilities are concentrated in the London area. In 1988, for example, 143 people were helped by the ILS: forty-two of them lived in London (Beardshaw, 1988).

Originally conceived by a disabled person, care-attendant schemes have evolved in response to some of the deficiencies of statutory provision with the aim of providing a more holistic user-centred service. In general, they are more flexibly organised, with assistance available outside office hours, and users and informal helpers are partly responsible for the training and supervision of volunteers. However, they are primarily a voluntary service. Provision is often unreliable and unpredictable (Begum, 1990) and ultimate control does not rest with users or their families (Mason, 1990). The FSSs, for example, are normally run by management committees comprising local dignitaries rather than by organisations of disabled people. In addition, their availability is largely determined by the willingness of statutory authorities to provide financial support (Beardshaw, 1988).

There has been an abundance of ideas from disabled people and their organisations which could easily overcome these difficulties, such as the Self Operated Care Scheme (SOCS) pioneered by Hampshire Centre for Independent Living (HCIL). The basic principle of the scheme is that a grant is paid to individuals who then employ their own personal assistants (PAs) in their own homes. The great advantage of the scheme is that the routine is decided by the disabled people themselves, 'which truly enables them to lead a life of their own choosing' (Brisenden, 1985, p. 10). In 1986 the HCIL devised a pilot scheme for disabled people who do not wish to be involved in the formalities of employing PAs, but want control of staff in their home. This involved a shared management arrangement with a third party. Members of the Derbyshire Coalition of Disabled People (DCDP) have experimented with a care cooperative involving 'professional' personal assistants and disabled people. These and similar schemes could be developed, but the major obstacle to their growth is the lack of Government support and funding (HCIL, 1990, p. 12).

Disabled people can arrange personal assistance privately using their own resources or disability benefits. But as we have seen in previous chapters, paying for private help is not a realistic option for the overwhelming majority of disabled people. They are, therefore, reliant upon unpaid informal helpers, some of the consequences of which are discussed in the following section.

The Carers' Movement and Respite Care.   The emergence of the carers' movement has added a further twist to the discriminatory spiral. The failure of the present system to provide appropriate support for disabled people not only discriminates against disabled people but also against those who are charged with the responsibility of providing that support, namely their families, friends and neighbours. Giving help to a disabled family member or friend can be both economically and socially demanding. Informal helpers are sometimes forced to give up their jobs and their social lives in order to provide support for those who need it. This is a situation which the overwhelming majority of disabled people neither want nor expect:

> Given free will and the ability to exercise that free will most adult disabled people would choose to respect and value the relationships that they enjoy with their relatives and friends rather than compromise them by imposing demands that exceed natural bounds (HCIL, 1990, p. 15).

The economic and emotional tensions ensuing from this largely enforced relationship have created significant socio-political divisions where there should not and need not be any. A strong and articulate 'carers' movement' has emerged which adds a further dimension to the discrimination encountered by disabled people.

Rock (1988) has noted that 'caring' today is big business, not in terms of paid work, but in organisation and campaigning. A number of carers' organisations regularly raise thousands of pounds for a growing membership to provide economic and social support for their members. The need for this support is not in doubt and many disabled people are thankful that they alone do not have to provide it. But many disabled people are expected to be grateful that someone is 'mindful' of their needs. As Rock (1988) notes, the word 'carer' is now synonymous with self-sacrifice and martyrdom, whilst the disabled person is often perceived as the cause of suffering and a burden. This view arises because most often the disabled person is the silent partner in the relationship (Rock, 1988, p. 4).

One illustration of the influence of the carers' movement is the increasing emphasis in official policy statements on the importance of 'respite care' as a valued feature of community-based provision (see the Government White Paper *Caring for People* [HMSO, 1989b]). It usually means moving disabled people out of their homes, while their regular informal helpers remain there temporarily freed of their 'care' responsibilities (Large, 1990a). The implications are that the 'overburdened, manipulated and abused, self-sacrificing' carers 'desperately' need a break from their 'overbearing, demanding, ungrateful and manipulative dependents', namely disabled people (HCIL, 1990, p. 14).

Thus respite care is another term for 'crisis management', but it would not be necessary if disabled people received adequate and stable personal support. The tensions which precipitate the need for crisis management would not arise if 'caring' or the provision of personal assistance were seen as a form of work with contracts of employment for both parties. While voluntary and unpaid personal assistants have to continue, often unaided, the need for respite care will increase and the position of the disabled person will continue to be both 'marginalised and invisible' (Rock, 1988, p. 4).

Conclusion

It is evident that the health and social support systems currently available to disabled people are a product of, and a major contributor to, institutional discrimination. They are organised around the traditional assumption that disabled people are unable to take charge of their own lives. This is clearly reflected in the ideology of community care as espoused by a succession of policy-makers and recent developments within the personal social services as a whole. It is particularly significant that demands by disabled people and their organisations for self-management have been ignored in official circles while the role of professionals has been re-emphasised and indeed strengthened. In terms of funding, services for disabled people are accorded a low priority within the present health and social support system, and the bulk of financial resources are spent on professionals' salaries and traditional facilities. The effect of this on disabled people's lives is usually negative.

Although the negative consequences of life in residential institutions are well known, many disabled people are still forced to endure it. Residential facilities continue to be supported by a variety of agencies at the expense of community-based ones. Disproportionate support for medical rehabilitation persists within the various welfare structures, while facilities which actively promote social integration go greatly under-resourced. Comprehensive assessments of disabled people and their families by professionals remain central to the process of service allocation, and professional power within welfare bureaucracies continues to go unchallenged. Although lip-service is paid to the idea of meaningful collaboration between service users and providers, notably with the introduction of the 1986 Act, this has yet to materialise. There is evidence of widespread disregard for the law within local authorities, which has largely been ignored by central Government, and organisations of disabled people have received little financial and political support.

Disabled people's opportunities for economic and social integration are severely restricted because of the lack of specialist information, appropriate technical aids and equipment, and a comprehensive personal assistance service. Although the 1986 Act required local authorities to give relevant information to disabled people in a suitable and appropriate format, in the main this has not taken place. In some cases information and advice is provided by user self-help groups, but official support has proved tenuous and unpredictable. Technical aids and equipment supply is split between a number of agencies in a way that creates confusion for all concerned. There is evidence in this area of widespread unmet need among disabled people and it was shown that some of the technical equipment currently available from the state sector does not make for maximum independence.

There is no national comprehensive personal assistance service for those disabled people who need it, and most of this work is done by unpaid, informal helpers, namely families and friends. Existing provision comes from a variety of sources, takes several forms and is mainly organised around supplementary help for informal helpers, the majority of whom go unaided. This policy discriminates not only against disabled people but against informal helpers. It has created unnecessary social and political divisions between the former and the latter, which compounds the discriminatory spiral in which many disabled people find themselves. Although there has been a number of solutions put forward by disabled people and their organisations which could easily overcome these problems, they have largely been ignored.

Current policies regarding health and social support systems for disabled people not only fail to provide them with the necessary services to live independently within the community, but also deny them the dignity of independence in personal relationships and in their own homes. Without a radical restructuring of the present system this is unlikely to change.

7

THE HOUSING, TRANSPORT AND BUILT ENVIRONMENT

Independent living for disabled people necessitates a physical environment which does not disable them. But because they have traditionally been excluded from the mainstream economic and social life of the community, a physical environment has been created which does precisely that. As a result 'ordinary' or mainstream housing, transport systems and public amenities and buildings are often out of bounds to disabled people. Indeed, it might be argued that institutional discrimination against disabled people is never more obvious than in this particular context. This chapter examines the discriminatory process in housing, transport and the built environment.

Housing

'Every individual has the right to live in an ordinary house in an ordinary street' (DCDP, 1986). In modern Britain this right is not extended to a large number of disabled people, simply because the overwhelming majority of British houses are built without consideration of their needs. 'Ordinary' or mainstream dwellings in both the public and the private sectors are designed explicitly for non-disabled people, in particular those who are 'male, fit and aged between 18 and 40' (Rowe, 1990). The housing needs of disabled people are rarely considered within the general area of housing provision and when they are it is usually within the 'ghetto' (Rowe, 1990) of so-called 'special needs housing' (Morris, 1990).

Although disabled people are 14 per cent of the adult population, only a tiny proportion of the general housing stock is accessible. It has recently been suggested that the total number of accessible dwellings in public and private hands currently stands at a mere 80,000 (Rowe, 1990, p. 4). Additionally, the demand for accessible housing is likely to increase dramatically in the near future because of the ageing population and the Government's stated commitment to community rather than residential 'care' for disabled and elderly people. A recent report edited by the Conservative MP Andrew Rowe concluded that 'there is no chance of the UK being able to keep as many of its ageing population in their own homes as the Government intends unless much more of the housing stock is physically capable of sheltering them' (Rowe, 1990, p. 7).

149

'Special needs housing' usually means small clusters of accessible homes set within mainstream housing estates where disabled people are cut off from their families, their friends and the able-bodied community as a whole. Besides having a potentially negative impact upon disabled people's ability to find employment (see Chapter 4), if only because the availability of this type of provision is so limited throughout the country, this policy also means that disabled people's opportunities for social interaction with non-disabled people are 'cruelly diminished', not only because their homes set them apart from the rest of the community but also because the houses of non-disabled people need to be visitable if a 'normal' social life is to be maintained. If the only homes which disabled people can enter are their own, then any socialising with non-disabled neighbours will have to be conducted there. Hence, the additional costs of entertaining neighbours will fall on 'those who are least able to bear them' (Rowe, 1990, p. 4).

In response to the growing dissatisfaction among disabled people regarding current housing policy, the British Council of Organizations of Disabled People (BCODP) held a national conference in July 1987. The delegates made a number of important practical recommendations for improvement, which, taken together, amount to a comprehensive national housing policy which would in time make all houses accessible to disabled people (see BCODP, 1987a). Similar recommendations were endorsed at a symposium in November 1990 on housing and independent living organised by BCODP and the housing charity Shelter which attracted 200 representatives from disability and housing groups up and down the country (Laurie, 1991).

However, these recommendations have been ignored. There are no Government directives to housebuilders to build more accessible homes, nor have housing policies been proposed which encourage public and private landlords to convert existing stock. Moreover, as the following sections show, the recent changes in housing policy make the likelihood of this happening in the foreseeable future seem more remote than ever.

The Role of Local Authorities. Successive studies show that disabled people rely far more on the public sector for their housing needs than the population as a whole (see for example Martin and White, 1988; Morris, 1988, 1990). The latest estimates suggest that approximately half of disabled households remain in the public rented sector, whereas the proportion for the population as a whole is a quarter (Morris, 1990). Two factors are mainly responsible for this. First, the poverty resulting from impairment (see Chapter 5) means that disabled people are less able to gain access to the private sector. Secondly, local authorities are the main providers of accessible housing (Morris, 1988, 1990).

Since the early 1970s local authorities have had a statutory obligation to accommodate the housing needs of disabled people when formulating housing policy. The 1970 Chronically Sick and Disabled Persons (CSDP) Act required local housing authorities to have regard to the special needs of 'chronically sick or disabled people' (Oliver, 1983). Hitherto local authorities have defined disabled people's housing needs by a medical need. Thus, rather than recognising disabled people's housing needs with a points system, either via a general waiting list or the transfer list, disabled people have to undergo a medical assessment. No other category of people seeking access to, or movement within, council housing is presented with this hurdle (Morris, 1991).

In 1974 the Department of the Environment (DoE) issued guidelines for purpose-built housing for disabled people which distinguished between 'wheelchair' and 'mobility' standard housing. The former are houses adapted throughout for wheelchair-users. Mobility housing consists of dwellings designed with certain features which adapt them fully for all but wheelchair-users, but they are accessible to them. Additionally, mobility houses can be easily adapted further if need be (see Morris, 1990).

A recent report by the housing charity Shelter has exploded the myth that housing associations have been more responsive to the housing needs of disabled people than local authorities. This is mainly because local authorities' housing programmes have been far larger than those of housing associations. Moreover, although housing associations expanded their operations during the 1980s, until fairly recently they have built fewer wheelchair and mobility homes not only as a percentage of their total housing stock but in absolute numbers (Morris, 1988). Also, while local councils have increased their total percentage of accessible houses in relation to their non-accessible housing stock, they are now building fewer because their housing programmes have been drastically cut by central Government. However, as Table 7.1 shows, local councils remain the main source of wheelchair and mobility accommodation.

It should also be remembered that much of the present accessible accommodation within the public sector is not compatible with disabled people's housing needs. Levels of provision vary greatly up and down the country, with marked differences in regional rates for both purpose-built housing and adaptations (Borsay, 1986). Also, due mainly to mistaken assumptions about households with a disabled member, there is an under-representation of two-, three- and four-bedroom properties. Apart from disabled people being as likely as non-disabled people to have families, many single disabled people need to accommodate a personal assistant in their home. This is rarely considered when their housing needs are being assessed. A report on the housing needs of disabled people in Hammersmith and Fulham showed a significant discrepancy between the supply of and the demand for multi-bedroomed accessible homes (Robinson, 1987). This is likely to be repeated throughout the country (Morris, 1988). Also, given the reduction in the amount of money which the Government will allow local authorities to invest in new housing stock, this situation is unlikely to change in the foreseeable future (Robinson, 1987).

However, this gap between supply and demand in the public sector is not surprising since up to now few local authorities have

Table 7.1. Provision of Wheelchair/Mobility and Mainstream Housing Compared, 1984–9

| | HOUSING ASSOCIATIONS | | | | |
	Mainstream housing	Wheelchair homes	% of total completions	Mobility homes	% of total completions
1984	13,538	92	0.6	112	0.8
1985	10,464	39	0.3	176	1.6
1986	9,883	65	0.6	190	1.9
1987	10,411	63	0.6	117	1.1
1988	9,958	44	0.4	106	1.0
1989	9,187	71	0.7	221	2.4
Total	53,451	374	0.6	922	1.7

| | LOCAL AUTHORITIES AND NEW TOWNS | | | | |
	Mainstream housing	Wheelchair homes	% of total completions	Mobility homes	% of total completions
1984	28,899	338	1.1	2,134	7.3
1985	22,935	250	1.0	1,593	6.9
1986	18,574	264	1.4	1,315	7.0
1987	16,000	197	1.2	1,061	6.6
1988	15,875	307	1.9	823	5.1
1989	12,931	110	0.8	884	6.8
Total	115,214	1,466	1.2	7,810	6.7

Note: There is no record of wheelchair/mobility homes being built by the private sector.
Source: Adapted from Tables 1.2 and 1.6 in DoE, 1987, pp. 2 and 12, and Table 1.2 and 1.5 in DoE, 1990, pp. 2 and 12.

displayed any serious concern about meeting the housing needs of disabled people. This was illustrated by the Shelter report *Our Home: Our Rights* (Morris, 1990) which examined the housing policies of a representative sample of twenty-one local authorities in England and Wales. It concluded that with few exceptions these authorities had very little data on the housing needs of disabled people within their areas. Most were unable even to provide adequate information on the numbers of disabled people living in institutions. Housing departments appeared to have little knowledge of 'either the demand which existed for housing among disabled people, or of what, if any, appropriate provision existed' (Morris, 1990, p. 23).

The survey showed that few authorities had a coherent policy for meeting the housing and housing-related needs of disabled people. Local authority housing departments generally failed to incorporate them into their policy initiatives or into the day-to-day running of their departments. Moreover, there was little evidence that the housing needs of disabled people had been considered when local authorities were setting up joint ventures of various kinds with either the private sector or housing associations (Morris, 1990).

Recent developments are unlikely to change this unsatisfactory situation. The White Paper *Caring for People* maintains that housing is crucial in the Government's community care programme. Under the new proposals local authorities have a clearly-defined duty to assess the housing requirements of disabled people individually in conjunction with their other needs. So that disabled people can remain in the community they are to be helped to make their homes 'places where it is possible to provide the care they need'. This is to be achieved through the new means-tested adaptation grant system (discussed below) which came into force with the 1989 Local Government and Housing Act (HMSO, 1989b).

The White Paper also suggests that people who are 'more severely disabled' might be 'helped' by a move into some form of specialised accommodation such as 'purpose-designed housing for people in wheelchairs, or core and cluster developments for people with mental handicaps' (HMSO, 1989b). In addition, local authorities' social service departments are urged to work closely with housing authorities, housing associations and all other types of housing providers in the development of 'a full and flexible housing policy' (HMSO, 1989b, p. 25).

This has serious implications for the future expansion of the supply of accessible homes. Because adapting a disabled individual's house does not signal a radical shift in housing policy, housing ghettos for disabled people are clearly central to the community care programme, and hitherto non-statutory bodies have proved extremely reluctant to provide suitable homes for disabled people.

Adapting Inaccessible Properties for Use by Disabled People. Because of the lack of accessible dwellings, the adaptation of existing homes in both the public and the private sectors is an increasingly common way of meeting the housing needs of disabled people. The OPCS surveys, for example, found that 24 per cent of all disabled adults had some adaptation to their homes (Martin, White and Meltzer, 1989). However, although such an *ad hoc* solution to the problem of inaccessible houses is not cost-effective (the cost of building accessible homes is about a third of that of adapting non-accessible ones [Yates, 1990]), it also does not address the central issue of discrimination in housing, but merely perpetuates it. This is because if the only dwellings which are adapted for use by disabled people are their own, then they represent little more than private prisons.

Moreover, there is substantial evidence that the current system of adapting inaccessible houses for disabled people is grossly inadequate. The OPCS surveys reported that for 35 per cent of all disabled people with 'locomotor' impairments and 42 per cent of those with personal assistance needs, their homes required adaptations (Martin, White and Meltzer, 1989). A national sample of 934 disabled young people living with their parents found that more than a quarter needed further housing adaptations (Hirst, 1982). A study of 111 families with a disabled member aged between 18 and 25 found that the housing of 56 per cent had been adapted in some way, but that only 9.5 per cent of those adaptations were judged satisfactory (Thomas *et al.*, 1989).

The present system of improvement grants is unsatisfactory for a variety of reasons. First, research shows that there are wide variations in local authority practice. For example, of the twenty-one local authorities which contributed to the Shelter survey mentioned above, only three had a specific policy on adaptations for homes occupied by disabled people. Although some authorities made budgetary provision for adaptations, this money was treated as revenue expenditure, when in fact it can be treated as capital expenditure, thus making more money available (Morris, 1990).

Such variation is mainly because official directives concerning grant allocation are unnecessarily complex and allow for considerable discretion locally. The 1970 CSDP Act gave local authorities powers to assist disabled people to carry out housing modifications, and the 1974 Housing Act made 'disability' one of the grounds on which 'house improvement' or 'intermediate' grants could be made. Both could be used to make dwellings more accessible. Initially these grants were confined to private sector homes, but in 1978 housing departments were asked to extend them to pay for the structural renovation of their disabled tenants' homes (Beardshaw, 1988). Subsequently, most local authorities increased their expenditure on improvement grants until 1984, but spending thereafter declined (Morris, 1990). The Shelter survey found that in most areas the number of adaptations being funded was very small. In 1987/8 one local authority made only one grant to a disabled owner-occupier, but in another, with a private sector half the size, ninety-one were awarded (Morris, 1990).

The system also allows for different interpretations of what are regarded as 'essential', 'necessary' or 'appropriate' adaptations. There are no definite guide-lines as to what is appropriate, and it may be argued that it is difficult to separate work that is needed to make a home more accessible from work that is necessary for general improvements (Morris, 1988). The problem is made worse because the procedure for grant allocation is long-drawn-out and bureaucratic, and involves a number of professional 'experts' from a variety of local authority departments including social workers, occupational therapists and housing officers — many of whom have little understanding of the requirements of disabled people. Additionally, problems of co-ordination and planning between local government departments often follow (Beardshaw, 1988; Morris, 1990).

Many households with a disabled person find that sufficient funding will only be made available to make specific areas of their home accessible. It is not uncommon for house adaptations to be limited to the ground floor (see Barnes, 1990; Morris 1990). This means that disabled people often cannot achieve optimum independence even within their own homes. In the London and Wycombe survey of 111 families of young disabled adults, for example, 38 per cent of those who had had adaptations made to their home felt that further modifications were necessary to make them more suitable for their disabled members (Thomas *et al.*, 1989). Other surveys of adapted accommodation suggest that this is not uncommon (Borsay, 1986).

Given this situation it is hardly surprising that disputes often occur between disabled households and the representatives of local authorities over what adaptations are appropriate. Sometimes disabled people or their relatives have threatened local authorities with adverse publicity before funding for suitable adaptations was forthcoming (Barnes, 1990; Oliver *et al.*, 1988).

Another major problem which disabled households have to face when making adaptations to their homes is the length of time it takes to get the work completed. The process is a long-drawn-out affair because applications have to be made and subsequently processed, housing needs are then assessed, plans are drawn up, planning permission is sought, and so on. In the London and Wycombe study delays of up to two years for the fitting of essential items such as grab-rails or a ramp to replace steps were common. Overall, 27 per cent of the sample experienced hold-ups in the supply and fixing of house adaptations (Thomas *et al.*, 1989). Moreover, delays and complications for more elaborate work such as house extension can take as long as five years from start to finish (Glendinning, 1986; Thomas *et al.*, 1989). These delays are not just inconvenient, but can cause great emotional upheaval and distress within the disabled household due to overcrowding, lack of privacy and generally unsuitable conditions making the disabled person more dependent (Oliver *et al.*, 1988).

The implementation of the 1989 Local Government and Housing Act will not change this situation. The guide-lines for the implementation of the new system are characteristically vague and leave much to the discretion of local officials. Local authority social service departments will play a 'key role' in the assessment of disabled people's housing needs in conjunction with housing departments and 'other relevant agencies', and housing departments will be responsible for the administration of the system through all stages, from initiation to post-completion. The final decision as to whether the adaptations are 'necessary and appropriate' rests with the housing department. Moreover, there is nothing in the new proposals that gives disabled people the right to have their whole house adapted to suit their needs (see DoE, 1990a).

Finally, many disabled people have hitherto incurred considerable economic hardship in order to make their homes accessible, and this will not change under the new system. Until the introduction of the 1989 Local Authority and Housing Act in 1990, improvement grants only covered 90 per cent of the amount required for modifications. Disabled people had to find the rest themselves. This could amount to a sizeable sum of money, particularly for households on low incomes. For example, it has been estimated that to make an average three-bedroomed mid-terrace house with front and rear access, costing around £44,000 at 1990 prices, accessible for disabled people would cost £24,000 (Yates, 1990). Thus, a family wishing to adapt such a house needed to find £2,400 — a difficult prospect given the financial circumstances of most disabled people (see Chapter 5). Moreover, the 90 per cent grant was available only in cases of financial hardship, otherwise people would receive 75 per cent and therefore their contribution had to be even higher (Morris, 1991).

However, under the 1989 Act disabled people wishing to adapt their homes may now qualify for a 100 per cent grant, but eligibility is determined by economic means-testing. Consequently, households with a disabled person will have to contribute any disposable income or savings which they might have in order to adapt their homes. It is also unlikely that the full extent of impairment-related expenditure will be taken into account when economic resources are being assessed for improvement grants. The Government also supports local 'care and repair' and 'staying-put schemes' run by statutory or voluntary bodies, which advise disabled and elderly people on how to use the 'capital tied up in their property' to finance 'repairs and adaptations' (HMSO, 1989b, p. 25). Hence any capital gains which disabled households may accumulate through buying their homes will be lost. In short, disabled people have to use up any surplus economic resources which they may possess to make inaccessible housing accessible — something that able-bodied people never have to do.

Owner-Occupation and Disabled People. The problem of non-accessible housing has been made considerably worse by the 'Right to Buy' policies of the 1980s, notably the 1980, 1985, and 1986 Housing Acts, and the widespread sale by local authorities of the 'better-quality stock', especially houses with gardens (Morris, 1988). Flats now constitute a bigger proportion of local authority-owned properties. This has particular implications for disabled people because the houses which were sold off are those with the greatest potential for modification. The council houses which are left are the least suitable (Morris 1988). Moreover, since local authority spending on building new homes and refurbishing old ones has markedly declined, adaptation of the existing stock is now the main source of accessible housing for disabled people (Morris, 1988).

Yet even the adaptation of non-accessible homes is also threatened by the sale of council houses. Throughout Britain it has become very difficult for disabled people to be transferred to council houses which can be readily adapted because they are mainly no longer in the public sector. Most of the houses sold under the Right to Buy scheme have gardens, and are thus the easiest to adapt and the most desirable. This situation will be made much worse if Government plans to sell off public-sector housing to private landlords are carried through (Morris, 1988; Ounsted, 1989; RADAR, 1987). The future prospects for both access into and transfer within council housing for disabled people are therefore uncertain. This can be demonstrated by the longer time that disabled people are registered on council, house waiting and transfer lists (Morris, 1988–1990).

Moreover, until the implementation of the 1988 Housing Act the policy of encouraging council tenants to buy their houses was not extended to disabled people living in accessible or adapted dwellings. The reason for this was that there is so little suitably adapted housing that it was felt that losing such stock from the rented sector through the Right to Buy scheme could not be justified. Although this policy was highly discriminatory, compounding the inequity between disabled and non-disabled council-house tenants, 'many people still hold this view' (Ounsted, 1989, p. 17).

However, tenants of charitable housing associations were not given the right to buy when it was extended to council tenants. A system of transferable discounts was set up instead. These gave people who were not allowed to buy their homes because their landlord was a charity the opportunity to obtain a sum of money in the form of a discount which would enable them to buy a house on the open market. This scheme did not include occupants of specially designed or adapted housing, and has been described as bereft of 'sense and fairness'. Subsequently, pressure was put on Government by a variety of organisations to include tenants of specially adapted homes within the provisions of the transferable discount scheme, and it was scrapped. It has not been replaced, and if a new scheme is introduced it is hoped that 'disabled people are given the same rights and opportunities as their able-bodied neighbours' (Ounsted, 1989, p. 18).

With the growth in owner-occupation, which now accounts for 63 per cent of all households, access to suitable housing is increasingly determined by the ability to pay. This has particular significance for disabled people who are either attempting to break into the owner-occupation market, or move within it. They suffer disadvantage in two ways: first, due to their lack of economic resources (see Chapter 5), it is still virtually impossible for them to get a mortgage without a secure income, and secondly, it is difficult to find accessible homes because both current and past housebuilders and developers have not built to a 'broader average' (Morris, 1990). Poor housing is also correlated with age, and many disabled people are above retirement age. In any measurement of housing deprivation — access to all parts of the house, level access to the street, adequate heating etc. — many disabled home-owners would be seen to score badly. (Morris, 1991).

Most of the existing housing stock in the private sector is unsuitable for many disabled people. Not one major British private housebuilder has adopted the minimum standards for accessible housing, namely mobility standards, and thus the stock of inaccessible housing continues to grow. Further, the tendency for many builders to construct low-cost first-time-buyer homes in which space standards are reduced has made this situation much worse. Moreover, 'other than some private sector sheltered schemes, there is no record of housing being built to wheelchair or mobility standard in the private sector' (Morris, 1990, p. 12).

Housing Associations. Although housing associations have a relatively poor record for providing accessible homes (Morris, 1988, 1990), they form a major part of the Government's proposals to create a new 'independent rented sector'. This has a number of serious implications for disabled people. First, evidence from the National Federation of Housing Associations on the new mixed funding system for housing associations shows that space standards are lower on these schemes than on other housing association developments (Ounsted, 1989). This marks a decisive shift away from designing for a 'broader average' (Morris, 1990).

Secondly, the private finance schemes which have been set up to fund housing associations' building programmes following the 1988 Housing Act threaten the very existence of the smaller housing associations which have hitherto provided accessible dwellings. Under the new system housing associations have to secure a larger proportion of their funding from the private investor in order to finance their operations. Since it is more expensive to build housing to wheelchair or mobility standards (Ounsted, 1989), those associations which do so will find it increasingly difficult to secure private finance. At the same time, the larger 'general needs housing associations' which soak up most of the private sector funding are ignoring the housing needs of disabled people (Morris, 1988; Ounsted, 1989).

Thirdly, under the new system housing associations are able to set their rents to take their capital costs into account (Ounsted, 1989). Hence, housing association rents will almost certainly rise accordingly. This will reduce housing opportunities for low-income households, particularly those with disabled members; as we have seen earlier, these are generally in the lowest income groups. If disabled or non-disabled family members are in employment, then they may be eligible for only partial housing benefit or none at all. Consequently, paying bigger rents which cover higher capital costs may simply not be feasible. Also, where existing tenants are unemployed and receiving housing benefit the increased rent will serve as an added incentive for them not to find a job since employment would almost certainly put this allowance at risk. The housing associations themselves have expressed concern that their function will be to accommodate people who can afford the new rent levels rather than those who cannot (Morris, 1988; Ounsted 1989).

Fourthly, there is a wide variation nationally in the coverage by housing associations. In some localities there are several housing associations operating, while in others there are none. Moreover, given that many of these organisations do not provide suitable homes for disabled people, this means that there are gaps in housing association provision in many local authority areas (Morris, 1988).

Finally, housing associations have a poor record of providing funds for adaptations. Housing associations rarely contribute to grants for adaptations to their own properties if local authorities make funds available (Morris, 1988). However, many housing association tenants have found that their local authority will not fund adaptations on the grounds that they are the responsibility of the association. At the same time the association will say that it has no funds for grants and that tenants should apply to local authorities. Thus, the tenants fall between the two. Housing associations have very seldom funded adaptations themselves (Prescott Clarke, 1982; Morris, 1990).

The Private Rented Sector.   Although the Government intends to expand the private rented sector it has a poor record of providing accessible homes for disabled people (Morris, 1988). Disabled people are also unlikely to be able to afford to rent private accommodation, since rents were deregulated with the 1988 Housing Act. Although existing tenants retain their rights, tenancies created after 15 January 1989 are not 'controlled'; they are only 'assured' and different terms apply (Ounsted, 1989). Landlords have an added incentive to harass existing tenants in order to create new lettings at higher market rates, which many disabled people, particularly older ones, would find difficult to withstand. It is evident that the private rented sector is a particularly important housing source for single elderly women, 12.5 per cent of whom hold unfurnished tenancies. These are controlled tenancies, and the incentive for landlords to remove such tenants is high. But the 'government's promises to tighten up the law on harassment have not been delivered in the Housing Bill' (Morris, 1988, p. 12).

There is evidence that the private rented sector does not accommodate the needs of disabled people. For example, 35 per cent of private tenants in one London survey wanted to move and the situation can only get worse because of the 1988 Housing Act (Morris, 1988). The most attractive type of letting for private landlords is the new 'assured shorthold tenancies' which can last for as little as six months, and where they can renegotiate the terms of the tenancy each time the previous agreement expires. A disabled tenant whose tenancy period has expired will have far more difficulty finding suitable new accommodation than an able-bodied person. Also, shorter tenancies make it less likely that properties will be adapted to suit the needs of disabled tenants (Ounsted, 1989).

Homelessness and Disabled People. The reduction of available local authority housing during the 1980s has meant that many disabled people find it increasingly difficult to find a home. Public sector rented accommodation has been cut by half since 1979 and the growing problem of homelessness is a direct result of the cutback of homes allocated on the basis of housing need (Morris, 1988). This has had an adverse effect on disabled people along with other groups with special housing needs. Table 7.2 shows that homelessness has increased far more rapidly among these groups than in the population as a whole.

Table 7.2.   Percentage Increase in Households Accepted as Homeless by Local Authorities between 1980 and 1986

Households accepted as vulnerable	*London*	*Other metropolitan*	*Non-metropolitan*	*England*
Elderly	71	43	46	53
Physical impairments	121	103	76	92
Mental illness	146	*	110	183
Other	754	283	251	383
All categories	70	48	54	57

Note: The number of people accepted as homeless because of mental illness by other metropolitan authorities declined from 330 in 1970 to 300 in 1986, in contrast to other categories where the increase has been steady. During the years in between the number fluctuated, rising at one point to 430.
Source: Adapted from Table 5 in Morris, 1988, p. 6.

It is evident from Table 7.2 that homelessness has increased much more among people with physical impairments and people with mental illness than among the general population. Although homeless disabled people appear to form a relatively small proportion of the total of people with housing need, there are many of the disabled population without homes who do not appear in these statistics.

'Hidden homelessness' is a problem rarely discussed in official circles. It refers to the tens of thousands of disabled people unable to leave hospitals or institutions, unable to leave a parental home or trapped within an inaccessible house. Under the local authority 'Code of Guidance', what is termed 'reasonable' is open to interpretation. People in 'residential care' or whose homes are inaccessible are assumed to be reasonably housed, and therefore cannot claim a statutory right to be housed under the homeless persons legislation. Moreover, local authorities do not cater for homeless people with physical impairments because Homeless Persons Units and temporary accommodation are rarely accessible (Morris, 1988, 1990).

Transport

However well designed and equipped a disabled person's home may be, without accessible transport it can quickly become a 'prison' (DCDP, 1986). Transport systems which are not fully accessible to disabled people contribute significantly to the barriers which confront disabled people in mainstream education, employment and social and leisure activities (Booth, 1988; Doyle, 1988; GLAD, 1986, 1988) and are thus a major factor in the discriminatory process.

The Government-sponsored Disabled Persons Transport Advisory Committee (DPTAC), set up in 1985 to provide 'informal advice and guidance' to the Department of Transport (DT) on transport and disabled people, estimated that between 10 and 12 per cent of the population as a whole are adversely affected by the 'unfriendly features of the transport environment' (DPTAC, 1989, unpaged). Moreover, transport systems earmarked 'special' are either segregated or 'inferior' to those on offer to the rest of society. They are limited in scope, poorly funded and fail to give disabled people full control over their transport needs (Findlay, 1990).

Private Cars.   Although the most popular form of transport in modern Britain is the private car, households with a disabled member appear to be only about half as likely as other households to possess a vehicle of their own (DPTAC, 1989, GLAD, 1986). There is a number of reasons for this. Cars are expensive to buy and run and motoring can be more costly for disabled people. Most cars are manufactured for the mass market, i.e. the able-bodied market, and are therefore inaccessible to many disabled motorists without appropriate adaptation. To have a car adapted inevitably costs money, and the more extensive the adaptations the more costly it is. This added expense is not limited to the initial purchase price for the vehicle but may also include running costs, maintenance and repair, and resale value. In addition disabled people are often forced to buy the more expensive cars for the features they have as standard, such as electric windows and electric rear-view mirrors, cruise control and automatic gearboxes. They also need to carry expensive mobile communications systems in case of breakdown. Many disabled people cannot afford this expenditure (Massie, 1988).

Additionally, disabled motorists often find that they have to pay more for vehicle insurance. Indeed, a recent survey found that some insurance companies are 'very reluctant to insure disabled drivers at all, most quote at increased premiums and very few insure on the same basis as able-bodied drivers' (*Same Difference*, 1989a, p. 1). Non-specialist companies often demand medical information about a disabled applicant's impairment before quoting. Some companies will then offer the same premium as they would an able-bodied applicant, but many will apply a loading, usually around 25 per cent, because the applicant is disabled (*Same Difference*, 1989a).

A small number of disabled people, 35,000 in all, are helped with the financial costs of motoring through the Motability scheme, but even here the extra expense can be considerable. Motability is a Government-sponsored charity which was set up in 1977 to help disabled people receiving Mobility Allowance (MA) gain access to private cars. However, MA is often difficult to obtain and many people who experience mobility problems do not receive it (see Chapter 5).

Through the Motability scheme disabled people or their immediate relatives are able to hire a car or buy one on hire-purchase. But to hire a car applicants must first surrender their MA to Motability and make an initial payment which can range from a few hundred to several thousands of pounds depending on the type of car chosen. The hire agreement includes maintenance, Automobile Association (AA) breakdown service, a 'low-cost' insurance policy and road tax, but when the agreement expires the car must be returned and a new initial payment found (Motability, 1990).

There is also an excess mileage charge which starts at 12,000 miles. The cost per mile between 12,000 and 15,000 miles is 5 pence, for 15,000 to 20,000 miles it is 8 pence and for over 20,000 miles it is 10 pence. So, the more the car is used the more it costs to rent. In addition, the hirer must pay for any necessary adaptations to the vehicle, as well as for their removal at the end of the leasing period. The range of adaptations is also limited because major ones are difficult to remove. If applicants cannot afford the initial payments or the cost of adaptations, Motability can offer help from its 'charitable fund', but this is not guaranteed (Motability, 1990).

Mainly because of the problems of modifying vehicles, people who need extensive adaptations have little choice but to opt for the hire-purchase scheme. New and used cars can be bought over a period of up to five years, but a substantial deposit is required for both and, as with leased vehicles, Motability does not help with the cost of adaptations. Moreover, the hire-purchase agreements do not include the cost of insurance, AA membership or maintenance. In addition, used vehicles sold under the scheme are subject to an inspection by the AA, the cost of which is charged to the seller (Motability, 1990).

Finally, because Motability is a charity, access to its services is something of a lottery; certainly it is not a right. The number of people it is able to help is determined by the funds it receives from Government and other contributors. Consequently, receiving MA does not automatically imply access to its services. Moreover, some of the funds allocated by Government to Motability have been invested to ensure the charity's survival. Thus even less money is available for would-be disabled motorists. As a result some disabled people do not receive the help they need (*Disability Now*, 1991).

Since the use of a private car is beyond the reach of many disabled people, it follows that if they wish to travel otherwise than on foot they will be overwhelmingly dependent on public transport — which, like mainstream housing, is constructed almost exclusively for the non-disabled traveller.

Buses.   For most of the population, disabled and non-disabled, journeys tend to be comparatively short, and buses provide a convenient and inexpensive means of travel. But research shows that the great majority of buses currently in use are not accessible to many disabled people. Deregulation resulted in the proliferation of smaller buses, many of which are more inaccessible than the orthodox versions, having steeper steps at the entrance and narrower aisles. Most of these vehicles are fairly new and unlikely to be replaced for a long time. A recent report by the Research Institute for Consumer Affairs (RICA), based on information from transport operators and users in eleven areas around Britain, indicated that getting on and off buses was the biggest problem for many disabled people. This was also the most frequently given reason for not using them (*Which*, 1990). A survey by the Greater London Association for Disabled People (GLAD) estimates that of the 450,000 Londoners who have problems using London Transport, 63 per cent use buses with 'difficulty or discomfort' and 20 per cent, 95,000 people, can not use them at all (GLAD, 1986).

To resolve this problem the DPTAC has recommended a maximum step height of 250 mm. (about 10 inches). Research shows that steps off the ground of more than 300 mm. (12 inches) are impossible for many people to use, but few buses on the roads have entrance and exit steps lower than this (*Which*, 1990). The DPTAC has also suggested that other features such as non-slip handrails, contrasting coloured edges to steps, non-slip flooring and low-level bell-pushes should be introduced (see DPTAC, 1988). But although some of the bus companies have started to modify their stock, this only accounts for a small number of buses actually on the road (*Which*, 1990). In London, only 500 of the 5,000 buses have these modifications, and most of these are limited to specific services known as 'Schedule X routes' (Wagstaff, 1990, p. 25).

For wheelchair-users the story is even more bleak. Very few buses on main routes are accessible to Britain's half-million wheelchair users; those services that are provided usually serve limited routes with restricted timetables: e.g. the much-publicised 'Airbus' service from central London to Heathrow airport, 'Carelink' which travels between London's main railway stations, and Yorkshire's 'Easybus', which is timed to give users about two hours in local towns. Moreover, although bus stops and bus stations are generally the responsibility of local authorities, the RICA survey reported that few bus stations had facilities for disabled passengers (*Which*, 1990).

Although it is frequently claimed that progress is being made towards all buses being more accessible (Frye, 1990; Massie, 1988), there is no legislation to make it compulsory. The European Commission has drafted a proposal titled 'Mobility Improvement for Workers with Reduced Mobility' which would make all 'new' and 'existing' buses, trains and trams accessible to disabled people. But it is unlikely to be implemented in its present form (Frye, 1991).

A further development at the European level is the resolution adopted by Ministers of the nineteen countries of the European Conference of Ministers of Transport. This is likely to become law, but it is limited to new buses only; at the same time, orders for new buses have fallen. This, according to the transport industry, is because of increased competition and the reduction in public subsidy since deregulation, outside London, in 1987/8 (Etchell, 1990). Moreover, the date for full implementation of this directive is *December 1997* (Frye, 1991). Thus, inaccessible buses will remain the norm rather than the exception for some considerable time to come.

Urban Railway Systems.   The GLAD report found that of the 465,000 Londoners who had problems in using public transport, only a quarter were able to use London's Underground at all, and only 10 per cent without difficulty. Wheelchair-users are actually barred from using certain sections of the underground system by four London Regional Transport (LRT) by-laws (GLAD, 1986) 'because of difficulties of emergency evacuation'. If wheelchair-users wish to use those sections of the tube which they are not barred from, then they are advised to give LRT twenty-four hours' notice, take an able-bodied companion with them and travel off-peak (*Which*, 1990).

Access to information on London's Underground is also a major problem for disabled people. The RICA study shows that indistinguishable train announcements in tube stations cause difficulties for people with hearing impairments, and people with visual problems said that there are too few announcements. In addition, automatic ticket barriers and the unpredictability of the lifts and escalators for reaching the platforms caused concern (*Which*, 1990). Similar situations exist in other parts of the country. Although five stations on the Merseyrail underground system have lifts and others have level or ramped access, some still have only steps or escalators. The Glasgow underground railway has no lifts or ramps and does not carry wheelchair-users (*Which*, 1990).

Although some of the newer urban railway systems have overcome some of these difficulties, the lack of understanding on the part of planners of the problems faced by disabled passengers still creates difficulties. For example, the Tyne and Wear metro system was designed to be accessible to disabled people. All forty-four stations and platforms are wheelchair-accessible. Good lighting, white platform edges and tactile surfaces have been used, yet there are few accessible toilets. Wheelchair-users can only find space in the trains at off-peak times and the gaps between rolling stock and platforms in some stations have caused problems (*Which*, 1990).

In the London Docklands Light Railway there is only one space in each of the two carriages per train for a wheelchair. This space is difficult to get into, and if it is already occupied by, for example, a baby buggy, wheelchair-users cannot then travel on the train. Also, the areas surrounding the stations are very inaccessible (Mason, 1991). The RICA study concluded that Britain's urban rail systems vary from accessible to 'no-go areas for wheelchair users'. They also presented a range of problems to other disabled travellers (*Which*, 1990).

Taxis.   Because of the difficulties disabled people face with other forms of public transport and the built environment (see below), many use taxis. However, not all taxis are user-friendly for disabled people and they are also expensive.

London taxis first licensed since February 1989 must be able to carry a wheelchair-user. However, this will not be compulsory for all London taxis until 1 January 2000 (*Which*, 1990). At the time of writing only 4,000 of the capital's 16,000 cabs are able to carry someone who uses a wheelchair (Frye, 1990). Outside London local authorities are responsible for licensing taxis. Over thirty councils, mainly those in big cities, are issuing 'new' licences for London-style taxis only, but only 'some' are insisting that operators use wheelchair-accessible vehicles (*Which*, 1990). Because of the shortage of accessible taxis, booking or hailing one can involve something of a wait (*Which*, 1990).

The majority of Britain's taxi fleets are still saloon cars, and therefore access can be a problem. Sliding from a wheelchair on to the car's seat is a possibility, but only if the driver is prepared to pull in close to the kerb. Some drivers are reluctant to lift the wheelchair into the boot of the car once the transfer has been made (Mason, 1991). All cars, even two-door saloons, can be adapted to make them fully accessible to disabled people, but this is something which licensing authorities do not appear to feel is necessary because it is not compulsory (*Which*, 1990). People with visual impairments complain that 'For Hire' lights are not easily seen and that they are unable to read the meter displays (*Which*, 1990). It is also apparent that some mini-cab drivers will not carry guide-dogs (VOADL, 1990).

Compared to other forms of public transport, travelling by taxi is expensive, especially on the low incomes that most disabled people have. Some local authorities have 'Taxicard' schemes which give reductions to people who are denied access to other forms of public transport. Many of the London boroughs have such schemes, which entitle card-holders to £9 worth of taxi travel for £1.25 (1990/1 prices). This takes passengers a distance of about 8 miles, depending upon traffic conditions. Users have to pay more if they are accompanied by a companion, and any excess is charged at the normal rate once the fare exceeds the £9 limit (see LRT, 1990). These charges are still higher than the cost of travelling by bus or tube. Finally, only a minority of areas throughout Britain have such schemes at present (*Which*, 1990).

Dial-a-Ride.   Because of the limitations of conventional transport a 'Dial-a-Ride' service has been set up for disabled people in several areas. Dial-a-Ride represents an *ad hoc* solution to the transport problems of disabled people. The seeds for it were first germinated by and within London's transport-starved disabled community during the late 1970s (Booth, 1988). London now has twenty-nine separate schemes. Funding is usually limited and comes from a variety of sources including local authorities, voluntary agencies and, in London, central Government. Most of London's schemes are organised locally and run partly by the people who use them, but this participation is being eroded by London Regional Transport's (LRT) regionalisation programme (*Hansard*, 1990d; Nichols, 1991).

Users have to telephone or write in advance to book a journey, and are then taken from door to door — but only on journeys where health or local authority transport is otherwise not available. Often minibuses are used, fitted with lifts or ramps. Fares vary, but are usually in line with local bus fares. These services are segregative in that they carry only disabled passengers (Findlay, 1990).

In common with all 'special' or segregated transport systems, journeys have to be booked well in advance and the services are usually available only at certain hours in the day. Demand is high and therefore telephone lines can be 'constantly engaged'. The RICA research reported that users had to order their journey between one day and two weeks in advance (*Which*, 1990). London Transport statistics show that in 1989/90 London Dial-a-Ride users were on average only able to obtain one return journey every 10.4 weeks (Nichols, 1991). In addition, because journeys are organised to carry a number of people, precise times are not always kept to (*Which*, 1990).

Long-Distance Coaches. Although coaches are one of the cheapest forms of long-distance travel and therefore one of the most attractive to people with low incomes, they present many problems for disabled people. Few inter-city coaches are wheelchair-accessible and consequently many disabled travellers who wish to travel long distances are denied this option for cheaper fares (Massie, 1988, 1990).

Very steep steps in vehicles present a major barrier to travellers with the slightest of mobility-related impairments. The RICA research found that the difficulty of getting on and off the coach and moving about on it, and the absence of appropriate toilets, deterred many disabled people from using coaches. National Express runs about 800 coaches throughout Britain. In 1990 only nine had a kneeling suspension which lowers the first step, plus a toilet level with the seating area. National Express told the RICA researchers that they would have 100 such vehicles on the road in 1991 (*Which*,

1990). As far as is known, there are no plans to make all National Express coaches accessible.

National Express says that its staff will help wheelchair-users able to travel in an 'ordinary seat', but requests seven days' notice prior to travel (*Which*, 1990). Non-disabled travellers do not have to do this, so why should disabled people? The RICA study concluded that coach services 'should and could serve disabled travellers much better than they do' (*Which*, 1990, p. 349).

The Railways. Although British Rail has been improving its ser vices to disabled passengers, practices which discriminate against them still remain the rule rather than the exception. Travelling in the guard's van with the baggage is an all too common experience for wheelchair-users (*Which*, 1990).

The improvements to British Rail services are still somewhat limited, being concentrated on Inter-City services and mainline stations. This is surprising considering that most people's journeys are relatively short, and most disabled people are in the lower income brackets and, therefore, unlikely to be able to afford these services. Nonetheless, 90 per cent of all new trains now boast wide-entry doors, automatic doors on the train and grab-rails fitted as standard. Also, passengers who use wheelchairs are now able to travel alongside non-wheelchair users (Hughes, 1990). However, it would be impossible for two or more wheelchair-users to sit together should they wish to, because the new rolling stock includes only single spaces in each coach (*Which*, 1990).

Few Inter-City trains yet have accessible toilets (*Which*, 1990). Although British Rail says that the new trains will all have them, this will still be unsatisfactory. Unlike non-accessible toilets, which are provided in each carriage, there would be only one accessible toilet per train (Hughes, 1990). It is conceivable, therefore, that a disabled passenger will have to travel the full length of an Inter-City train in order to use the toilet.

The future is even more depressing for travellers on provincial services, where trains with similar facilities to those described above will not be used extensively for some years yet (*Which*, 1990). Moreover, on the new Sprinter trains wheelchair-users will have to travel in the 'vestibule or, in some cases, the seating area' (Hughes, 1990). On Network South East British Rail admits that it will be well into the twenty-first century before all their trains are 'modern'. 'In the meantime the guard's van looms large for people who have to travel in their wheelchair' (*Which*, 1990, p. 349).

Inaccessible stations are also a major problem for disabled people. There are only 130 stations which British Rail says have 'top-class access and facilities' for disabled travellers. For the remainder development is selective, with priority being given to 'low-cost facilities benefiting a large group'. These include induction loops at booking office windows for people with hearing impairments, and white markings on platforms and stairs to assist people with visual impairments (Hughes, 1990). Local stations offer the least facilities. There are hundreds of unstaffed or partly staffed stations which British Rail advises disabled people not to use. This can mean travelling further and in the wrong direction in order to get a train from a station with the necessary facilities (*Which*, 1990).

Finally, to avoid problems British Rail suggests that disabled people contact their area managers well in advance if they need 'special arrangements' or 'help' when travelling. This will usually mean that on arrival at the station the disabled person will be escorted like a child on to the train by a member of British Rail staff (*Which*, 1990). Hence, under the present system not only are disabled travellers denied the spontaneity of rail travel which can be enjoyed by non-disabled travellers, but traditional assumptions about disabled people not being able to look after themselves are emphasised and reinforced.

Air Travel. Because of the expense many disabled people will never be able to travel by air, but for those who can afford it the experience can be degrading and humiliating. Booking a flight is usually the first major problem. Travel agents frequently do not know about the levels of support and access currently available. Also, before disabled people are allowed to fly the booking agent must complete the 'International Air Transport Medical Information Form', or one similar to it. This asks for medical information about the disabled traveller's impairment. It also contains personal questions like 'Does he smell?' (Wood, 1990). These questions are often put to the disabled person in public places. It is hardly surprising that disabled people find the booking procedure embarrassing and intrusive (*Same Difference*, 1990).

The Association of British Travel Agents (ABTA) justifies this form by saying that the airlines need as much data as possible to provide an adequate service. But as the airlines cannot tell whether the form has been completed correctly, they also cannot assess accurately the disabled traveller's needs. Moreover, airlines do not appear to use this information because disabled travellers may be subjected to a further set of similar questions on arrival at the air terminal (*Same Difference*, 1990).

Most aircraft do not have suitable access for disabled travellers and it is usual for them to be carried on to the plane. Moreover, it is not uncommon for airlines to be unprepared for disabled passengers even when they have been given all the relevant information well in advance. People who use electric wheelchairs are kept waiting to board the plane while the chairs are separated from their batteries (*Same Difference*, 1990).

Unlike able-bodied passengers, disabled people are not permitted to sit anywhere on the plane because safety regulations stipulate that they should not be seated where they might hold up an emergency evacuation. This means that they are seated away from emergency exits, where they will not impede the evacuation of their able-bodied fellow passengers in the event of an accident (*Same Difference*, 1990).

The Built Environment

As well as accessible housing and transport, disabled people need the same degree of physical access to public amenities and buildings as non-disabled people if integrated living is to become a reality. However, a fully accessible physical environment is a rarity in modern Britain.

We have shown elsewhere that the successful integration of disabled children and students into mainstream schools, colleges and universities is severely hampered by inaccessible buildings, and institutional discrimination against disabled people's employment is compounded by a mainly inaccessible architectural infrastructure. It follows that the difficulties created for disabled people by an inaccessible environment will extend into every area of economic and social life.

Research into the experience of disability has repeatedly shown how greatly an inaccessible environment contributes to the difficulties faced by disabled people and their dependence upon others (e.g. Barnes, 1990; CORAD, 1982; Morris, 1989; Oliver *et al.*, 1988; SJAC, 1979). One study focusing on this particular issue was conducted by the RICA for the magazine *Which* during 1989. A random sample of thirty disabled people in various parts of the country were asked to keep diaries for a typical week in their lives. They recorded what happened when they went shopping, to the bank etc. Overall, respondents completed or attempted to complete a total of 293 routine daily tasks, and encountered 300 problems of one form or another. On 30 per cent of occasions respondents were unable to 'have done what they wanted without someone else's help' and on one occasion in ten 'they had to give up' (*Which*, 1989, p. 498).

It should be noted that the respondents in this survey were all disabled people who were not asked to perform functions which were not usual for their particular lifestyle. It is likely, therefore, that they were each aware of the problems posed by the environment and only attempted to do things which they believed they were able to do. If they had been asked to attempt activities which were considered 'normal' for an able-bodied person it is highly probable that the number of problems encountered would have been far higher. To illustrate this point, one of the respondents with a visual impairment reported that she had encountered difficulties in a post office — after she had telephoned in advance to tell them she was coming (*Which*, 1989, p. 498). On the whole, able-bodied people do not expect access problems in a post office and certainly do not feel it necessary to telephone in advance to let staff know when they are coming.

Legislation, Access and the Built Environment.   The 1970 CSDP Act adopted an explicitly voluntarist approach to problems of physical access. It 'requests' anyone in charge of buildings or premises to which the public are to be admitted to make adequate provision for disabled people. 'Provision' is not defined in the Act but according to the Silver Jubilee Access Committee (SJAC) it is taken to mean 'not only new constructions but also the conversion of existing ones' (SJAC, 1979, p. 3).

The 1970 Act requests that public toilets and toilets in premises open to the public meet the needs of disabled people; Section 8 of the Act applies these requirements to all universities and school buildings. The Chronically Sick and Disabled Persons (Amendment) Act 1976 extended this 'provision' to places of employment (SJAC, 1979). The access sections of the 1970 Act and the Act of 1976 only applied to England, Scotland and Wales; for Northern Ireland, provision came two years later with the introduction of the CSDP (Northern Ireland) Act 1978 (SJAC, 1979).

The initial impact of this legislation was limited, to say the least. This was because under the CSDP Acts provision needed to be made only 'so far as it is in the circumstances both practical and reasonable'. There was no definition of this phrase in the Acts and subsequent Department of Health and Social Security (DHSS) circulars did not dwell on this point (SJAC, 1979, p. 4). Consequently those with the responsibility for implementing the legislation, namely local authorities, were free to interpret it almost as they pleased.

Following the findings of two Government-sponsored reports on access and the first abortive attempts to introduce anti-discrimination legislation (see Appendix), the Government decided to use the building regulations to ensure that part of the access provision outlined in the CSDP Acts was enforced. The SJAC report *Can Disabled People Go Where You Go?* (1979) showed that in general local authorities had not responded positively to the access requirements of the new legislation. Indeed, the Committee on Restrictions against Disabled People (CORAD) report of 1982 found that for many disabled people access difficulties were the 'fundamental cause and manifestation of discrimination' (CORAD, 1982, p. 9). There followed a Government initiative which culminated in the inclusion of Part M in the Building Regulations in 1985 which came into force in 1987 (DoE, 1990b).

Part M stipulates that 'reasonable provision' must be made to give disabled people access to new premises to which the public are admitted, such as shops, offices, factories and schools, and to the parts of those buildings to which it is 'reasonable to provide access'. For shops and offices, access requirements apply to the whole structure, but in other cases they apply only to the floor of the premises which contains the main entrance. The Department of the Environment (DoE) has stated that the reason for limiting the range of premises in which all floors were to be made accessible was because there was no British Standard (BS) giving guidance on means of escape for disabled people (DoE, 1990b). One year after the implementation of Part M, this was resolved with the publication of 'BS5588: Part 8: Means of Escape for Disabled People' which gives appropriate instructions for this particular eventuality (BSI, 1988).

There are a number of problems with these regulations. Many new public buildings are only required to be accessible at the level of the main entrance. In hotels, for example, this might only apply to the reception area around the foyer (SIA, 1987). Buildings built before 1987 are not covered by Part M unless they have been extended or have had their use changed. Where buildings are extended, for whatever reason, or converted for a different use, the legislation only demands that access should not be made worse. Developers do not have to make existing structures more accessible. For instance, if a large extension is added to a small inaccessible building it need not be made accessible, or if an inaccessible warehouse is converted into a shop, access does not have to be improved. Moreover, Part M was only intended to improve physical access for people who have difficulties walking, but does not cover the needs of those with visual or hearing impairments or people with impairments which restrict the use of the upper limbs. Finally, Part M does not cover the seemingly ever-growing number of public buildings which have been 'listed' with the DoE because of their historical or environmental value, and which, under the present system, will never be accessible to disabled people. Similar regulations apply in Scotland and Northern Ireland, although the legislation there also applies to extensions and conversions, but they only apply to the ground floors of buildings (*Which*, 1989).

The Reality of Access to the Built Environment.   To find out how effective Part M is in practice, the RICA study asked an architect (whether able-bodied or not is not known) to inspect a number of new buildings. It was concluded that access to them was possible for most disabled people but a number of problems remained. There were closed heavy-duty fire-doors which were difficult to open, and poorly designed details and fittings, including such furnishings as tables, rubbish bins and fire extinguishers which restricted the mobility of wheelchairs and provided trip hazards (*Which*, 1989). Since with modern technology fire-doors do not normally need to be kept closed, both these problems could easily be overcome through increased disability awareness training among architects and planners.

As for the built environment generally, the RICA researchers asked access groups in Birmingham, Brent, Eastbourne, Exeter, Milton Keynes, St Helens and Sunderland to inspect their main shopping areas. In particular, they were asked to look at access to and facilities within a variety of buildings including banks, building societies, chain-stores, supermarkets, fast-food restaurants, pubs, cinemas, post offices, town halls, DSS offices, Citizens Advice Bureaux (CAB) and main streets. Among the common problems were buildings which were inaccessible to people with mobility problems because they had steps to the door and no ramps or hand-rails; heavy doors which were difficult to open; plate glass doors and glass frontages on buildings which were badly marked (a real hazard for people with visual impairments); and inadequate parking facilities (*Which*, 1989).

In most of the twenty-eight banks visited, cash dispensers were too high for wheelchair-users and difficult for people with visual impairments to use because of poor design. Counters were also a problem for wheelchair-users, and not all banks had induction loops or other devices to help people with hearing impairments. A similar situation was reported in building societies. Few of the twenty-one chain-stores visited had parking facilities or changing rooms big enough for wheelchair-users, and only ten had lifts, one of which was judged to be unusable by people in wheelchairs because the controls were too high. Moreover, only one of these stores had an accessible toilet. Although all fourteen pubs inspected were considered accessible, only three had accessible toilets for both sexes — one had an accessible toilet for men but not for women. Access to the seven libraries surveyed was not a problem but inside not all sections were accessible: some were not on the ground floor and only six had lifts, two of which were considered too small for wheelchairs, while one was a goods lift (*Which*, 1989).

Access to toilets was a major problem in restaurants. Only five of the fourteen visited had toilets which could be used by disabled people. Many of the restaurants were found to have fixed seating and tables which made movement difficult for anyone with mobility problems. One of the town halls inspected was accessible only via steps, and two of the seven DSS offices did not have accessible toilets. Getting in and out of supermarkets was not considered a problem but the facilities inside were frequently lacking. Eight of the eighteen supermarkets did not have any seats, which is important for people who have difficulty walking, only three had accessible toilets and fewer than half had baskets or trolleys which could be used by wheelchair-users. Some of the CAB offices were inaccessible, two of the seven post offices had steps and no ramps. Cinemas were found to be virtual no-go areas for disabled people unless they went with an able-bodied companion, booked in advance, were prepared to make special arrangements such as going in at a set time and, in many cases, were prepared to see only what was showing on the ground floor. All fourteen inspected had steps, less than half had accessible toilets and only one had an induction loop for people with hearing impairments (*Which*, 1989).

Each of the seven inspection teams visited the main street in their particular town. Good parking facilities are essential to many disabled people, but only one of the towns had sufficient spaces. One of the areas visited had no sloped kerbs at key crossing points to help wheelchair-users cross the road. The researchers concluded that provision for people with visual impairments was especially poor, since only two of the seven towns had raised lumps on the pavements to indicate where to cross (*Which*, 1989).

One of the most significant examples of institutional discrimination against disabled people in the physical environment which the RICA study did not address concerns pedestrianisation. Many towns and cities now have pedestrian zones and shopping precincts where vehicle use is prohibited. These vary in size from huge areas in major cities to schemes just a few metres long in small towns. Moreover, according to the Department of Transport (DT) it is likely that as car ownership increases so too will the number of pedestrian zones — particularly in busy shopping areas (DTWO, 1987). However, while pedestrianisation might be acceptable to people who can walk without difficulty, it causes major problems for those who cannot.

Many towns which have introduced pedestrian zones have denied access to disabled people with mobility-related impairments by refusing to exempt Orange Badge holders from the vehicle restrictions. Under the Orange Badge scheme disabled drivers are entitled to concessionary parking in many areas, including town centres. But because this scheme is widely abused by able-bodied motorists, several local authorities have refused to allow Orange Badge holders into traffic-free areas. To prevent this abuse the Government has agreed to amend the scheme, and a draft set of proposals was produced in April 1990 (DT, 1990a), but it has not so far been implemented.

Although some authorities allow Orange Badge holders to use their cars in traffic-free zones, others have banned them completely. By way of compensation they are providing special parking spaces in multi-storey car parks and electric wheelchairs for 'shop-mobility' schemes. Under these schemes disabled individuals must park their cars and transfer to wheelchairs which are intended to be used by all disabled people to do their shopping. This overlooks the fact that most wheelchairs are individually modified to suit the needs of their owners. To transfer to a wheelchair which is not one's own can be as uncomfortable for the user as it is for an able-bodied person to wear badly fitting shoes. Able-bodied people would not put up with such discomfort in order to go shopping, so why should wheelchair-users? An alternative approach adopted by some authorities has been to ban Orange Badge holders at certain times of the day. Others have introduced local permits that favour their own disabled residents but ban everyone else. This would effectively signal the beginning of the end of the Orange Badge system (Chittenden, 1990).

This discrimination has been vehemently opposed by disabled people and their organisations. Throughout 1990 demonstrations of disabled people against the exclusion of disabled drivers from pedestrian precincts were seen in several British cities. A civil disobedience campaign was mounted in Chesterfield which resulted in the prosecution of two disabled motorists, Ken Davis and Jack Fitton. Ironically, at their trial they both had to be carried up a flight of steps in their wheelchairs to get to a makeshift magistrates' court because the usual court-room was inaccessible. They were then fined £79 and £61 respectively, which they declined to pay on principle (DCDP, 1990). Their fines were subsequently paid by an unknown source. One reason for this might be that apart from prison hospitals most of Her Majesty's Prisons are also inaccessible to disabled people (Masham, 1990).

It will be apparent from the above that there is local variation in access to the built environment and that much of the responsibility for this rests with local authorities. They are responsible for the implementation of Part M regulations and must draw attention to them when issuing planning permission for new buildings. The authority's Building Control Officer is usually responsible for this task, but some councils also employ an Access Officer, who will monitor planning applications, advise on the alteration of existing buildings, and generally ensure that public buildings in the council's area are accessible to disabled people. However, relatively few local authorities employ Access Officers. In a recent survey, of the 265 local authorities which responded to a postal questionnaire only thirty-six employ a full-time Access Officer and only sixteen of these are themselves disabled (ACE, 1991).

Some local authorities support local access groups, of which several emerged during the 1980s. These vary in size, take several forms and perform a variety of tasks. Some consist wholly of voluntary members while others include volunteers and local authority employees. Some have only disabled members while others do not. Some are controlled by local councils while others are autonomous. Many are involved in monitoring planning applications, advising developers, advising local authorities on access issues and the publication of access guides, while others concentrate on campaigning and pressure group activities. Unfortunately, the existence of an access committee does not necessarily mean that local councils respond to the needs of disabled people. For example, Leeds Access Committee celebrated twenty-one years of existence in 1989 (*Forum*, 1989), but the central lending library, reference library and museum are inaccessible (LADC, 1983) and large areas of the city's shopping facilities have been pedestrianised with the exclusion of Orange Badge holders (Anderson, 1990).

Clearly the effectiveness of these groups will largely depend on the willingness of local authorities to make access a reality. On this point the RICA study concluded that local authorities could do much to give disabled people better access to both public- and private-sector buildings in their area. This could be achieved by the employment of more Access Officers and increased consultation with disabled people (*Which*, 1990).

But local authorities receive little direction and encouragement from central Government to improve access. These issues are dealt with nationally by the Centre for an Accessible Environment

(CAE), previously known as the Centre on Environment for the Handicapped, and the Access Committee for England (ACE). There are no equivalent bodies to ACE in Scotland, Wales and Northern Ireland, where environmental issues are covered by their own national councils on disability.

The CAE was created in 1969, with funding from Government, to provide advice on the environmental needs of disabled and elderly people. It is run mainly by professionals appointed by the Department of Health (DoH), who advise architects and planners on the design of modern buildings. In response to the growing need for a central organisation to serve the increasing number of local access groups throughout the country, the Government set up ACE fourteen years later. Its main aim was to bring together disabled people, architects and representatives of the building industry to form an independent policy advisory committee.

However, it is apparent that ACE is anything but independent. From the outset it has been the responsibility of CAE, as regards both funding and the appointment of its members, and until 1990 the organisations shared office space — they now share the same building. Indeed, two directors of the Committee have resigned reportedly because it is subject to excessive control by CAE (*Same Difference*, 1990d, p. 2). In view of this situation, the Government gave ACE more control over its finances in the autumn of 1989, but abolished the Director's post and replaced it with a one-day-a-week Chairman and a Policy Officer. In addition, guide-lines were issued for its primary function. In a letter to the Chair of CAE the Minister for Disabled People stated that ACE should be 'something quite different from a pressure group', with its members not representing any particular interest or group but addressing issues on an 'informal basis' (*Same Difference*, 1990d, p. 2). Given this situation it is no wonder that access remains a major problem for disabled people.

Proposals for Amendments to the present Building Regulations.
The Department of the Environment (DoE) has recently announced proposals in 1990 to amend the Building Regulations to improve access for disabled people. These proposals recommend extending access to all storeys of new 'non-domestic' buildings, including those which have been internally rebuilt with only an external wall or walls remaining of the pre-existing structure. They would also extend access to include alterations and extensions to structures originally subject to access regulations. It is also proposed that the new regulations should cover access requirements for people with visual and hearing impairments. This would mean the introduction of textured

surfaces and induction loops etc. (DoE, 1990b). These proposals are to be put before Parliament sometime in 1991 and if approved could be in force one year later.

While these proposed amendments are welcome, they have only a limited impact on access for disabled people. They only apply to non-domestic structures, hence houses and flats which are inaccessible will still be built. As with Part M, the amendments will only apply to buildings completed after their implementation. Existing owners will be under no obligation to make their premises accessible to disabled people, and there is nothing in the new regulations about 'listed' buildings — they are allowed to remain inaccessible. Finally, structures will still be erected which are not accessible to people with impairments in their upper limbs or with non-visible impairments whose needs are not even mentioned in the new proposals. Thus for the foreseeable future the majority of disabled people will still not be able to go where able-bodied people go.

Conclusion

This chapter has shown how the physical environment — mainstream housing, transport and the architectural infrastructure — has been constructed without reference to the needs of disabled people.

The first section showed how the housing needs of disabled people have been and continue to be largely ignored within the general area of housing policy. Accessible homes are only a tiny percentage of the total housing stock, and many of them are in public-sector 'special needs' housing ghettos which maintain and emphasise the traditional economic and social divisions between disabled and non-disabled people. This is mainly because most disabled people do not have the financial resources to enter the private sector and because local authorities have, since the 1970s, had a legal obligation to accommodate disabled people's needs. Recent developments in the Government's housing policy are unlikely to change this situation. There are no Government initiatives to encourage public- or private- sector developers to build accessible housing. The 1980s saw a reduction in housebuilding generally, with the result that fewer accessible homes were built, individual disabled households were encouraged to use any resources which they might have to adapt their homes to suit their individual needs, and 'special needs' housing remained central to the Government's community-care programme.

In addition, Government efforts to encourage home-ownership and generate an independent rented sector make the widespread availability of accessible housing even less likely in the future. The sale of council houses has meant that fewer adaptable properties are available for disabled people to move into. Most housing associations have proved reluctant to meet the housing needs of disabled people and those which have done so are being squeezed out of existence by the new housing association financing system. Private landlords have never been great providers of suitable housing for disabled people, and the recent deregulation of rents is likely to make them still less so. The culmination of these policies is a disproportionate rise in homelessness among disabled people.

It was then demonstrated that all modern transport systems are to varying degrees inaccessible to disabled people. This affects their choice of transport, the amount they have to pay to travel, and their dependence on others in order to travel any distance. The cost of buying and running a private car is often more expensive for disabled than for non-disabled motorists. The most convenient and inexpensive forms of local public transport, namely buses and urban railway systems, are entirely inaccessible to many disabled people. As a result they are forced to rely on such methods of getting around as taxis or segregated 'special' services which are either more expensive or provide a generally inferior service which denies them direct control over their transportation needs. As for long-distance transport, each of the three systems discussed — coaches, railways and airlines — provides a largely sub-standard service for disabled travellers. The cheapest form of long-distance travel, namely coaches, is the least accessible and they all require considerable advance warning before they can accommodate disabled people's needs. Moreover, although there is much talk from policy-makers and transport providers about making public transport more accessible for disabled people, it is clear that it will be the twenty-first century before public transport becomes widely accessible.

Disabled people's ability to perform even the most routine of daily tasks is thus severely diminished because of a predominantly inaccessible built environment. To some extent this problem was officially recognised in the 1970s, when the Government adopted an explicitly voluntarist approach in an attempt to resolve it. However, despite some improvement, the data show that on the whole this policy has failed. A wide variety of public and private buildings around Britain is inaccessible to disabled people, and although there are building regulations which stipulate that structures erected after 1987 should be made accessible, major problems still remain. One of the most important is the growing shift toward pedestrianisation and traffic-free zones in city centres. It is important not only because they preclude people with mobility difficulties and bring into full focus the way in which disabled people's needs are ignored by architects and town planners, but also because pedestrianisation demonstrates clearly that legislation which simply tinkers with the Building Regulations will not eradicate discrimination against disabled people in the context of the built environment. It is probable that many of the new pedestrian precincts will have been created after 1987 and therefore should not in themselves be inaccessible to people with mobility-related impairments. So if access to the built environment for disabled people, along with accessible housing and accessible transport, is to become more than the empty rhetoric of policy-makers, local and national, then the Government should take the lead and introduce legislation making it compulsory.

8

LEISURE AND SOCIAL LIFE, AND THE INFLUENCE OF THE MEDIA

This chapter considers the impact of institutional discrimination on the leisure and social activities of disabled people. It shows that disabled people's ability to participate in mainstream recreational pursuits and establish 'normal' social contacts and relationships is severely restricted as a result of the economic, environmental and social barriers discussed in previous chapters.

Work and Leisure. Contrary to popular belief, many disabled people have less leisure time than their non-disabled contemporaries. Also, their capacity to participate in recreational pursuits is greatly reduced if they are not in work.

Broadly, leisure is perceived as the opposite of paid work. It represents a period of free time and enjoyment when people can engage in activities of their own choice. This poses something of a problem for people who have no paid work with which to contrast leisure. Those most obviously affected are women at home and retired and unemployed people, but for them leisure is still defined as time over which they have control. For women at home, for example, leisure is contrasted with domestic work. This is also true for the other groups mentioned above, whose lives are largely organised around what working people regard as leisure (Abercrombie and Warde *et al.*, 1988).

Since the 1939–45 war there has been a general decrease in the amount of time people spend in paid work and a corresponding increase in leisure time. For industrial workers the working week has been reduced by about four hours, and now stands at around forty hours (HMSO, 1991). Non-manual workers tend to have a shorter working week, averaging something like thirty-seven hours (Abercrombie and Warde *et al.*, 1988).

Opportunities for leisure may have been created by the availability of free time, but some variation is available to different groups of people. For example, according to Government estimates, in 1989 retired men had the most leisure time with ninety-three hours per week, followed by unemployed men with eighty-eight hours. The corresponding figures for women were eighty-two and seventy-two hours. Men in full-time employment had forty-four hours of free time per week and similarly employed women eleven hours less

(HMSO, 1991) because women's domestic workload is generally much greater than men's. There are no separate figures for free time available to disabled people but it is probably a similar variation among different groups. For example, disabled men, whether in work or not, are likely to have more leisure time than their disabled women counterparts.

Table 8.1. Time Use in a Typical Week, 1989

Hours spent on	Full-time Employees male	female	Economically inactive women	Retired
Employment and travel	48.9	43.6	0.4	0.7
Essential (domestic and personal) activities	25.9	42.2	65.3	30.8
Sleep	49.0	49.0	49.0	49.0
Free time	44.2	33.2	53.3	87.5
Free time per weekday	4.7	3.2	7.1	12.3
Free time per weekend day	10.4	8.5	9.0	13.1

Note: Comparable figures for unemployed disabled or non-disabled people or gender differences for retired people are not available.
Source: Adapted from Table 10.2 in HMSO, 1991, p. 170.

It is also probable that many disabled people, irrespective of gender, will have less free time than their non-disabled equivalents. Generally, essential domestic and personal activities take longer to complete as impairment increases, particularly for those who rely on personal and domestic assistants for routine daily functions. People with personal assistance needs who are in full-time employment often face problems in balancing time between personal needs, work and leisure pursuits. This is made worse when they do not have complete control of those services and have continually to negotiate with local authorities or other agencies to maintain and refine their personal assistance packages to suit their individual needs (Oliver *et al.*, 1988).

People's ability to enjoy leisure time is closely related to their employment status. In general, we are socialised into the belief that work is good and idleness reprehensible. Consequently, people who are excluded from the workplace often find it extremely difficult to organise their lives around leisure (see Fagin and Little, 1984;

Parker, 1979; Willis, 1985). This is as true for disabled people as for non-disabled people. For example, research documenting the experience of people who had acquired spinal cord injuries found that employment was an important factor associated with expressed levels of satisfaction with leisure activities. The majority of people who were not working felt that they had too much leisure time and insufficient meaningful and enjoyable activity to fill it. Moreover, those in part-time work reported less satisfaction with their leisure activities than those in full-time work (Oliver *et al.*, 1988).

Although disabled people are able to obtain from statutory authorities such as the Department of Employment (DE) vital equipment like lightweight wheelchairs and reading aids to overcome disability in employment, there is no equivalent provision for leisure activity. Consequently, unemployed disabled people are denied access to technical aids unless they buy them themselves or go cap-in-hand to charities. Moreover, although disabled people with jobs are able to use any equipment supplied by the DE for recreational pursuits, this provision can be withdrawn once employment ceases (see Chapter 4).

Income and Leisure.   Apart from access, which is discussed later, a major source of dissatisfaction among disabled people over leisure must almost certainly stem from their lack of financial resources. People's ability to enjoy recreation is closely related to the amount of money they can spend (Abercrombie and Warde *et al.*, 1988; Parker, 1979; Willis, 1985). As people have become more affluent, their spending on leisure has increased accordingly. Between 1966 and 1976, for example, consumer expenditure of all kinds rose by 21 per cent in real terms (Parker, 1979). In 1989 British households spent almost 16 per cent of their total weekly budget, £35.01, on a range of leisure-based activities and items such as alcohol consumed outside the home, eating out, books, television sets, video recorders, holidays, public entertainment (cinema and theatre admissions etc.) and sports goods, not including clothing (HMSO, 1991).

As we have seen in Chapter 5, the majority of disabled people do not have sufficient income to cover the full cost of impairment-related expenditure, let alone leisure activities. So in general their standard of living is judged to be much lower than that of non-disabled people, and there is a definite relationship between impairment and the inability to buy desired items, particularly among unmarried disabled people below retirement age (Martin and White, 1988).

Home-Based Leisure Activities.   Although there is an enormous variety of leisure pursuits available, the greater part of most people's leisure activities take place at home. Watching television, visiting or entertaining friends, listening to the radio, listening to music and reading are generally the most popular (HMSO, 1991). The same is also true for disabled people (Barnes, 1990; Brimblecombe *et al.*; 1985; Oliver *et al.*, 1988), although their choice of home-based leisure pursuits is often reduced.

If one considers the most popular recreational activity in Britain, television (HMSO, 1991), although the content of many programmes is implicitly or explicitly 'disablist'* and therefore offensive to many disabled people (see below), gaining access to them can be a problem for the deaf community. Apart from programmes specifically for people with hearing impairments and disabled people generally, relatively few mainstream programmes are accessible to the non-hearing population. The proportion of programmes transmitted with subtitles for people with hearing impairments for all channels is currently about 12.5 of total output for pre-recorded programmes and 14.5 per cent if live broadcasts including the news are included (DBC, 1990).

There is also some variation from week to week depending on the type of programme being transmitted. To gain access to this service, people with hearing impairments must have a television equipped to receive Teletext, which is more expensive to buy than an ordinary set. Although the number of subtitled programmes is due to increase gradually over the next few years, it is unlikely to exceed more than 50 per cent of the total output. This is because subtitling is expensive and 50 per cent is the figure which TV companies must reach by 1998 under the Broadcasting Act 1990 (HMSO, 1990a). Finally, subtitled programmes are not always accessible to people with hearing impairments who use English as a second language. Consequently, to make television programmes fully accessible to all members of the non-hearing community there is a need for sign language to be transmitted at the same time as subtitling (RNID, 1990). For the present this is not on the political agenda.

Socialising with friends in a domestic environment is the second most popular leisure activity in Britain (HMSO, 1991), but it is often a problem for disabled people. As we have seen in Chapter 7, the majority of Britain's housing stock is not accessible to many disabled people and their opportunity to be entertained in someone else's home is therefore often out of the question. Moreover, since some disabled people live in houses which are only partly accessible, entertaining friends in their own homes is often difficult,

---

*The word 'disablist', while answering the obvious need for an equivalent to 'sexist' and 'racist', has not yet become common parlance like the other two words. This fact in itself has some bearing on our discussion.

particularly if they want to entertain in private away from other family members (Barnes 1990; Oliver *et al.*, 1988).

Reading is one of the most popular home-based leisure activities. Sixty-five per cent of the population read a daily newspaper, 72 per cent a Sunday newspaper, 3 per cent general magazines, 6 per cent magazines specifically for women and 81 per cent of the 26 per cent of the adult population who use public libraries borrow books (HMSO, 1991). Yet newspapers and magazines are rarely, if ever, published initially in an accessible form for people with visual impairments. Newspapers are not produced in Braille and only a few magazines are available in this medium. Voluntary agencies such as the Talking Newspaper Association will provide taped versions of these publications, but they are usually a summary or digest of the original and are delivered weekly (RNIB, 1990a). Hence, users of the service are denied access to the entire publication and can only get it some time after it has been available to the non-disabled population. Such virtual censorship would not be acceptable to the non-disabled population and is unacceptable to many people with visual impairments (Press, 1991).

As for books, new publications are not in accessible forms and if disabled people with visual impairments wish to read them then they must apply to one of the voluntary agencies which provide this service. Examples include the Calibre Tape Library, Monument Tape Library or the Royal National Institute for the Blind's (RNIB) Talking Book service for fiction, or the Central Cassette Library at Peterborough for non-fiction (RNIB, 1990a). Although access to books is not impeded in the same way as for newspapers and magazines, people often have to wait some time to receive the book of their choice because of consumer demand. Many local libraries provide a selection of large print books and some carry taped versions, but these selections are usually extremely limited (Press, 1991). Moreover, it is also important to remember that access to libraries is frequently a problem, not only for people with visual impairments, but for disabled people generally (see Chapter 7).

Leisure Activities outside the Home.   As noted in the last chapter, disabled people's ability to enjoy leisure activities outside their homes is severely restricted because of an inaccessible physical environment, with a lack of accessible transport and buildings. A succession of studies shows that all leisure and social activities are heavily weighted in favour of car-owners/drivers and those with ready access to the car of their family or a friend (Barnes, 1990; GLAD, 1988; Oliver *et al.*, 1988; Rowe, 1973). In the GLAD study, 58 per cent of the people interviewed used their own, their family's or a friend's car for social activities requiring transport, and only 15 per cent used public transport. Those dependent on specialised transport systems such as local authority transport 'participated in the fewest leisure activities outside the home' (GLAD, 1988, p. 3).

Because car use is so important for leisure and social activity, and because public transport is so difficult for disabled people to use, those who wish to go out but have no car because of the cost or because they cannot drive are forced to rely on family or friends to drive them about. Apart from the obvious 'dilution of independence' which follows, this means that social and leisure activities often have to be arranged around times when drivers are available. This restriction on both spontaneity and freedom of choice is a frequent source of frustration for all concerned (Oliver *et al.*, 1988).

Spontaneity and choice are also severely affected by the inaccessibility of public buildings. Many pubs and restaurants pose major problems for disabled people. Moreover, 'the majority of museums and galleries, cinemas, concert halls and theatres remain inaccessible, at any rate in some respects to wheelchair-users and to many other people with disabilities' (Carnegie Council Review, 1988, p. 15). The same is true of most football grounds, race courses and other sporting stadia. To use these facilities, wheelchair-users and people with mobility-related impairments are frequently advised to 'phone in advance' for appropriate arrangements to be made (see Crouch *et al.*, 1989; McCart, 1991; Plumb, 1990). But many disabled people choose not to go where they cannot manage by themselves, and therefore tend not to venture into 'unknown territory' but rather to stick to tried and tested areas and places (Oliver *et al.*, 1988).

Transport and physical access are not the only hurdles which disabled people must confront before they can enjoy mainstream leisure pursuits away from home. Not only is there ignorance, but even apprehension is felt toward disabled people by many representatives of the mainstream leisure industry which cannot be explained simply by the problem of access. Moreover, although rarely discussed in print, there is a widely-held belief throughout the entertainment business that the presence of disabled people can discourage non-disabled customers.

At present this problem is made worse because there is no legislation ensuring that places of entertainment are made accessible to all sections of the community. The current safety and fire regulations simply state that 'in a society which values the rights and amenities available to all, fire regulations should not be used to place unnecessary restrictions on the ability of disabled persons, particularly those whose mobility is impaired, to use places of entertainment' (HMSO, 1990b, p. 20). However, these regulations only 'recommend' that licensing authorities 'encourage' the licensee to make suitable arrangements. Hence, local licensing authorities and leisure industry management are free to discriminate as they choose.

Examples can be found throughout the leisure industry. In theatres, for instance, the widely-acclaimed *Access in London: A Guide for Those who Have Problems Getting Around* (1989) shows that although attitudes among theatre staff are changing, discrimination is still detectable. The guide provides clear evidence of practical improvement and the survey team, which included disabled people, was often given a friendly welcome. However, in some places 'positive talk seemed to substitute for material change' and in others the researchers' enquiries were 'not welcomed' (Crouch *et al.*, 1989, p. 118). The guide gives evidence of widespread discrimination by concert hall, theatre and cinema managers. For example, some places do not allow wheelchair-users to visit them if they are not accompanied by an 'able-bodied companion'. Where disabled people are allowed to attend unaccompanied, they are often assigned a non-disabled steward to watch over them in case of emergency. This effectively means that disabled people are denied the opportunity to enjoy themselves without an escort. Indeed, some cinemas refuse to admit wheelchair-users at all (Crouch *et al.*, 1989, pp. 131–2). Similar examples can be found throughout Britain (see Plumb, 1990). Moreover, the management at the country's most popular tourist attraction, Madame Tussaud's in London, discourage visitors who use wheelchairs at busy times and insist that fire regulations require that no more than three such visitors be allowed in the building at the same time. Wheelchair-users are urged to telephone first 'to be sure of getting in' (Crouch *et al.*, 1989, p. 109).

Institutional discrimination against disabled people is also prevalent throughout the hotel and catering trade. A recent report produced by the English Tourist Board, *Tourism for All* (Baker, 1989) draws attention to some of the relevant issues. Besides focusing on the need for better access to tourist attractions and the development of better travel facilities, it recommends that more hotel rooms be made accessible and calls for the application and extension of the building regulations (Baker, 1989).

This report goes into some detail recommending the provision of holidays for low-income groups; many disabled people are unable to go on holiday because of lack of money (Martin, White and Meltzer, 1989). It points out that Britain now lags behind the rest of Europe in this and suggests that Government should cease to regard it as some kind of undeserved charity but rather as a fundamental right to be enjoyed by all. It also comments that successive governments have displayed an 'extraordinary meanness' in stopping the benefits of people on holiday, on the basis that they are not available for work during this time (Baker, 1989).

The report does not discuss in any detail attitudes toward disabled people within the hotel trade. One writer has recently commented that this is a serious omission. 'Much of it is born out of ignorance, and ignorance breeds fear and enmity. It is not so very long ago that someone said to me "You don't want to have those people in your hotel"' (Dillon, 1990, p. 20).

Discrimination against disabled people within the leisure industry is sometimes quite blatant. It is not uncommon for them to be refused entry to places of entertainment simply because they have an impairment. The usual rationalisation is that their presence prevents non-disabled people from enjoying themselves. In 1990 a disabled skittles team was banned from a local pub because its members were perceived as 'mentally handicapped'. The landlord justified the decision on the grounds that he had received complaints from other customers and was worried about 'the level of supervision' (Harper, 1990, p. 14).

Some sections of the leisure industry claim that they are aware of these problems and are doing something about them, but more often than not this is mere rhetoric. For example, the Arts Council publicly acknowledged the extent of discrimination within the leisure industry in 1985 with the publication of the Carnegie Council's first report, *Arts and Disabled People*. This report made a number of specific recommendations for changes to existing Arts Council policy, including the recommendation that grant aid to arts organisations be made conditional on improvements for disabled people (Carnegie United Kingdom Trust, 1985). A consultation paper followed, entitled *Access to the Arts*, and *A Code of Good Practice on Arts and Disability* was issued to all organisations receiving Arts Council grants. The *Code of Good Practice* obliges arts organisations not to discriminate in employment, to improve the accessibility of venues and to seek the active involvement of disabled people in future developments. The Council also set up an Arts and Disability Monitoring Committee consisting mainly of disabled people. Its main role is to advise on initiatives to improve the participation of disabled people in the arts (Carnegie Council Review, 1988).

The subsequent Carnegie Council Review *After Attenborough*, published in 1988, found that the main recommendations made by the first report were not being implemented and that, as a result, little progress had been made toward improved opportunities in the arts. In particular, very few recipients of Arts Council funds had made efforts toward improving access (Carnegie Council Review, 1988). In the same year the Arts Council was severely criticised by members of its own Arts and Disability Monitoring Committee for applying for an exemption certificate under the employment quota scheme, which meant that the Council would not be liable to prosecution for failing to meet the minimum of 3 per cent disabled staff (see Chapter 4). Also, the Council's headquarters in Piccadilly was inaccessible to disabled people (*Same Difference*, 1990b). Subsequent developments have included the relocation of the Arts Council's head office in new premises which are at the time of writing (February 1991) being made accessible, at least as far as possible since the new building is listed (see Chapter 7), and a new initiative on recruitment. However, the Council does not apparently anticipate meeting the 3 per cent quota in the foreseeable future because it has reapplied for an exemption permit from the Department of Employment (Harp, 1991). It is clear that if institutional discrimination against disabled people throughout the mainstream leisure industry is to disappear, then fine words are simply not enough.

Segregated Leisure Activities.   There are a number of segregated recreational and social activities specifically for disabled and elderly people. These include day centres, adult training centres (ATCs), also known as 'social education centres', and social clubs (Martin, White and Meltzer, 1989).

The National Survey of Day Services (Carter, 1981) estimated that during the mid-1970s there were 2,600 day centres and ATCs of one form or another operating each week up and down the country. The number has since increased markedly, although it is not possible to obtain an accurate picture of this expansion because statistics are not collated in a coherent form by the various service-providing agencies (Tester, 1989). Day services are provided by local authorities and a variety of voluntary organisations for disabled and elderly people; agencies providing services specifically for elderly people 'tends to mean disabled elderly people' (Martin, White and Meltzer, 1989, p. 62).

The OPCS surveys found that in the mid-1980s 5 per cent of all disabled adults attended day centres or ATCs. However, use of these facilities varies with age and severity of impairment. Indeed, attendance at all segregated facilities is highest among people with high levels of impairment and among the younger age-groups. Eight per cent of disabled adults aged under fifty attend day units, compared with 2 per cent aged fifty to sixty-four, 4 per cent aged sixty-five to seventy-four and 7 per cent aged 75 or over (Martin, White and Meltzer, 1989, pp. 62-3).

Since day centre attendance is not compulsory and is often regarded as one of the least desirable options for disabled people (HCIL, 1990; Oliver, 1983), particularly for those below retirement age (Barnes, 1990; Carter, 1981; Jowett, 1982; Kent *et al.*, 1984), it is important to note that many people are introduced to the idea of day centre use by staff and careers officers at special schools and colleges as an alternative to employment (see Chapter 3). Some younger disabled people look to day centres to escape the debilitating social isolation which often accompanies impairment (see below), and others are directed into them by medical professionals to assist in their 'rehabilitation' (Barnes, 1990; Carter, 1981).

Most day centres are outside city centres in suburbs and four out of every ten are in the grounds of residential institutions, usually hospitals or residential homes (Carter, 1981). The buildings normally used are one of two types: either large gymnasium-like structures or the modern purpose-built variety, both of which tend to make them stand out from the rest of the community (Barnes, 1990; Durrant, 1983). Many also have their own highly distinctive transport system which ferries disabled people from their own homes to the day centre and back again at night. Added to the fact that most day services cater exclusively for overtly disadvantaged minorities, this lends weight to the claim that they are highly segregative (Barnes, 1990; Oliver, 1983).

However, it may be argued that day centres provide a range of activities and services, both social and educative, which fulfil users' social needs and give them a level of autonomy and independence unavailable in the community at large. But mostly these facilities cannot give disabled people the confidence and skills to achieve these goals outside the centres. This is because most units are run by able-bodied people for disabled people, are inherently paternalistic and/or operate under predominantly voluntary principles. Thus users are generally freed of all obligations and responsibilities while in the centres. Elsewhere in society this is a situation normally reserved for either very young or very old people (see Barnes, 1990).

Moreover, because of the extent of institutional discrimination against disabled people in society generally, many users' experience of life outside the centres is limited to the family home. Thus partial institutionalisation, with users coming to accept that life outside their homes is limited and should preferably be lived within an institutional setting, is likely to result. This has particular significance for disabled day centre users who often rely on ageing family members for personal assistance needs: partial institutionalisation is likely to lead to institutionalisation proper, with users coming to accept that for disabled people life inside an institution is both acceptable and inevitable (Barnes, 1990).

Day centres therefore go against the idea of an integrated society, although they are presented by the carers' lobby and many welfare professionals as an essential ingredient of the 'community care' programme. They serve as a segregated alternative to mainstream social and recreational facilities and so perpetuate dependence rather than alleviating it. Indeed, many people use day centres as their only way of gaining access to the essential support services on which they depend (see Chapter 6). They are a significant drain on economic and human resources which could be put to far better use elsewhere (HCIL, 1990).

Similar criticisms apply to special clubs for disabled people. According to the OPCS survey 6 per cent of disabled adults under fifty, 3 per cent of those aged between fifty and sixty-four, 3 per cent of those between sixty-five and seventy-four, and 2 per cent of those aged seventy-five and over use these clubs (Martin, White and Meltzer, 1989, p. 63). However, the OPCS researchers did not distinguish between segregated clubs for disabled people and voluntary associations of disabled people, and thus it is difficult to ascertain respective attendance figures. Consequently the OPCS figures should be treated with caution. We are concerned here with clubs for disabled people, not voluntary associations of disabled people, which are discussed in the following chapter.

Special clubs for disabled people are, like day centres, run by a variety of agencies including local authorities and voluntary organisations. Some special schools also run this type of club, but in general clubs linked to special schools differ from those in mainstream schools by being much more subject to adult control, in both membership and attendance (Anderson and Clarke, 1982). They are also often exclusive to people connected with the school in some way, and so are even more segregative than other clubs for disabled people. In addition, many are open only in term-time, so their users who depend on them for social contacts tend to be stuck for something to do in the holidays (Anderson and Clarke, 1982).

Many social clubs for disabled people are run by local authority social service departments and are often linked to day centres and other municipal facilities. Transport is usually provided, and users can be transported to and from the club in specially adapted local authority vehicles. These clubs are often used in the evening by the same people who visit the day centres during the day (Barnes, 1990). There is also a wide variety of national and local organisations for disabled people with specific leisure interests. Two examples are Sports for Young Disabled Women, which organises climbing and other outdoor activities, and Riding for the Disabled, which arranges horse riding sessions for disabled people generally (*Forum*, 1990). Although such clubs fulfil a very real social need, their existence does little to break down the barriers between disabled and non-disabled people in the leisure industry as a whole. Indeed, because they provide an alternative to mainstream recreation they might be said to perpetuate these divisions. Moreover, as with other segregated facilities, many disabled people are directed toward these clubs by social workers and other professionals (Barnes, 1990).

There is one national organisation which claims to bring together the disabled and non-disabled sections of the community specifically for leisure and social activity. It runs a national network of so-called Physically Handicapped and Able-Bodied (PHAB) clubs. There is relatively little empirical data on the activities of these clubs nationally, but one recent study suggests that some of them are organised in conjunction with special schools and local authorities and that, despite their name, most members are disabled people. The only non-disabled people involved are helpers or relatives of users. Moreover, the age-span of members ranges from small disabled children to elderly disabled people and the clubs close at 9.30 p.m., far earlier than most social clubs used by the general public. Finally, the study also shows that many of the disabled people using these facilities do so because they have access to nothing else (Barnes, 1990).

Social Relations and Disabled People.   From studies of the experience of disability it appears that in general disabled people express only marginal dissatisfaction with their social lives. Those with acquired impairments often find that satisfaction in this area only comes after some time, with a change in expectations and the development of new interests (Morris, 1989; Oliver *et al.*, 1988). In general, dissatisfaction is greatest among the younger people (Martin, White and Meltzer, 1989), because young people generally are far more concerned with peer group relationships than family ones and rely more on activities outside the home for social contacts (McRobbie, 1989). Older disabled people tend to be less dissatisfied with their social contacts, which are usually well established and centre around family and neighbours rather than outside activities such as pubs or clubs. An important fact is that people who acquire impairments often find that the number of their non-disabled friends diminishes after the onset of disability (Barnes, 1990; Morris, 1989; Oliver *et al.*, 1988).

Although a number of studies report high levels of social isolation among young disabled people (see for example Barnes, 1990;

Thomas *et al.*, 1989), there are relatively few which contrast their social lives with those of their non-disabled peers. Two which did are Anderson and Clarke's *Disability and Adolescence* (1982) and Brimblecombe's *The Needs of Handicapped Young Adults* (1985). Both studies found the social lives of disabled young people and their non-disabled equivalents to be significantly different.

Anderson and Clarke compared the leisure and social activities of thirty-three non-disabled young people and 119 young disabled people aged between 14 and 18. Sixty-three of the latter were or had been in mainstream schools and the rest in special education. They found that most young people with impairments spent more time engaged in solitary leisure activities such as watching television or listening to music than their non-disabled peers. One-third said they never saw friends outside school, compared to only 10 per cent of the non-disabled young people. They were also more likely to go out with siblings or parents than were the latter. Nearly 75 per cent of the sample with impairments normally went out with one or more members of their family, while the non-disabled young people nearly always went out with their peers. The researchers concluded that the level of social contact the young people had was closely linked to their difficulties with mobility. Those who had the most problems in getting about were also more isolated socially (Anderson and Clarke, 1982). Similar findings have been recorded by other studies of the social lives of disabled people generally (Martin, White and Meltzer 1989; Oliver *et al.*, 1988; Thomas *et al.*, 1989).

Anderson and Clarke also reported that social isolation was higher among disabled young people who attended special schools, of whom 60 per cent never socialised with friends outside school, over half had never been to a friend's home, and only a quarter had made such a visit in the previous month. The majority of this group only had friends who were themselves young people with impairments. Consequently on both sides of the relationship there were difficulties in making social contact. As noted in Chapter 3, these problems are compounded because special schools generally have a larger catchment area than mainstream schools, and therefore pupils attending them often live a long way from each other. By contrast, young people, with and without impairments, attending mainstream schools had friends living within walking or wheeling distance from home (Anderson and Clarke, 1982).

The Brimblecombe analysis compared the lifestyles of 385 disabled young adults aged 16–25 with those of their non-disabled equivalents. The study demonstrated that in this particular age-group non-disabled people are three times more likely to be living independently from their parents and to be employed and married than their disabled contemporaries, among whom they also found social isolation to be widespread. Three times more disabled than non-disabled people never went out socially in an average week, and almost double the number of cases, 52 per cent as opposed to 28 per cent, went out on two days or less. Only 3 per cent of the non-disabled young people never went out with friends. The disabled young adults were less likely to be involved in 'normal' social activities, such as going to the pub, generally associated with people in this age-group. As a result many felt there was a 'shortfall' in their social lives. When compared to the non-disabled people interviewed, twice as many of the disabled people said that they often felt 'lonely, miserable or that life was not worth living, three times as many of them were not able to say they often felt happy' (Brimblecombe *et al.*, 1985, p. 63).

Apart from the problems of gaining access to mainstream leisure activities, there is a number of reasons why establishing and maintaining social relationships is more difficult for disabled than for non-disabled people. Those who need personal assistants (PAs) are at a particular disadvantage because most do not have complete control over them. Going out to visit friends, for example, needs careful planning. Consequently, as with leisure activities, spontaneity and choice are greatly reduced. People who are forced to rely on friends and relatives for such services find that this reliance can be a big constraint on an active social life (Oliver *et al.*, 1988), as well as causing tension between them and those acting as unpaid PAs (HCIL, 1990).

The importance of employment for social contact is well known (Fagin and Little, 1984), particularly for older people (Abercrombie and Warde *et al.*, 1988). Moreover, studies of the experience of disability show that disabled people in work are more satisfied with their social life than those without work (Morris, 1989; Oliver *et al.*, 1988). Indeed, one of the main reasons many disabled people want to work is to gain access to a 'normal' pattern of social activity (Barnes, 1990), even though when they work they may not have time to meet friends outside working hours (Oliver *et al.*, 1988).

Studies of the social experiences of disabled people also suggest that many see their effect on others as limiting their social lives (Barnes, 1990; Martin, White and Meltzer, 1989; Oliver *et al.*, 1988). The Oliver study reported that a few individuals believed they were a burden to their friends, which held them back from 'normal activities, and from being able to engage in social activities in a carefree and spontaneous manner' (Oliver *et al.*, 1988, p. 63). Some disabled people have reported that while friends are happy to see them in their own homes they are clearly unhappy to be out with them in public. The public image of disability, which disabled people have to come to terms with every day of their lives, is sometimes said to be 'hard for friends to confront' (Morris, 1989, p. 105).

A significant aspect of social life for many disabled people, which is also directly affected by public perceptions of disability, is that of personal and, particularly, sexual relationships. This vital area of life is one which many disabled people find hedged around with numerous restrictions, and this is naturally a cause of great concern (Barnes, 1990; Hurst, 1984; Morris, 1989) and dissatisfaction (Oliver *et al.*, 1988).

Although the lack of spontaneity and choice in leisure activity generally does much to inhibit disabled people's ability to participate in this form of social interaction, cultural factors are significant here. Although economic and environmental factors make initial encounters more problematic for disabled people than for non-disabled people, many disabled individuals see themselves as an unattractive proposition for potential sexual partners. The institutionalised animosity against their having children (see Chapter 2), society's obsession with the 'body beautiful' (Morris, 1989) and the widespread belief that sexual activity is limited to specific actions, namely completed coitus and multiple orgasm (a view only now being seriously questioned because of the AIDS epidemic) make these relationships particularly difficult for many disabled people. In short, they are widely perceived as 'sexually dead' (Hooper, 1990). This affects their ability to establish not only short-term sexual relationships but long-term ones as well (Barnes, 1990; Oliver *et al.*, 1988; Morris, 1989).

The Media

Much of the above can be attributed to the persistence of traditional misconceptions about disability and disabled people. Indeed, 'the pre-conceived attitudes towards, assumptions about and expectations of disabled people are one of the biggest barriers to equal opportunities' (Reiser and Mason, 1990, p. 98). As we saw in Chapter 2, stereotyped assumptions about disabled people are based on superstitions, myths and beliefs inherited from earlier times. They are inherent to our culture, and part of the reason why they persist is that they are continually reproduced through television, radio, films, advertising, books and both local and national newspapers.

The way disability-related issues are presented in the media not only offends many disabled people but is also a major barrier to integration. Just as racist or sexist attitudes, whether explicit or implicit, are acquired through the 'normal' learning process, so there is evidence that 'disablism' is learned in this way too. On the basis of a photograph study, children have been found not to react badly to 'abnormal' looks until they are at least eleven years old, and thus 'discrimination against funny-looking people' is not some innate result of evolutionary forces, but is a socially learned phenomenon (*New Society*, 1985).

While the communications media alone cannot be held responsible for this, their impact cannot be overlooked. In 1988/9, for example, 98 per cent of British households had a television set and between 1985 and 1989 British people spent an average of 24.75 hours a week watching it and 9.75 hours listening to the radio. Nearly 14 million households have at least 1 video recorder and the British Videograph Association estimated that in 1989 378 million people rented videotapes while video sales were in the region of 38 million (HMSO, 1991). Although there is some dispute over the level of influence of the mass media on our perceptions of society, there are few who argue that it does not have any (see for example Broadcasting Standards Council, 1989). Moreover, in 1977 Biklen and Bogdana identified ten commonly recurring negative stereotypes of disabled people in the mass media. These included the disabled person as pitiable and pathetic, as an object of curiosity or violence, as sinister or evil, as the super cripple, as laughable, as her/his own worst enemy, as a burden, as non-sexual and as being unable to participate in daily life (Biklen and Bogdana, 1977). These stereotypes are particularly evident on television, in the newspapers and in the advertising industry.

Television. Although misrepresentation of disability is prevalent throughout the media as a whole, it is particularly so on British television. Research by the Broadcasting Research Unit (BRU) shows that although disabled people are under represented on television, when they are depicted it is usually within the context of one of the above stereotypes (BRU, 1990).

The BRU researchers analysed the peak-time television programmes broadcast by all four British television channels over a six-week period during 1988. They found that disabled people appeared in only 16 per cent of all the factual or current affairs programmes analysed. This proportion rose to 24 per cent when news programmes were included. The most common feature of factual reporting on disabled people concerned medical treatment. This was the theme in 16 per cent of such broadcasts analysed. In 11 per cent the focus was on the special achievements of the disabled person and in 9 per cent on the cure for the particular impairment displayed. The emphasis on medical treatment was even greater — 22 per cent — when news programmes alone were examined. Not one of the forty-four game shows observed contained a disabled person (BRU, 1990). The general absence of disabled people from mainstream television programmes, along with the traditional association between disability and medicine, reinforces the idea that they are incapable of participating fully in everyday life, while at the same time feeding the notion that they should be shut away and segregated (Reiser and Mason, 1990).

The BRU study found that disabled people were portrayed in fictional programmes but they represented a mere 0.5 per cent of all the characters portrayed. When only speaking characters are considered the percentage rises to 1.4. This contrasts strongly with the number of disabled people in the population as a whole, which according to the OPCS survey stands at 14 per cent (Martin, Meltzer and Elliot, 1988). Only 8 per cent of soap opera episodes and 9 per cent of situation comedies contained someone with an impairment. The BRU researchers did not analyse the way in which disabled people are perceived as objects of humour on British television. The widespread practice of ridiculing people with impairments finds expression in cartoon characters such as Mr Magoo, an elderly man with a visual impairment which causes him much misfortune, as well as the comedy routines of a host of contemporary television comedians (Reiser and Mason, 1990). Also, the portrayal of disabled people on British television is not representative of the disabled population as a whole. For example, 65 per cent of the disabled people on television are male, 95 per cent are white and over 50 per cent are aged 25–40 (BRU, 1990). In reality, the majority of disabled people are women, more than 5 per cent are not white and the likelihood of impairment increases with age (see BRU 1990; Martin, Meltzer and Elliot, 1988).

The genre most likely to include disabled characters on British television is that of crime and thriller films. In contrast to drama programmes, feature films are more than twice as likely to include disabled people. Of 134 feature films examined, seventy-two proved to contain disabled characters, of whom fifty-three were in major or minor speaking parts, and twenty-five made the circumstances of disability an important issue. In more than half of the latter, thirteen films, it was judged to be 'sentimental'. In only eight was the issue of prejudice and discrimination raised (BRU, 1990).

The most commonly used stereotypes are the disabled person as a criminal, as barely human and as powerless and pathetic. Disabled people appeared as criminals in six of the seventy-two films studied, as subhuman in five and as pathetic in seven. Disabled characters are also brought into films 'to enhance the atmosphere of a film when it needs to be one of deprivation, mystery or menace'. In short, they are introduced not because they are ordinary and like others but to suggest precisely the opposite, 'that they are not ordinary people' (BRU, 1990, unpaged).

When the portrayal of disabled characters is compared and contrasted with that of able-bodied characters, it is 'immediately' apparent that the former are of lower status. They are less likely to be in white-collar or professional employment and more likely to be unemployed. The attitudes displayed toward disabled characters are also markedly different from those toward non-disabled characters. Disabled characters are much more likely to evoke sympathy, pity, sadness, fear or a patronising attitude (BRU, 1990). Non-disabled characters are more likely to evoke respect or attraction. As to the relationships portrayed, disabled characters are far less likely to be involved in sexual relationships with other characters and more likely to be loners, and indeed are usually presented as incapable of sexual activity. Battye (1966) referred to this as 'the Chatterly syndrome' following D. H. Lawrence's novel *Lady Chatterly's Lover*, which recounts a sexual liaison between a member of the landed gentry and a lowly gamekeeper. Lady Chatterly takes an able-bodied lover mainly because her husband acquired his impairment from war injuries and is therefore, as perceived by Lawrence, sexually inactive (Battye, 1966).

In addition, disabled characters are portrayed as difficult to get on with, moody and introverted; they are their 'own worst enemy'. They are also far more likely than non-disabled characters to be the victims of violence and to be dead by the end of the programme, reinforcing the view that disabled people are helpless and dependent (Reiser and Mason, 1990). Most important, 'seldom was any suggestion made in these films that society, social arrangements or social attitudes and values had any bearing upon the fate of these people' (BRU, 1990, unpaged).

The BRU research also showed that, where dramatic fiction is concerned, American programmes are more likely than their British equivalents to portray disabled people as 'sociable, extrovert, moral and non-aggressive and less likely to be dependent, sad, moody or difficult to get on with'. Additionally, the attitudes evoked by the American disabled characters display more respect and less aggression than in the British productions. Disabled people in American programmes are much more likely to have an emotional relationship (62 per cent) than were similar characters in British productions (26 per cent) and those in British productions are more likely to have no relationship at all (23 per cent as opposed to 12 per cent) (BRU, 1990).

Surprisingly, around the end of the 1980s this misrepresentation of disability and disabled people on television was acknowledged officially. For example, the Government-appointed Broadcasting Standards Council stated in its Code of Practice that there is a need for programmes and advertising (see below) which give a 'fair reflection of the parts played in the everyday life of the nation by disabled people' (Broadcasting Standards Council, 1989, p. 45). This would mean, first, a shift away from the presentation of disabled people in factual programmes in a way which gives non-disabled viewers 'a sense of the superiority of their condition, or the emotional enjoyment of their generous sympathy', and, secondly, a concerted effort by writers and producers to include more disabled characters, preferably played by disabled actors, in fictional programmes. Also, these characters should be part of 'the drama of life' and not used 'in either a sinister or a sentimental fashion' (BRU, 1990, unpaged). Whether the television companies will be prepared to do this remains to be seen.

Newspapers. The British press can be separated into at least two distinct groups, namely the 'quality' broadsheets such as *The Times* and the tabloids like the *Sun* and the *Daily Mirror*. While the first group has a reputation for accurate in-depth reporting, the latter is often short on news but high on sensationalism. The treatment of disabled people often brings out the worst in the newspapers 'not only from the tabloids, but also from the so-called "quality press" as well' (*Same Difference*, 1990c, p. 3).

The use of 'disablist' language is common in the British press. For example, terms like 'the disabled' and 'the handicapped' still often appear despite campaigns to raise the awareness of journalists. The term 'cripple' is also freely used, particularly in stories of the 'brave cripple' variety where disability is used in a sentimental and pitiful guise. Reports in all sections of the press generally misrepresent the experience of disability mainly because they are printed for their sensation value rather than their accuracy. Common examples include items about the sexual impotence of recently disabled men, disabled individuals who 'bravely manage' to achieve despite their 'handicap', and the celebrity who understands the 'plight' of disabled people, or who is willing to make unprecedented personal sacrifices to help a disabled friend or a particular group of disabled people (*Same Difference*, 1990c). It is also common for journalists to heap excessive praise on disabled individuals, particularly children, for carrying out a perfectly normal act (Reiser and Mason, 1990).

Although some sections of the British press are prepared to sink lower than others in their portrayal of disabled people, abuses of language and image are common throughout the whole range of newspapers. Disabled people are seen as legitimate 'fodder by a sensation-hungry press eager for an easy story and unwilling to consider the harm that may be done to the public image of disabled people' (*Same Difference*, 1990c, p. 4).

However, in 1990 the editors of the major national newspapers agreed on a voluntary Code of Practice on representation, to ensure that people are 'fairly represented' in the press and not exploited for their news potential. This is widely regarded as little more than a public relations exercise. A further development following the creation of the Code has been the appointment to all the major newspapers of a 'readers' representative' or Ombudsman to deal with complaints and exert pressure for change when readers point out problems, but offensive material has to be actually published before action can be taken. The umbrella organisation for dealing with complaints about the British press is the Press Complaints Commission, which has hitherto been notoriously slow to deal with complaints and appeared reluctant to exercise its limited powers (*Same Difference*, 1990c).

The Advertising Industry.   In general, there are two ways in which the advertising industry contributes to the discriminatory process. First, disabled people are excluded and sometimes deliberately ignored by advertising agencies (Levy, 1990). Secondly, some advertisers, notably charities, present a particularly distorted view of disability and disabled people in order to achieve their stated aims (Campbell, 1990a). Either way, disabled people are the losers.

As for the exclusion of disabled people from mainstream advertising, apart from concealing disability and disabled people from the community as a whole, this is a clear denial of the role of disabled people as consumers. Although this could be understandable on the grounds that on the whole disabled people have less spending power than the rest of society, they still buy things no matter how little money they have. It is a situation which many disabled people find offensive (Levy, 1990).

The omission of disabled people from mainstream advertising campaigns is not limited to the private sector. For example, the Government, fast becoming one of Britain's biggest advertisers, with its programme having reached £88 million, is one of the worst offenders in this respect. A Government spokesman recently stated that the Department of Social Security's (DSS) own commercials do not address disabled people or include them as actors. Moreover, even if they were included, in the present circumstances they would have no influence on how they are portrayed (Levy, 1990)

On the few occasions when aspects of disability are used in mainstream advertisements, they are usually of a kind that deeply offends disabled people. A notable example was an 'epilepsy' advertisement for Yorkshire Television devised and created by the advertising agency Young and Rubican. It consisted of a picture of wavy lines accompanied by the caption 'Some people will have a fit when they see this'. It was withdrawn only after a number of complaints by viewers to the Advertising Standards Authority (Levy, 1990). While this might be seen as a vindication of the present system of regulation, the damage had already been done before the advertisement was removed. Considering the widespread ignorance surrounding epilepsy and the discrimination experienced by people who have this type of impairment (see Sutherland, 1981), such a situation should have been avoided in the first place.

The portrayal of disabled people in charity advertising is a major bone of contention for many disabled people and their organisations. Indeed, the depth of feeling against the cynical exploitation of stereotypes by charities has resulted in the formation of the Campaign to Stop Patronage, an organisation of disabled people dedicated to the abolition of this particular form of discrimination. It gained widespread publicity after a well-attended demonstration against the 1990 Telethon, an annual television event in which charities appeal for public funds on behalf of disabled people and other disadvantaged groups (*Disability Now*, 1990). The use of disablist imagery by charities was not discussed by the BRU research in any great detail because these organisations were not allowed to advertise on television at the time of that study. Since then, however, the situation has changed with the lifting of restrictions on charity advertising on independent television and radio by the Independent Broadcasting Authority in 1989, following Home Office approval.

Reiser and Mason (1990) have noted that the disabled person as pitiable and pathetic is probably the stereotype most commonly used by charities. They point out that for many years one of these organisations allowed their campaign to use the absurd sight of little girls wearing calipers sitting outside shops begging. They also note that although many charities are responsible for public misinformation surrounding disability and disabled people, they receive much of their financial support from Government sources (Reiser and Mason, 1990).

However, although still widely used, the disabled person as pitiable and pathetic is not the only negative image extensively used by charities. Campbell (1990a) has identified three distinct phases in the evolution of disablist imagery as promoted by the more progressive elements in the charity industry. These are the 'philanthropic' phase, the 'courageous and the exceptional' phase and the 'ability not disability' phase. The 'philanthropic' phase refers mainly to the more traditional fund-raising activities of the socially well placed who concerned themselves with the care and protection of the 'poor unfortunates'. Disabled people were presented as objects of pity who were rarely seen since most of them were shut away in institutions (Campbell, 1990a).

As many of these establishments began to close during the 1970s, causing disabled people to become more visible in the community, some of the more 'enlightened' charities adopted a different approach. They focused on the 'courage and bravery' of individual 'super-cripples' in their efforts to enlist public support for their activities. The majority of 'ordinary' disabled people were ignored and remained as socially isolated as ever (Campbell, 1990a). However, the growing strength of the disability movement in the 1980s precipitated a further shift in these organisations' exploitation of disabled people. Now, after largely superficial consultations with specific representatives of the disabled community, the 'negative' elements of disability, namely individual impairments, are to be ignored and the more 'positive' aspects emphasised and celebrated, in particular the 'normal' or 'able-bodied' abilities of individual disabled people (Campbell, 1990a).

While this development might be seen as something of an improvement on earlier disabling imagery, it will do relatively little to remove institutional discrimination against disabled people. There is a number of reasons for this. First, the emphasis on 'ability not disability' is an attempt to suppress difference; it is a denial of the status of the disabled person and disabled culture. Secondly, the new 'positive images' of disabled people fail to reflect the racial, sexual and cultural divisions within the disabled community as a whole. In the current economic and social climate, disabled people do not fit neatly into able-bodied perceptions of normality (Campbell, 1990a).

Thirdly, the use of the concept 'normality' tends to obscure the need for change. Logic dictates that if disabled people are perceived as 'normal', then there is little need for the introduction of policies to facilitate their integration into 'normal' society. Fourthly, there is an inherent contradiction in the assertion that disabled people are basically 'normal' but at the same time have to get others, notably non-disabled people, to beg on their behalf for the basic necessities of life. This makes the claim to normality untenable because 'normal' people are rarely dependent for their livelihood on the benevolence of others. Finally, and most important, the focus of this 'new' approach remains squarely on disabled people rather than on the 'disabling society in which we all live' (Campbell, 1990a, unpaged). Consequently this shift in emphasis can be seen as little more than a cynical marketing exercise by charities to conceal the fact that they themselves are a fundamental part of the disabling process.

The main problem with these and other media images of disabled people is that they have been devised and produced by non-disabled people. Indeed, it is only very recently that disabled people have had any say in how they are presented on television or in the press. To rectify this the British Council of Organizations of Disabled People (BCODP) is working on the production of a code of ethics to enable advertisers and others in the media industry to avoid disablist imagery (BCODP, 1991). In addition, groups of disabled people have produced two examples of advertisements for television which present a more positive image of disabled people; both focused on the need for equal rights for disabled people and both were featured on the BBC's *Comic Relief* programme on 15 March 1991.

Reducing Discrimination in the Media. It is clear that if disablist imagery in the media is to be reduced then major changes are needed. Apart from the developments mentioned, representatives of the disability movement have suggested a number of ways this might be achieved. First, there should be heightened involvement of all personnel throughout the media, including broadcasting companies, newspapers and advertising agencies, in comprehensive disability awareness courses designed and presented by disabled people. This is particularly important for those who are actually responsible for programme production, newspaper content and major advertising campaigns (Campbell, 1990b).

Secondly, there should be a greater effort to recruit and train more disabled people to work in the media industry. Corporate awareness of disability-related issues is likely to be less of a problem if disabled people are integrated at all levels into media organisations. A few tentative moves in this direction have been made by the main television companies, but in the media generally there is still a long way to go. Channel 4 has set up a media training course for disabled people at the North East Media Centre in Gateshead (Davies, 1990) and the BBC has a trainee assistant producer scheme for its programme *One in Four* (Campbell, 1990b).

Thirdly, there is a need for an overriding framework or policy statement for both the broadcasting and print media, as well as the advertising industry. Such a document should be drawn up by a representative group of disabled people working in conjunction with representatives from each of the areas concerned, namely, the Broadcasting Standards Council, the Press Council and the Advertising Standards Council. These bodies would then take the role of monitoring committees to monitor output. If these committees are to be 'empowering' and not simply 'tokenistic' (Campbell, 1990b), they would also need to be given authority to impose sanctions on those who disregard the agreed policy.

This authority must come from the Government. It is notable that some of the countries which have anti-discrimination legislation also have strict guide-lines for the presentation of disability in the media. In Ontario, Canada, there are stringent regulations for the portrayal of disabled people on television which stipulate that they should be integrated into mainstream programmes and advertisements, and not simply used only when a specific disabled person is needed (Government of Ontario Communications, 1989). Given the prevalence of disablist imagery in the British media, particularly when compared to some other countries, and the extent of institutional discrimination against disabled people throughout British society, similar measures must surely be needed in Britain too.

Conclusion

As we have seen in this chapter, disabled people's opportunities for participating in leisure activities and establishing 'normal' social relationships are much inferior to those of non-disabled people. Although there is some variation in the amount of leisure time available to different sections of the community, disabled people, particularly those dependent on personal and domestic services, have less than their non-disabled equivalents. At the same time those who have the most leisure generally enjoy it least.

There are several reasons for this. Because of the centrality of work to our culture, most unemployed people find it difficult to fill their time; this is true particularly of disabled people because some of the technical aids on which many depend are only provided for those with jobs. An important but related factor is disabled people's lack of financial resources; this applies to those with and without jobs because they all tend to have less disposable income than their non-disabled contemporaries. This is especially significant when it is remembered that over the last few years the link between people's ability to enjoy recreation and the amount of money they have to spend has become of ever-greater importance. It is also evident that the choice of leisure activities available to disabled people, both inside and outside the home, is less than that available to the general population. Among home-based leisure activities, examples include the absence of television programmes accessible to the deaf community and the lack of reading materials for people with visual impairments. Outside the home an inaccessible physical environment is a major barrier to leisure activities. Transport and access difficulties cannot be over-emphasised here, because both contribute so greatly to disabled people's dependence on others for access to leisure. This reliance means that spontaneity and choice are further reduced.

Although physical access to mainstream recreational facilities is itself a major problem for disabled people, it is suggested that there is also a degree of antagonism toward them among staff who work in the entertainment industry. This finds expression in such ways as the interpretation of fire regulations by local licensing authorities and entertainment managers, who implicitly or explicitly dissuade disabled people from using mainstream leisure venues, the reluctance of hotel and catering personnel to make their premises accessible to disabled customers, and occasional overt expressions of prejudice by leisure industry workers. Institutional discrimination against disabled people within the leisure industry has been acknowledged in official circles for some time, but a number of voluntary measures that have developed to combat it are so far largely ineffective. In addition, there are segregated social and recreational activities specifically for elderly and disabled people, which provide relief from the social isolation of some sections of the disabled community, but these cannot be considered an acceptable substitute for accessible mainstream facilities. However, there is plentiful evidence that use of these organisations induces rather than diminishes dependence, and that their very existence acts as a barrier to facilities that are provided for the general public.

This situation inevitably affects the social lives of disabled people, who generally experience a reduction in social contacts after the onset of impairment. Social isolation is highest among younger people, who generally rely far more on external sources for social contacts than their older counterparts. Hence, institutional discrimination in the leisure industry has marginally more impact on younger disabled individuals. Overall, however, public perceptions of disability add to the difficulties all disabled people find when making social contacts, especially in personal and sexual relationships. Cultural factors are important here. Much of the responsibility for the persistence of disablist imagery clearly lies with the media, notably television, newspapers and the advertising industry, especially in charity advertising. On the whole the British media present a distorted view of disabled people to the general public, which not only undervalues their role in society but keeps alive the ancient prejudices and fears which surround impairment. The practices of television and the advertising industry in Britain appear to be less enlightened than those in other countries. Once again, those in authority are aware of the true state of affairs and have made commitments to do something about it, but rhetoric has outstripped results. The initiative from the disability movement might go some way to resolve this problem but to be effective it needs Government support.

9

POLITICAL LIFE

There are few more basic rights in a democratic society than the right to participate in the political process. Indeed, according to T.H. Marshall (1950), along with civil and social rights this is one of the three basic rights of citizenship. Yet although Britain is one of the oldest democracies, there are many barriers in the way of disabled people who want to exercise this right. This chapter examines these barriers and shows how disabled people have overcome them through the formation of their own organisations and the adoption of more direct forms of political action.

The Democratic Process and Disabled People

The Electoral Register. It has recently been suggested that one of the most fundamental ways in which disabled people can exercise control over their own destinies is through participation in elections (Fry, 1987), in particular by exercising their right to vote (Ward, 1987). Yet a number of studies of what happens in elections have found that many disabled people are not eligible to vote simply because they do not appear on the electoral register (Fry, 1987; MIND, 1989; Ward, 1987).

There are several reasons for this, many of which can be directly related to traditional assumptions about disabled people's inability to assume social responsibility (Borsay, 1986a). Unlike non-disabled people, some sections of the disabled population, particularly those living in long-stay hospitals, may still not even be allowed to vote. Historically, people living in institutions, especially hospitals for people with mental illness or learning difficulties, have not been registered to vote. They were excluded by the Representation of the People Act 1949, Section 4 (3), as being 'patients' and not 'residents'. However, this ruling was successfully challenged by three so-called 'patients' from Calderstones Hospital in 1979–81. As a result, the Representation of the People Act 1983 now allows residents in such hospitals to vote, but 'only under certain narrowly defined conditions'. These conditions do not apply to similarly impaired people living in the community, or to any other section of society (Ward, 1987).

Under the conditions imposed by the Representation of the People Act 1983, residents in hospitals for people with intellectual impairments 'may' be entitled to vote provided they complete a 'Patient's Declaration' form on or by October 10 each year. This enables their names to be entered on the electoral register. However, although the form is written in particularly 'formal' and 'complex' language, residents must complete it themselves unless they are unable to do so because of visual or other physical impairments (Fry, 1987; Ward, 1987). Additionally, the form has to be countersigned by a member of the hospital staff who must be present when it is filled in. Staff may assist residents if they have difficulty reading or writing, but the residents must sign the forms themselves. In short, unlike all other members of the community, disabled people living in these establishments have to prove themselves capable of voting before they can be allowed to do so (Ward, 1987).

There are other problems associated with this system. For electoral registration purposes long-stay hospitals are not considered as residences. Consequently, residents in these establishments who wish to vote must register their home address on the Patient's Declaration form. This has several negative implications. First, if residents register to vote they cannot do so in the area where they are living, namely the constituency in which the hospital is located. Thus they are deprived of influencing events in the locality surrounding their present home. Secondly, because hospital residents are eligible to vote elsewhere, local candidates, whether in local or parliamentary elections, tend not to visit hospitals. So residents may also lose their basic right to meet and question their potential elected representatives. Thirdly, residents may never be able to vote in person but may have to rely on a postal vote (see below) if they are registered for an address some distance away. Access to this facility has to depend either on hospital staff or others being aware of by-elections and local elections in other areas of the country, or on their own diligence in making the appropriate arrangements for postal voting every time there is an election (Ward, 1987).

In some hospitals, inevitably, residents' participation in elections is determined by the attitudes and practices of the staff. For example, medical personnel are sometimes asked who they 'feel' will be able to cope with the registration process. In one hospital residents were not given the appropriate help when completing the registration form, and in another residents lost their right to vote because they were attending an Adult Training Centre (ATC) and thus were not actually in the hospital building during the daytime of October 10 (the last date in the year for registration) when the registration process was taking place. In a third case, people who had previously voted lost their right to vote simply because registration through a Patient's Declaration has to be done in person and at the hospital. On the day of registration residents were elsewhere. The hospital could have made arrangements for people to register to vote on a number of occasions before October 10 to avoid this problem (Ward, 1987).

There are large variations in the numbers of residents in hospitals for people with intellectual impairments who do not appear on the electoral register, and although the situation has improved in recent years there is little room for complacency (MIND, 1989). In 1984, 1985 and 1988, MIND investigated the number of people in 'psychiatric' hospitals in the North-West who appeared on the electoral register. The latest analysis shows that there are still wide variations, 2.8 to 15.6 per cent, from one institution to another (MIND, 1989). The situation has improved since MIND began this research, which also asked hospital staff to examine their policies on this issue. In 1988 ninety-two more people were registered than in the previous year. However, only 329 of the 4,349 residents in these hospitals are registered to vote; hence the vast majority of residents remain disenfranchised. The study shows that 'electoral registration figures continue to reflect differences in staff practices and in particular senior staff's attitudes to patients' rights' (MIND, 1989, p. 1).

Disabled people residing in the community, whether in staffed or unstaffed residential homes or in private houses, all have an automatic right under the present system to vote once they reach eighteen, provided that they are listed on the electoral register. For this to happen they, or the 'head of the household' (which includes the head of residential accommodation as well as private houses), must enter their names on a special form delivered to every home, to be completed by October 10 or, at the very latest, December 15 each year. The names from these forms are then entered on to local electoral registers by February the following year. Failing this, individuals can still vote provided that their particulars are entered on a different form obtainable from the local authority electoral registration officer (neither of these forms is currently available in Braille or large print for people with visual impairments). The names from these forms are then entered on a supplementary electoral register which is compiled monthly. People who appear on this register are usually eligible to vote one month after submitting the form. People are only able to vote in local and parliamentary elections if their names appear on the current electoral or supplementary register (Ward, 1987).

Again, disabled people who live in staffed or sheltered accommodation are sometimes denied the right to vote because of the mistaken practices or the ignorance of staff. One study which looked at the policies of five local authority social service departments (SSD) and twelve health districts (HD) covering the South-West Region found that registration was more common in SSD than in HD establishments. There were also wide variations between different authorities and even between different units in the same area (Ward, 1987). Although residents in local authority homes have a right to be registered, many are not; it is apparent that officers in charge of homes 'are making their own decisions about who should be eligible for inclusion in the electoral register, when they complete the standard electoral registration form for their establishment each October' (Ward, 1987, p. 7).

A similar situation was also found to exist in private and voluntary homes. The right to be entered on the electoral register and subsequently to vote may be dependent solely on the awareness and integrity of those in charge. Data collected from five private homes and one voluntary home suggested that many residents might be disenfranchised. The proportion of people living in these establishments registered to vote varied from none in one voluntary and two private homes, to all in two other private homes and just over half in a private home. One proprietor of several other private homes is reported as saying, wrongly, that 'his residents were not legally entitled to vote'. It is thus true to say that 'the level of understanding about residents' rights in this area clearly leaves much to be desired' (Ward, 1987, p. 8).

Given such ignorance among 'professional experts' it is not surprising that the general public are no better informed. Many people living at home with their families seem not to get entered by their head of household on the electoral registration form. Interviews with disabled people reveal that many are even unaware whether they have been registered to vote or not (Fry, 1987; Ward, 1987). It is likely that this problem, particularly for people categorised as having 'learning difficulties', stems partly, at least, from low expectations by other family members or from a mistaken belief that disabled relatives are not entitled to vote, along with a lack of information from day centres, ATCs and/or other services (Ward, 1987). This problem may have been made worse following the implementation of the Poll Tax, exemption from which could be sought by, or on behalf of 'severely mentally impaired' people. Whatever the situation officially, the Poll Tax and electoral registration were quite separate and distinct. Omission from the former does not imply disqualification from the latter; in the public mind the two are interlinked (Ward, 1990). At the time of going to press, the Poll Tax is apparently to be abolished and replaced by a so-called 'Council Tax'. Whether the interlinking referred to disappears with the discredited Poll Tax remains to be seen.

Physical Access. Getting registered to vote is only the first of many problems faced by disabled people who wish to exercise their democratic rights. Major problems ensue as a result of the lack of physical access in terms of getting to the polling station, getting into the polling station, getting into the polling booth and actually marking the ballot paper (Fry, 1987).

A study documenting the experiences of seventy disabled people in five Parliamentary constituencies in various parts of England and Wales found that inability to get to the polling station because of a lack of accessible transport was frequently cited as a reason for not voting. Inaccessible polling stations also presented a major barrier. Data from interviews with disabled people suggest that some do not register to vote precisely because of the physical difficulties of voting (Fry, 1987; Ward, 1987). In addition to steps and heavy doors on the way into the building, the polling booths themselves are too narrow for some types of wheelchair. A study of twenty polling stations in just one parliamentary constituency during the 1987 General Election showed that only four of these were considered fully accessible, six had 'minor' difficulties such as 'kerbs or steps', seven had 'major difficulties' like high steps or heavy doors which were not propped open, and three were said to be 'virtually impossible' (Fry, 1987). This cannot really be surprising, since there is no legal obligation on local authorities to ensure that polling stations are fully accessible. Section 18 of the Representation of the People Act 1983, as amended by schedule 4 paragraph 4 of the Representation of the People Act 1985, only places an obligation on local councils 'so far as it is reasonable and practical' to designate as polling stations places which are accessible to disabled people (Home Office, 1989).

Because of access difficulties many disabled people are forced to depend on others, such as close relatives, friends and/or professional helpers, if they want to exercise their democratic right to vote. However, as we have seen in earlier chapters, activities which heighten disabled people's dependence on other people, particularly family and friends, often deter them from participating. Thus, while some disabled people are willing to enlist the help of others in order to vote, many are not. In addition, some disabled people are not able to vote simply because they have no one to help them (see Fry, 1987). Many of these problems would, of course, not arise if disabled people needing help had access to and control of the services of a personal assistant (see Chapter 6).

Help might also be needed in marking the ballot paper, yet the help available under the present electoral system is limited. The presiding officer may give a disabled person assistance with voting. Rule 38 of the Parliamentary Elections Rules in Schedule 1 to the Representation of the People Act 1983 requires the presiding officer to mark the ballot paper of someone who is 'illiterate or prevented from voting in the usual way if asked to do so', although some presiding officers are not fully conversant with this issue. It was reported in 1987 that on at least one occasion a disabled individual was denied the right to vote by the presiding officer, who considered him incapable of voting because he could not read or write (Ward, 1987). The presiding officer is not under any statutory duty to assist disabled people in other ways, such as getting into or leaving the polling station. Only people with visual impairments are allowed to vote with the assistance of someone else. Moreover, any person assisting in this way must first complete and sign a form issued by the presiding officer at the polling station to confirm that s/he meets the statutory criteria. To be able to help a person with a visual impairment to vote an individual must be either entitled to vote in the same election or be a close relative, namely a parent, sibling or spouse, and be aged eighteen or over (Fry, 1987). This must place an unnecessary burden on those closest to people with visual impairments.

Postal or Proxy Voting. It could be argued that these problems can be easily overcome by disabled people voting by post or by proxy, namely getting someone else to vote for them. Either of these two methods is offered as an alternative for people who have difficulties voting. However, to be eligible applicants must be (*a*) registered as 'blind' with the local authority; (*b*) in receipt of Mobility Allowance (MA) or (*c*) unable 'reasonably' to be expected to go to the polling station in person, or vote there unaided due to physical impairment. Where the applicant is registered 'blind' or receiving MA, the application need not be signed or 'attested' by someone else, provided that the name of the local authority or the reference number of the MA is given. Other applications, however, have to be attested by a medical doctor, a Christian Science practitioner or a registered first-level nurse. With people living in residential institutions of any sort, the form may be attested by the person in charge of the accommodation (see Registration of Electors forms RPF 7B; RPF 9A: PB0).

Disabled individuals wishing to vote by either of these latter two methods must therefore first obtain the appropriate form from their local Electoral Service Office; secondly, fill it in; thirdly, get it signed by at least one other person; and, finally, return it to the address where they are registered to vote so that it arrives there two and a half weeks before polling day. Registration forms are not particularly easy to understand and complete (Ward, 1987), and many individuals, particularly if living in a residential home, are unlikely to know the address of the Electoral Registration Officer for the area where they are registered to vote. Moreover, if more than one election occurs in a year (e.g. a local government and a Parliamentary election), then the individual must go through the whole process at each election (Ward, 1987).

Although some disabled people might find these alternatives acceptable, others do not. Research shows that while some find applying for postal or proxy votes a daunting prospect, others do not know how to go about it, find that the process of application is too complex, or are unhappy about having to get the form signed by a doctor (Fry, 1987). Some disabled people also object to the idea of postal votes because it necessitates voting before everyone else and therefore before the political campaign is over (Fry, 1987). In the final analysis, while postal and proxy voting are in particular circumstances a necessary component in the democratic process, they can never be and should not be seen as a substitute for the provision of facilities which make it possible for disabled people to vote in person at the same time as everyone else.

Lack of Political Information.   It will be evident from the above that it is far more difficult for disabled people to exercise the most fundamental of democratic rights, namely voting, than for non-disabled people. This raises the question whether disabled people have the same access to political information as non-disabled people. The limited evidence available suggests that they do not.

Evidence from studies documenting the participation of disabled people in elections suggests that disabled people are largely ignored by those involved in mainstream politics, both nationally and locally. For example Fry (1987), reporting on the 1987 General Election, found that disabled people with visual or hearing impairments 'had no access to much of the election material taken for granted by others' (Fry, 1987, p. 15). Telephone enquiries to each of the three main political parties in March 1991 revealed that both the Conservative and Labour Parties did produce taped versions of their respective election manifestos, but the availability of this material was not widely publicised. As for other political information such as *Hansard*, this is not published in accessible forms for people with visual impairments. The only way they can gain access to this and other published political material is by request to the Royal National Institute for the Blind (RNIB), but as we have seen in Chapter 8 this has a number of important limitations.

As for the non-hearing community, British sign-language interpreters have been visible at all the national party conferences for the past four years. They were present at the Labour Party conference of 1985 for the leader's speech, and the facility was later extended to cover the entire conference. The two other main political parties have provided similar services since 1988. However, although the proceedings of the House of Commons have been televised since 1989, they are still not fully accessible to the deaf community. Although the Select Committee on Broadcasting & C (previously known as the Select Committee on Televising the House) discussed this issue with representatives of organisations of and for the deaf community at some length, the matter remains unresolved. Although all but one of the Committee are in favour of making the televising of Parliament accessible, it has been opposed by the broadcasting authorities largely on grounds of cost (Blagden, 1991). This contrasts with the situation in parts of Canada and the United States, where the cost of making live political broadcasts accessible to the non-hearing community is borne by Government (Blagden, 1991a).

Locally, the situation is less clear-cut. None of the major parties is apparently prepared to impose standards of accessibility on the material put out by local politicians. Whether or not political information is produced in accessible forms for disabled people is apparently subject to the discretion and resources of local officials, and there is no evidence to suggest that they exercise this discretion. Indeed, disabled people even found difficulty in obtaining information about the accessibility of local political meetings, both from local party headquarters and from political canvassers, and it was found that local candidates rarely visited residential institutions for disabled people (Fry, 1987). It has also been noted that although local councillors might visit local authority homes for disabled people as part of their specific duties, few seemed to visit in order to put forward their political views at election times (Ward, 1987). Although one health authority made a point of inviting local and parliamentary candidates to canvass people in long-stay hospitals for people with intellectual impairments, few took up the offer. On the other side, there is evidence that representatives from political parties have offered to visit hospitals and residential homes to discuss political issues with residents, but these offers have been rejected by staff. A number of reasons have been offered to justify this: for example, political figures have been refused admittance on the grounds that they have a 'captive' audience, or because staff do not consider it either 'appropriate or worthwhile' to discuss political issues with residents (Ward, 1987). On one occasion a visit had been suggested by one of the main political parties, but the manager had declined the offer on the grounds that it would be unfair because none of the other parties had made similar requests (Fry, 1987).

Lack of information is increasingly being regarded as a major barrier to citizenship, not only for disabled people but for the population as a whole. Indeed, the recent House of Commons Commission on Citizenship, commenting on the widespread ignorance among British people on these matters, noted that opportunities for learning to be a citizen need to be expanded both in schools and after statutory schooling (House of Commons Commission on Citizenship, 1990). It may be argued that this is especially pertinent to disabled people since many of them receive an education inferior in quality to that received by non-disabled people (see Chapter 3). But there is little evidence to suggest that this is being provided. For example, there has been little attempt by staff in residential institutions to provide education on 'citizenship rights' like voting. Although Ward's study in the South-West of England shows that these facilities were being provided in some ATCs and Social Education Centres and through advocacy schemes, such services are not 'extensive or widespread' (Ward, 1987).

The Party System. Apart from the problems described, disabled people's ability to participate within the current party system and thus get disability-related issues on to the political agenda are restricted in other ways. First, because a large proportion of local constituency meeting-places and headquarters is inaccessible to disabled people, it is very difficult for them to become grassroots party activists (Mason, 1991). Secondly, it is very difficult for disabled people to offer themselves as candidates at local and national elections because environmental and social considerations make both campaigning and door-to-door canvassing almost impossible (Oliver and Zarb, 1989; Oliver, 1990).

Thirdly, and most important, even if these barriers to political participation were removed, there is little or no opportunity within the present party system for disabled politicians, or indeed non-disabled politicians, to put issues perceived by disabled people as disability-related on to the political agenda. This is because each of the main parties claims to represent all sections of the community and politicians working within the party system are expected to do the same. They are not expected or indeed allowed to represent overtly one specific section of the community or to reflect their interests. While it is true that there are examples of both local and national disabled politicians, they are not, nor do they claim to be, representative of disabled people's organisations or of disabled people. In general they are career politicians with particular knowledge in an area of general concern; for example, David Blunkett, the Labour parliamentarian with a visual impairment, is a specialist in local government.

There is little evidence that the present party system has served the disabled population well, particularly where anti-discrimination legislation (ADL) is concerned. This issue has been forced on to party political agendas by disabled people and their organisations (see Chapter 1) but whereas nine bills have been introduced in Parliament (see Appendix), all have been defeated. This has usually been through covert action, but was once overt, through the operation of the party political system; that is through a sustained unofficial campaign by Government whips to ensure that their party members voted it down (Oliver, 1985, 1990; Oliver and Zarb, 1989). Thus many disabled people have become disillusioned with the current party system (see Fry, 1987).

Pressure Group Politics and the Political Emancipation of Disabled People

Single-Issue Pressure Group Politics. Since party politics has largely failed to accommodate disabled people and their concerns, it is necessary to consider whether other conventional forms of political participation, in particular single-issue pressure group activity, have been any more successful. Hitherto they have not, largely because this form of political action has been dominated by traditional organisations *for* rather than organisations *of* disabled people.

British people have long organised themselves into pressure or interest groups to influence politicians and political parties in order to defend or advance their own particular interests. This form of political participation has increased dramatically since the early 1970s (Townsend, 1986), and especially during the 1980s (Patten, 1990; House of Commons Commission on Citizenship, 1990), and today there are hundreds of these organisations of various sizes operating both locally and nationally.

Although theoretically pressure groups are supposed to have equal access to those in power, some are manifestly more influential than others. Broadly these organisations can be divided into two. First, there are 'competitive groups' whose members come from a variety of economic and social backgrounds but share a particular interest, such as the Anti-Vivisection Society and the Child Poverty Action Group. Secondly, there are 'corporate groups', whose members share a common economic and social status within the community; examples include business and professional associations such as the Confederation of British Industry and the British Medical Association, and trade unions (Borsay, 1986; Cawson 1982). Since in most cases the latter have considerably more standing within society as a whole and usually more economic power, it is they who have the most impact upon the Government. The majority of disability organisations are of the first variety, and so their influence on policy-makers is relatively limited (Borsay, 1986a; Oliver and Zarb, 1989; Oliver, 1990).

However, there are other reasons why the majority of disability organisations have only a marginal effect upon the political decision-making process. First, most of them are registered as charities, which bars them from direct and overt political activity. Since the seventeenth century it has been illegal for the 'beneficiaries' of charities to be members of their management councils, so it is difficult for disabled people to control these organisations, or for charities to engage openly in politics (Williams, 1989). Secondly, many of these organisations, which for many years have acted as both charities and disability pressure groups, have built up close working relationships with official policy-makers, which gives them a degree of credibility but relatively little power (Borsay, 1986).

The credibility of such organisations is based on tradition rather than any claim to being representative of disabled people. We have noted at several points throughout this study that until fairly recently the overwhelming majority of disability organisations have been organisations for rather than of disabled people. Although historically the former have represented the interests of disabled people in Government and are used and supported by them for this express purpose, they frequently lack direct links with disabled people and are generally inadequately accountable to them (see especially Chapters 2 and 6), The key decision-makers in these organisations are usually salaried professionals who put forward their own views on the needs of disabled people rather than the perceptions of those they claim to represent (Finkelstein, 1980; Large, 1981; Oliver, 1984, 1990; Oliver and Zarb, 1989; Reiser and Mason 1990; Wood, 1990).

Apart from the fact that many of these organisations continue to undermine the empowerment of disabled people through their fundraising strategies (see Chapter 8), in terms of their political activity there are several examples of their being unrepresentative of disabled people's views, notably in the failure of the Royal Association for Disability and Rehabilitation (RADAR) and the Spastics Society to lend initial support to the demand for anti-discrimination legislation (ADL). Indeed, it was pressure from individual disabled people and from organisations controlled and run by them which forced public about-turns on this issue (Oliver and Zarb, 1989; Oliver, 1990). In addition, in 1990 both RADAR and the Spastics Society were severely criticised by disabled people for not giving support to Britain's biggest disability demonstrations, which were held in London, Manchester and Glasgow on October 12 to demand full citizenship rights and a 'proper income' for disabled people (*Disability Now*, 1990d).

A further dimension of pressure group activity is that of minority group politics. Following the success of the Civil Rights Movement and Women's Movement in the United States in the 1960s, it has been suggested that disabled people should demand the right to full citizenship on the basis of their own particular needs as a 'minority group' (Hahn, 1986). Such an approach would mean that disabled people would be accommodated within the existing political framework simply as one more special interest group. The decision-making process would remain intact, but the demands of disabled people would be given a political legitimacy which they now lack (Liggett, 1988).

However, in order to gain even this dubiously privileged position disabled people would have to accept 'the disabled and non-disabled distinction' and the notion of 'the normalising society'. Consequently, the price of political participation as a minority group would inevitably involve

> special pleading and . . . move away from the strategies disabled people have chosen for themselves, that is the personal and public affirmation of disabled identities and the demands that disabled people be accepted by and integrated into society as they are; that is, as disabled people (Oliver and Zarb, 1989, p. 225).

Apart from such an approach legitimating institutional discrimination against disabled people in certain circumstances, there is little or no evidence that policy-makers are responsive to this or any other form of conventional pressure group activity. This can easily be demonstrated from the campaign for a national disability income.

The Campaign for a National Disability Income. As we saw in Chapter 5, the campaign for a national disability income began in 1965 with the formation of the Disablement Income Group (DIG). This group provided a major focus for pressure group activity and published plans for a national disability income comprising two distinct elements: a disablement costs allowance and an income maintenance scheme. Ten years later, fifty voluntary organisations came together as the Disability Alliance (DA), which now embraces over ninety groups. The two organisations produced similar proposals which were later updated (DA, 1987; DIG, 1987). Additionally, the DA proposals incorporate a separate independent benefit for people who 'care' for a disabled person. The Disablement Income Group maintains that if disabled people were given a proper, adequate income, it would not be necessary to pay personal assistants (PAs) separately (see Chapter 5).

It is not easy to assess the success or failure of the activities of these pressure groups (Oliver and Zarb, 1989), largely because all the major political parties have made public commitments to the establishment of such a scheme (DA, 1987), but have hedged their pronouncements with get-out clauses such as 'when economic circumstances permit' and 'as a matter of priority'. In addition, while disabled people have witnessed some minor improvements in their financial circumstances through the 1970s and 1980s, usually connected to the performance of the economy, there have also been major reversals. Moreover, a national disability income has yet to become a reality, and recent changes to the benefit system suggest that this is unlikely in the foreseeable future (see Chapter 5).

There are several reasons why this campaign has been unsuccessful. First, both organisations have suffered from the problem, already mentioned above, that as registered charities they have been unable to campaign in an overtly political way. As a consequence, they have had to divide their resources into two elements in order both to retain their charitable status and to proceed with their political activities. Also, both the DIG and the DA have found it necessary to set up information and advisory services to help disabled people through the maze of benefits to which they are entitled. Finally, they have conducted research to demonstrate that the financial circumstances of disabled people are substantially worse than that of their non-disabled peers. Hence, neither organisation has been able to concentrate solely upon pressure group activities (Oliver and Zarb, 1989; Oliver, 1990).

It has been argued that both organisations have a somewhat naive view of contemporary politics. This perception is based on three assumptions: first, that evidence must be produced to show that disabled people experience poverty; secondly, that plans for a national disability income must be expertly costed to show that the financial burden on the economy will only be marginal; and thirdly, that pressure must be sustained to convince political decision-makers of the validity of the argument. Often referred to as the 'social administration approach', such a strategy can be criticised for its assumptions about consensual values and rational decision-making, its simplistic view of the workings of politics and its failure to acknowledge, let alone consider, the role of ideology (Oliver and Zarb, 1989; Oliver, 1990).

What the income approach to disability appears to ignore is that hitherto political decisions have not been based on specific issues unless there has been some immediate return for the economy, regardless of the consensus on the need for a national disability income. Indeed, the introduction of such a scheme would mean paying people not in work an income enabling them to have a similar lifestyle to those who are. Such a scheme would have significant consequences for a society which requires its citizens to produce enough goods and services to maintain the material life of the population. It would also undermine the ideological foundation of such a society, namely a work ethic emphasising the value of those who work and denigrating those who do not. Clearly, the question of whether a national disability income is achievable within the context of contemporary Britain has not been seriously considered (Oliver and Zarb 1989; Oliver, 1990).

This apparent failure to address such basic issues has stimulated criticism of both the DIG and the DA from the more 'populist' organisations of disabled people, notably the Union of Physically Impaired Against Segregation (UPIAS). The two principal criticisms of this approach are, first, that it concentrates on the symptom (the poverty of disabled people) and not the cause (the disabling society in which we live), and secondly, that both organisations have moved away from representing disabled people and instead present an 'expert view of the problem'. Such an approach, if followed to the logical conclusion, would make matters worse rather than better (UPIAS, 1976).

Furthermore, it has been argued that a 'narrow incomes approach' would necessarily involve some kind of assessment procedure which would simply legitimate and perpetuate the discriminatory policies of the past. Disabled individuals wishing to claim the disability income would be required to present themselves for assessment by 'social administrators'. They would have to appear 'passive, nervous and deferential' in order to conform to the expert view of disability; in other words, they would have to reinforce all the traditional assumptions associated with disabled people and thus relinquish any claim to economic and social equality. Such an approach can only enhance the power of professionals and justify the continued subordination of disabled people. A few of the more privileged disabled individuals might be cast into the role of token 'expert', but the strategy as a whole would perpetuate the historical and traditional situation whereby disabled people 'are made dependent upon the thinking and decisions of others' (UPIAS, 1976, p. 18).

The debate about expert and mass representation in pressure group politics continued throughout the 1980s with some 'experts' claiming that these groups can be representative in certain circumstances, particularly in discussions with Government officials and policy-makers (see Townsend, 1986). But, like UPIAS before it, the British Council of Organizations of Disabled People (BCODP) denies the claims of such groups to be representative of disabled people in any way. They argue that 'expert' representation can only be counter-productive, and that the only way forward is to involve disabled people fully in their own political movement.

The Political Emancipation of Disabled People.   Because of the perceived failure of conventional political avenues to address disability-related issues as they define these issues, disabled people themselves have resolved this problem in a number of ways. These include the development of 'self-help/populist' groups within the context of the disability movement and the adoption of a more direct form of political participation.

As noted in Chapter 1, the groundswell of initiative from within the disabled community during the 1960s and 1970s became centred around the idea of independent living. Much of the inspiration for this initiative came from abroad, particularly the United States. The American Independent Living Movement (ILM) was especially important because it provided both an ideology and a practical solution to the problems faced by disabled people. The reasoning behind the ILM was that the obstacles to disabled people's empowerment were seen as hostile physical and social environments, and existing services restricting rather than enabling them. The ILM set about attempting to change this, first, by defining the problem in this way, and secondly, by setting up alternative kinds of service provision controlled by disabled people themselves. Learning about these achievements, discovering that disabled people in Europe were struggling to achieve similar goals and establishing links with organisations of disabled people in the developing world through Disabled People's International (DPI) all added to disabled people's knowledge and power.

This collective awareness precipitated the emergence and proliferation throughout Britain during the following decade of a variety of self-help groups such as the Spinal Injuries Association (SIA) and the Greater Manchester Coalition 'of Disabled People (GMCDP). Initially a response to the apparent failure of the British welfare system to integrate disabled people into mainstream economic and social life, many of these groups had as their primary aim to enable members 'to solve their problems themselves and not have them solved for them'. However, because of the extent of institutional discrimination and the opportunities these organisations provided for disabled people to express their views, a further aim quickly emerged; namely to identify the needs of the membership as a whole and articulate them, to statutory agencies and to political parties, at a local and a national level (Oliver and Hasler, 1987).

This shift in emphasis is the more remarkable considering the great variety within the disabled population as a whole, e.g. in social class, age, sex, family circumstances and clinical conditions. One writer (Borsay, 1986) has suggested that the traditional medical definitions of disability have created 'artificial fissures between disease categories' which tend to obscure common social needs. Moreover, as we saw in Chapter 5, the present benefit system also fosters economic and social divisions within the disabled community.

However, a particular form of self-help which began in the United States and provides the most concrete example of how disabled people have responded to institutional discrimination, is the Centre for Independent Living (CIL). Now firmly established throughout Britain and indeed the world, CILs represent a unique attempt to achieve self-empowerment as well as being a form of direct action aimed at creating new solutions to problems defined by disabled people themselves (Oliver, 1987).

It is these organisations alone which have provided an effective framework for the political and cultural emancipation of disabled people in modern Britain. Moreover, as noted in Chapter 1, since 1981 an increasing number of these groups have chosen to come together under the banner of BCODP. Indeed, BCODP was established by these organisations as the democratic and representative voice of disabled people. Its executive committee is elected annually from member organisations and is directly accountable to them via the quarterly BCODP council meeting and the Annual General Meeting. Moreover, BCODP is about to implement a regionalisation programme which will heighten this accountability, and at the same time provide a better framework for mutual support between member organisations both nationally and locally (BCODP, 1991a).

The success of BCODP is entirely due to disabled people themselves (Hasler, 1991). Its conception and subsequent development have been achieved without extensive financial support from Government (see Chapter 6), or from the traditional organisations for disabled people. On the contrary, BCODP and the disability movement as a whole were criticised from the start as being elitist, isolationist, unrepresentative and Marxist by numerous academics and by experts from organisations for disabled people (see Goodall, 1988; Harrison, 1987; Holden, 1990; Williams, 1983). Yet through the 1980s BCODP and its member organisations produced a wealth of policy initiatives which, when implemented, will benefit not only them but the disabled population generally. Furthermore, these strategies owe as much to the political ideologies of the right as they do to those of the left. These include enabling disabled people to free themselves from unnecessary and costly bureaucratic regulation; to earn a living rather than live off the state; to achieve a degree of personal autonomy comparable to that of their non-disabled peers; and to expand their role as consumers. Moreover, the arguments put forward by BCODP and its member organisations have profoundly influenced those bodies which originally saw it as upstart and unnecessary (Hasler, 1991). This can be demonstrated from the crucial issue of equal rights for disabled people, and the need for ADL to secure those rights (see Chapter 1).

These initiatives not only established BCODP and its member organisations as the only true and valid voice of disabled people in Britain, but they also stimulated a growing number of disabled individuals to adopt a disabled identity and take a more direct approach to political participation. Here too, much of the inspiration for this radicalisation stems from America, in particular the strategies adopted by the Civil Rights Movement and the Independent Living Movement. In the United States the Civil Rights Movement of the 1960s had an enormous influence on the securing of disabled people's rights and the way in which those rights were secured. Indeed, when traditional legal channels were exhausted, 'disabled people . . . learned to employ other techniques of social protest'. These included organised boycotts, sit-ins and street demonstrations (De Jong, 1983, p. 12).

The excessive paternalism of the welfare state, along with the absence of a strong British Civil Rights tradition, caused disabled people in Britain to be more cautious in their tactics. However, this situation changed dramatically in the late 1980s. Despite the barriers which confront disabled people in the built environment (see Chapter 7), they have taken to the streets in increasing numbers to protest against institutional discrimination in all its forms. Since the 'Rights not Charity' march of July 1988 there have been many demonstrations and civil disobedience campaigns by disabled people and their supporters all over the country on a range of issues including inaccessible transport, an inaccessible environment, the exploitation of disabled people by television companies and charities, and the poverty which accompanies impairment. To focus the public's attention on these and other injustices, disabled people are now prepared to risk public ridicule, arrest and even imprisonment (see DCDP, 1990; *Disability Now*, 1990a, 1990b, 1990d; Findlay, 1990; Hasler, 1991). Moreover, while disabled people continue to experience the institutional discrimination described in this study, this type of direct action is likely to intensify rather than diminish.

Conclusion

This chapter has shown how institutional discrimination serves to prevent disabled people from participating in politics through the normal channels. It has also demonstrated that disabled people have resolved this situation through the formation of their own organisations, and the adoption of a more radical approach to political involvement.

The first part showed that many disabled people are denied the basic right to vote because they do not appear on an electoral register. A number of reasons were given for this, many of which grew out of past discrimination. Unlike any other section of the indigenous adult population, some of the disabled population are presented with unreasonable bureaucratic hurdles before they can even exercise their right to vote. Moreover, disabled people living in long-stay hospitals are not allowed to vote in the area where they are currently living. Many disabled residents in these and other institutions are prevented from voting because of the discriminatory policies and ignorance of the professionals who work in them; this ignorance is not confined to professionals. Although all disabled people living in the community are entitled to vote, many in practice are denied this right because of the ignorance of those on whom they are forced to depend.

We have also seen that environmental factors prevent a significant number of disabled people from exercising their political rights. Although inaccessible transport, polling stations, and polling booths present major problems for many disabled people, there is no statutory obligation on local authorities to ensure that these facilities are accessible. Furthermore, although it has been officially acknowledged that some disabled people might need help when voting, the help currently available is extremely limited. Postal or proxy voting is an unsatisfactory substitute for voting in the usual fashion because of the complexity of the application process, and because people are expected to vote before the rest of the electorate. Also, disabled people do not have the same access to political information as non-disabled people. This applies to material provided by the main political parties both nationally and locally; information generated via the communications media and data available from local authorities. It was suggested that conventional political institutions such as the present party system have not served the disabled population well.

The second part of the chapter focused on pressure group politics. It was shown that hitherto traditional single-issue pressure group activity has failed to address disability issues as disabled people define them, mainly because this type of political activity has been dominated by traditional organisations for disabled people which, although part of the political establishment, have relatively little power. They are also not representative of disabled people's views, being dominated mainly by non-disabled professional experts. This was demonstrated by their protracted and unsuccessful attempt to secure a national disability income for disabled people — a policy which would not remove discrimination against disabled people, but legitimate and perpetuate it. Disabled people responded by forming their own organisations which, although not explicitly political, have provided both an ideology and a practical framework for their political emancipation. Part of an international movement to secure equal rights for disabled people, the policy initiatives developed by these organisations have profoundly influenced both the traditional organisations discussed above and the disabled population as a whole. This is evident from the support for anti-discrimination legislation expressed by all the major organisations for disabled people (discussed in detail in the opening chapter), and the willingness of an increasing number of disabled people to identify with the disability movement and adopt a more radical approach to remove institutional discrimination in all its forms.

10

CONCLUSION: THE CASE FOR ANTI-DISCRIMINATION LEGISLATION

This study has highlighted the extent of institutional discrimination against disabled people in contemporary Britain. It paints an alarmingly depressing picture. Because each of the chapters has concluded with a detailed summary there is little need to repeat them here. This conclusion therefore concentrates on the argument for anti-discrimination legislation.

Clearly, the traditional ideological justifications for discrimination are well entrenched within the core institutions of our society. After more than a century of largely state-sponsored education, disabled children and young people are still not legally entitled to the same type of schooling as their non-disabled peers. The overwhelming majority of British schools, colleges and universities remain unprepared to accommodate disabled students within a mainstream setting. Thus, many young people with impairments have little choice but to accept segregated 'special' education which is both educationally and socially divisive, and which fails to provide them with the necessary skills for adult living. Moreover, by producing educationally and socially disabled adults in this way the 'special' education system perpetuates the false assumption that disabled people are somehow inadequate, and thus legitimises discrimination in all other areas of social life, particularly employment.

Discriminatory attitudes and institutionalised practices which work to the disadvantage of disabled people in employment are well established within the British labour market. They are conspicuous in the policies and practices of employers and employment agencies, public and private. As a result, disabled people are more likely to be out of work than non-disabled people, they are out of work longer than other unemployed workers, and when they do find work it is more often than not low-paid, low-status work with poor working conditions, thus accelerating the discriminatory spiral in which many disabled people find themselves.

The overwhelming majority of disabled people and their families are forced to depend on welfare benefits in order to survive. Further, the present disability benefit system does not even cover the cost of impairment and effectively discourages those who struggle for individual autonomy and financial independence. The inevitable outcome is a life of extreme economic deprivation and excessive bureaucratic regulation and control; in other words, poverty and dependence.

This dependence is compounded by the present system of health and social support services, most of which are dominated by the interests and concerns of the professionals who run them and the traditional assumption that disabled people are unable to take charge of their own lives. While disabled people may no longer be forced to live in residential institutions, their opportunities for economic and social integration are severely restricted due to a lack of information, appropriate technical aids and a comprehensive personal assistant service. Hence, many are compelled to rely on informal unpaid helpers — usually family or friends. Current provision, therefore, denies disabled people not only opportunities to live independently within the community, but also the dignity of independence within the context of personal relationships and the family home.

This cycle of dependence is intensified by a largely hostile physical environment in housing, public transport and the built environment generally. Although the need for personal mobility has become increasingly apparent in recent years for all sections of society, particularly for work, disabled people continue to be confronted with inaccessible homes, transport systems and public buildings.

Moreover, along with unemployment, a lack of money and a heightened and unnecessary dependence on others, environmental factors are crucial in excluding disabled people from the kind of leisure and social activities which the non-disabled community takes for granted; indeed, some sections of the leisure industry are evidently unwilling to cater for disabled people. Discrimination is compounded for disabled people who are women, and members of ethnic minorities and the gay community.

Until quite recently disabled people did not have a credible collective voice to articulate their views and so successive Governments have been able to avoid and even deny the extent of institutional discrimination against disabled people. But a large part of the responsibility for this lies with a succession of British Governments. Although there is a growing consensus in democratic countries that disabled people have the same basic human rights as non-disabled people, and that Governments should ensure that disabled people are able to achieve a standard of living equal to that of their fellow-citizens (UN, 1988), this has not yet come about in the British Isles. Yet Britain was one of the first western nations to establish the notion of basic human rights for disabled people in law with the setting up of the welfare state in the early 1940s; everything that has happened since has been a gradual retreat from this position. Although the British Government endorsed the United Nations Programme of Action Concerning Disabled Persons in 1982, it has consistently refused to implement policies which would enable disabled people to attain a lifestyle comparable to that of their non-disabled neighbours.

As we have seen, the Education Act 1944 specified that disabled children should be educated alongside their peers and the Disabled Persons (Employment) Act 1944 attempted to secure employment rights for disabled people. But non-enforcement of these tentative rights, coupled with the gradual but intensifying drift from rights-based to needs-based policies, has served to underline the traditional individualistic approach to disability, the very opposite of what is needed. This is evident in each area discussed in this study.

In education, while reiterating the principle of integration, the Warnock Report and the 1981 Education Act both explicitly emphasised the importance of the concept of Special Educational Needs within the education system as a whole. This is a policy which has justified not only the continued segregation of a substantial part of the student population, but also the exclusion of minority languages and cultures from the mainstream sector, in particular the language and culture of the non-hearing community. In the crucial area of employment, the data show that the Government's lack of commitment to the employment quota scheme and its obvious preference for voluntary policies of persuasion have not only resulted in a failure to provide disabled people with meaningful employment, but also emphasised the traditional divisions between disabled and non-disabled workers.

Although it has been officially acknowledged that disabled people and their families receive significantly lower incomes than the rest of the population (due to institutional discrimination in the labour market and the additional costs which impairment incurs), recent changes to the disability benefits system will not change this situation. Indeed, the shift away from statutory entitlement in favour of discretionary awards distributed by semi-independent organisations with limited budgets, following the introduction of the 1988 social security reforms, signals a significant erosion of disabled people's rights as well as an intensification of unnecessary bureaucratic regulation and control.

A similar situation exists regarding health and social support services for disabled people. Although the transition from rights-based to needs-based provision can be traced back to the 1948 National Assistance Act, it has intensified in recent years. Although the 1948 Act placed a duty on local authorities to provide residential accommodation and some services for disabled people, it also acknowledged the historical involvement of charities in these areas and so permitted the local authorities to designate responsibility for provision to voluntary agencies if they so wished. An inevitable outcome of this was a proliferation of residential institutions of one form or another run by charitable trusts and private agencies, and the failure of local authorities to develop appropriate community-based services. Moreover, contrary to the views of some non-disabled observers (Topliss and Gould, 1981), the 1970 Chronically Sick and Disabled Persons Act did little to change this situation.

The 1980s saw a further retreat from the notion of rights as a result of the inclination toward voluntary rather than statutory-based services of a succession of policy-makers in both local and central Government. While the introduction of the 1986 Disabled Persons (Services, Consultation and Representation) Act paid lip-service to the idea of meaningful collaboration between service users and providers, there is evidence of widespread disregard for the law within local authorities which has hitherto been ignored by central Government (see Chapter 6). Moreover, it has recently been announced in the House of Commons that key sections of the 1986 Act which would have secured the right of disabled people to have an advocate had they needed one, and given them the right to ask local authorities for services and to have a written statement on their needs assessment (see Chapter 6), are not to be implemented (*Hansard*, 1991a). Clearly, despite the talk of choice and consultation emanating from a growing number of politicians of both left and right, current provision is still controlled by mainly non-disabled professionals who decide what services disabled people should have, when they should have them, and how they should be delivered.

Although there is an increasing shortage of accessible homes, there are no policy initiatives to remedy this in either the public or the private sector, and segregated special-needs housing remains central to the Government's community care programme. The prevalence of special-needs transport systems is also likely to remain the norm rather than the exception because, even though the Department of Transport supports the desirability of accessible public transport systems in principle, it is clear that it will be well into the twenty-first century before they become anything like a reality. Moreover, although policy-makers have endorsed disabled people's rights of access to public buildings with the recent amendments to the Building Regulations, it is clear that these measures will not eradicate discrimination within the context of the built environment, particularly in the leisure industry where inaccessible buildings exclude disabled people to a large extent from mainstream recreational pursuits.

Indeed, the rhetoric of individual needs is central to the arguments of those who have successfully opposed measures to reinforce the rights of disabled people. First, it has been suggested that defining disability would present major problems in disagreements over equal rights. In 1983, for example, one Government supporter noted that to establish that discrimination had taken place the 'extent of the disablement would have to be proved, which can be very distressing' for a disabled person (*Hansard*, 1983, p. 1250). Such a position seems somewhat hollow since until recently policy-makers appeared content to allow disabled people to have their impairments measured in this way in order to receive the benefits and services to which they are entitled. Nonetheless, given the strength of feeling against discrimination among disabled people and their desire to remove it this is likely to be one test that many would welcome.

Secondly, on discrimination in perhaps the most important area of all, employment, the Department of Employment's consultative document *Employment and Training for Disabled People* reiterated an argument which has been repeated constantly by opponents of anti-discrimination legislation throughout the 1980s. It states: 'A major difficulty is that disability, unlike race or sex, can be relevant to job performance and what to some might seem like discrimination may in reality be recruitment based on legitimate preferences and likely performances' (DE, 1990, p. 30). This implies that discrimination is indeed acceptable on the grounds that disabled workers are not as productive as non-disabled workers.

Such arguments are difficult to understand particularly when, since the early 1970s, successive Governments have spent a large amount of public money telling employers the opposite, namely that given the appropriate equipment (which the Government is willing to provide — see Chapter 5) disabled workers are as productive as non-disabled workers. Further, the same publication reports. 'There is clear evidence that most people with disabilities can be as productive as the general population. . . . Even severe handicap, whilst clearly giving rise to difficulties, has frequently been overcome' (DE, 1990, p. 14).

Thirdly, it has been suggested that an anti-discrimination law would be complex to draft and therefore uncertain in its application (DE, 1990). This point is difficult to understand in the light of developments abroad and the fact that, as noted in the Introduction to this work, there is support for the drafting of such legislation within the legal profession. If this type of legislation would present major problems for those charged with interpreting it, this would surely not be the attitude of lawyers.

There is a fourth argument that anti-discrimination legislation would exacerbate traditional divisions between disabled and non-disabled people; this point is often used in relation to employment, for example 'the relationship between people with disabilities and employers might be damaged and the task of persuasion made much harder' (DE, 1990, p. 39). However, it is difficult to see the logic in this, considering that all the evidence hitherto has shown widespread support for anti-discrimination legislation among the general public (see Chapter 1). Also, since most employers have proved particularly unresponsive to policies of persuasion (see Chapter 5), it is probable that anti-discrimination legislation could only have a positive effect on the employment of disabled people.

This continual denial of equal rights to disabled people by successive British Governments is all the more astonishing when other disadvantaged groups have some protection under the law, and when legislation to combat institutionalised disablism is becoming increasingly common throughout the western world. The overtly unequal treatment accorded to disabled people in Britain has prompted an almost universal demand from disabled people and their organisations for similar legislation in Britain, and it is a demand which is likely to increase in strength.

What these organisations are demanding is comprehensive anti-discrimination legislation which (a) establishes a suitable framework to enforce policies ensuring the integration of disabled people into the mainstream economic and social life of the community, such as the employment quota scheme, and (b) provides public confirmation that discrimination against disabled people for whatever reason is no longer tolerable. This would be legislation emphasising social rights rather than individual needs, and focusing on a disabling society and not individual disabled people.

For such legislation to be truly effective, disabled people would inevitably need access to the kind of medical and other information which historically has been used to justify their economic and social subordination. Thus an essential addition to anti-discrimination legislation would be laws facilitating freedom of information going beyond providing access to information held on computers and in local authority files. Locked medical cabinets would need to be opened and the unofficial documents which are kept as ways of avoiding information disclosure, as with current practices which require information to be provided to parents under the statementing regulations of the Education Act 1981, would need to be made available.

There will also be a need for some kind of mechanism offering disabled people individual and collective redress. This can only be accomplished by the adequate funding of the nationwide network of organisations controlled and run by disabled people themselves. As we have seen, it is these organisations which have put the issue of institutional discrimination on to the political agenda, and which are best fitted to ensure its eventual eradication.

The abolition of institutional discrimination against disabled people is not a marginal activity; it strikes at the heart of social organisations within both the public and the private sectors. It would not be possible to confront this problem without becoming involved in political debate and taking up positions on a wide range of issues. It is imperative, therefore, that any mechanism for enforcement should remain independent of Government influence and control. Indeed, as Gregory (1987) has shown, one of the chief reasons for the relative failure of the Sex Discrimination Act 1975 and the Race Relations Act 1976 to remove sexism and racism in Britain has been the semi-autonomous status of the Equal Opportunities Commission and the Commission for Racial Equality. Their semi-autonomy has become a double-edged weapon in the hands of unsympathetic Governments: because they are independent, they can be ignored, and because they are not independent, they can be subdued through Government control of funds and appointments. Hence, both organisations have been forced to concentrate on policies of education rather than enforcement — the opposite of what is needed.

However, none of these policies by itself is likely to prove successful. First, anti-discrimination legislation without freedom of information and a supportive network of disabled people will simply benefit the legal profession. Secondly, access to information by itself will almost certainly expose disabled individuals to further professional mystification and exploitation. Thirdly, support for organisations of disabled people without an appropriate framework guaranteeing basic human rights would effectively neutralise the only collective voice that disabled people have in this country. But an integrated policy similar to that suggested above would provide a means of addressing institutional discrimination effectively and thus eliminating it.

It could be argued that institutional discrimination against disabled people is so entrenched within British society that it is unrealistic to think that its eradication is possible. Those who take this view need to be reminded that no-one in contemporary Britain lives in the 'real world'. They need to be made aware that all human beings live in a socially created world and that institutional discrimination is nothing more than a social creation and as such can be got rid of. While the policies outlined above might not remove institutional discrimination overnight, they would certainly contribute significantly to its demise.

APPENDIX

CHRONOLOGY OF ATTEMPTS TO INTRODUCE ANTI-DISCRIMINATION LEGISLATION RELATING TO DISABILITY

1. On 6 July 1982, the Rt Hon Jack Ashley MP introduced the Disablement (Prohibition of Unjustifiable Discrimination) Bill, under the Ten-Minute Rule. It was given an unopposed first reading but was lost, along with all other uncompleted business, at the end of the session.

2. On 11 February 1983, the Disablement (Prohibition of Unjustifiable Discrimination) Bill, a Private Member's Bill introduced by Mr Donald Stewart, failed to secure the necessary 100 votes for the Closure (77 voted in favour, none against, but 100 votes were needed to end the debate and vote for or against giving the Bill a second reading).

3. On 18 November 1983, an entirely new Bill, the Chronically Sick and Disabled Persons (Amendment) Bill, Part 1 of which was concerned solely with making discrimination against disabled people unlawful, failed to be given a second reading. It was another Private Member's Bill, and was introduced by Mr Robert N. Wareing. This time there were more than 100 voting for the Closure but a Government whip ensured defeat — 164 for and 210 against — and no vote was therefore taken on the question of the Bill being given a second reading.

4. Also on 18 November 1983, Lord Longford announced that he would take over the Bill and introduce it in the House of Lords. Lord Longford's Chronically Sick and Disabled Persons (Amendment) no. 2 Bill was given an unopposed second reading on 16 December 1983. Amendments were made to the Bill and it was given an unopposed third reading on 3 April 1984. Minutes later, however, it was defeated by 68 votes to 49 on the motion that the Bill do not pass.

5. Lord Longford's Bill sought to make discrimination against disabled people unlawful and to set up a commission to investigate cases of alleged discrimination, to conciliate where necessary and to issue guidance on avoiding discrimination. Following the blocking by the Government of Mr Wareing's Bill, Lord Campbell of Croy introduced his Disabled Persons Bill to establish a commission to investigate cases of disadvantage and discrimination without making discrimination unlawful.

6. Lord Campbell's Disabled Persons Bill was given an unopposed

second reading with Lord Longford's Bill on 16 December 1983, passed through all its stages with minor amendments, and was given an unopposed third reading and passed on 12 April 1984. Lord Campbell made it known that he did not propose to promote his Bill any further; it was therefore lost at the end of the session.

7. Mr Wareing introduced a Ten-Minute Rule Bill, the Disabled Persons Rights Bill, on 3 April 1987. It was not opposed, but did not get a second reading.

8. On 6 June, 1989, Mr Wareing also attempted to include a new clause into the 1989 Employment Bill to prohibit discrimination against disabled people. Although the motion was given a second reading, its inclusion was rejected by a majority of 90 votes — 169 MPs voted for and 259 against.

9. On 6 February 1991, Mr John Hughes presented the Disability Discrimination Bill (Bill 78) before the House to make certain kinds of discrimination on grounds of disability unlawful. The Bill was given a first reading and ordered to be read a second time later in the year. At the time of going to press the Bill had not been written and a dalt for its second reading had not been fixed.

(Data supplied by Peter Large and Mike Oliver)

SELECT BIBLIOGRAPHY

ABBERLEY, P. (1986) 'The Concept of Oppression and the Development of a Social Theory of Disability', *Disability, Handicap and Society*, 2, 1, 5-19.
—— (1990) *Handicapped by Numbers: A Critique of the OPCS Disability Surveys*, Bristol Polytechnic, Bristol.
ABERCROMBIE, N., WARDE, A., BOOTHIL, K., URRY, J. and WALBY, S. (1988) *Contemporary British Society*, Polity Press, Cambridge.
ACE (1988) *Advisory Centre for Education [ACE] Special Education Handbook*, ACE, London.
—— (1989) 'Ace Attacks Exemption Clauses', *Special Children*, 31, June/July 1989, p. 3.
—— (1991) 'Access Officers — National Survey: Summary of Designated Officers', Action Committee of England, London.
ANDERSON, B. (1990) Statement, August, Leeds Forum of Disabled People and Equal Opportunities Unit, Leeds.
ANDERSON, E. and CLARKE, L. (1982) *Disability and Adolescence*, Methuen, London.
AUDIT COMMISSION (1986) *Making a Reality of Community Care*, HMSO, London.
BAKER, M. (1989) *Tourism for All*, English Tourist Board, London.
BALDWIN, S. (1985) *The Costs of Caring*, Routledge and Kegan Paul, London.
BALOO, A., McMASTER, I. and SUTTON, K. (1986) *Statutory Sick Pay*, Disability Alliance and Leicester Rights Centre, London.
BANTON, M. (1983) 'Categorical and Statistical Discrimination', *Ethnic and Racial Studies*, 6, 3, 269-83.
BARCLAY REPORT (1982) *Social Workers: Their Role and Tasks*, Bedford Square Press, London.
BARKER, C., WATCHMAN, P. and ROWAN-ROBERTSON, J. (1990) 'Social Security Abuse', *Social Policy and Administration*, 24, 2, pp. 104-19.
BARNES, C. (1990) *Cabbage Syndrome: The Social Construction of Dependence*, Falmer Press, Basingstoke.
BARTON, L. (1986) 'The Politics of Special Educational Needs', *Disability, Handicap and Society*, 1, 3, pp. 273-90.
BARTON, W. R. (1959) *Institutional Neurosis*, John Wright and Sons, Bristol.
BATTYE, L. (1966) 'The Chatterley Syndrome', in HUNT, P. (ed.), *Stigma*, Geoffrey Chapman, London.
BCODP (1986) *Disabled Young People Living Independently*, British Council of Organizations of Disabled People, London.

237

—— (1987) *Summary on the Report of the Audit Commission*, British Council of Organizations of Disabled People, London.

—— (1987a) *Disabled People Looking at Housing*, British Council of Organizations of Disabled People, London.

—— (1991) *Images of Disabled People in Advertising and the Media: Proposals for Research*, British Council of Organizations of Disabled People, London.

—— (1991a) *Draft Proposals for the BCODP Regionalization Programme*, British Council of Organizations of Disabled People, London.

BDA (1984) *Deaf Discrimination*, British Deaf Association, London.

BEARDSHAW, V. (1988) *Last on the List*, Kings Fund Institute, London.

BEGUM, N. (1990) *Burden of Gratitude: Women with Disabilities Receiving Personal Care*, Social Care Practice Centre/Department of Applied Social Studies, University of Warwick.

BIKLEN, D. and BOGDANA, R. (1977) 'Media Portrayal of Disabled People: A Study of Stereotypes', *Inter-Racial Children's Book Bulletin*, 8, 6 and 7, pp. 4–9.

BLAGDEN, F. (1991) *Report to the Advocacy and Information Committee (Televising of Parliament)*, Royal National Institute for the Deaf, London.

—— (1991a) Personal communication.

BLAINE, R. (1989) 'A Mystery in Two Acts', *Special Children*, 31, June/July 1989, pp. 5–6.

BLAXTER, M. (1981) *The Meaning of Disability* (2nd edn), Heinemann, London.

BMA (1990) *Briefing Note: Compensation For Medical Injuries Bill*, October 1990, British Medical Association, London.

BONE, M. and MELTZER, H. (1989) *The Prevalence of Disability Among Children*, OPCS, London.

BOOTH, T, (1988) 'Accessible Public Transport — When Will the Dream Become a Reality?', *International Disability Studies*, 10, pp. 81–3.

BORSAY, A. (1986) *Disabled People in the Community: A Study of Housing, Health and Welfare Services*, Bedford Square Press/NVCO, London.

—— (1986a) 'Personal Trouble or Public Issue? Towards a Model of Policy For People with Physical and Mental Disabilities', *Disability, Handicap and Society*, 1, 2, pp. 179–97.

BOWE, F. (1978) *Handicapping America*, Harper and Row, New York.

BRECHIN, A. and LIDDIARD, P. (eds) (4th imp. 1985) *Look at it This Way*, Hodder and Stoughton in association with the Open University Press, Milton Keynes.

BRIGHOUSE, T. (1989) *Ending Segregation in Local Schools: Possible Approaches to this Task*, The Centre for Studies on Integration, London.

BRIMBLECOMBE, F. S. W. Tripp, J., Kun, D., Smith, R., Wadsworth, J., Lawrence, C., and Creber, G. (1985) *The Needs of Handicapped Young Adults*, Paediatric Research Unit, Royal Devon and Exeter Hospital, Exeter.

BRINDLE, D. (1990) 'Benefit for Disabled who Cannot Cook a Meal', *Guardian*, 13 Nov., p. 23.

BRISENDEN, S. (1985) *A Charter for Personal Care*, HCIL, Hampshire.

—— (1986) 'Independent Living and the Medical Model of Disability', *Disability, Handicap and Society*, 1, 2, pp. 173–179.

BROADCASTING STANDARDS COUNCIL (1989) *Annual Report 1988-89 and Code of Good Practice*, Broadcasting Standards Council, London.

BROWN, C. (1985) *Black and White Britain*, Gower Press, Aldershot.

BRU (1990) *Images of Disability on Television*, Broadcasting Research Unit, London.

BSI (1988) *British Standards 5588. Part 8: Means of Escape for Disabled People*, British Standards Institute, London.

BUCKLE, J. (1984) *Mental Handicap Costs More*, DIG, London.

BURRELL, E. (1989) 'Fostering Children with Disabilities: The Lessons of the Last Ten Years', *Foster Care*, Sept., 59, pp. 22–3.

CAMPBELL, J. (1990) Personal communication.

—— (1990a) 'Developing Our Image – Who's in Control?', Paper presented to the 'Cap in Hand' conference, Feb. 1990.

—— (1990b) Untitled paper given at 'A Seminar on Creating a Positive Image: The BBC and Disability', 25 Oct. 1990.

CAMPLING, J. (1981) *Images of Ourselves*, Routledge and Kegan Paul, London.

CANTER, H. and BARNITT, R. (1982) 'Losing Control: Observations from a DHSS Research Project on Residential Provision for Disabled People', *Social Work Service*, Autumn, pp. 15–24.

CANTLEY, C. and HUNTER, D. (1985) 'People Processing Toward a Typology of Selected General Practitioner Referral and Admission Practices', *Ageing and Society*, 5, pp. 276–88.

CARNEGIE COUNCIL REVIEW (1988) *After Attenborough: Arts and Disabled People*, Bedford Square Press, London.

CARNEGIE UNITED KINGDOM TRUST (1985) *Arts and Disabled People: The Attenborough Report*, Carnegie United Kingdom Trust, Bedford Square Press, London.

CARTER, J. (1981) *Day Centres for Adults: Somewhere To Go*, George Allen and Unwin, London.

CAWSON, A. (1982) *Corporatism and Welfare: Social Policy and State Intervention in Welfare*, Heinemann, London.

CENTER, Y. and WARD, J. (1987) 'Teachers' Attitudes towards the Integration of Disabled Children into Regular Schools', *Exceptional Children*, 34, 1, pp. 31–48.

—— (1989) 'Principals' Attitudes towards the Integration of Disabled Children into Regular Schools', *Exceptional Children*, 34, pp. 149–61.

CHINNERY, B. (1990) 'Soapbox', *Social Work Today*, 17 May 1990, p. 27.

CHITTENDEN, M. (1990) 'Disabled Ready to Risk Jail to Fight against Car Ban', *Sunday Times*, 15 April 1990.

CLARKE, A. and HIRST, M. (1989) 'Disability in Adulthood; Ten Year

Follow up of Young People with Disabilities', *Disability, Handicap and Society*, 4, 3, pp. 271–86.

CII Journal (1978) August, pp. 134–43.

CLUNIES ROSS, L. (1984) 'Supporting the Mainstream Teacher', *Special Education Forward Trends*, 11, 3, pp. 3–11.

COLLINS, R. (1988) 'School Chiefs Bar Boy in Wheelchair', *Sunday Times*, 11 Sept. 1988.

COLVIN, M. and HAWKSLEY, J. (1989) *Section 28; A Practical Guide to the Law and its Implications*, National Council for Civil Liberties (NCCL), London.

COMMISSION OF THE EUROPEAN COMMUNITIES (1988) *Report from the Commission on the Application of Council Recommendations 86/379/EEC of 24 July 1986 on the Employment of Disabled People in the Community*, Office for Official Publications of the European Communities, Luxembourg.

COMMUNITY CARE AND THE BENEFITS RESEARCH UNIT (1990) *The New Poor*, Community Care and the Benefits Research Unit, London.

CONFERENCE OF INDIAN ORGANIZATIONS (1987) *Double Bind; To be Disabled and Asian*, London Conference of Indian Organizations.

Contact (1990) 'Working the System', *Contact*, 64, Summer, p. 32.

COOPER, D. (1989) *Building on Ability*, Training Agency, Sheffield.

—— (1990) *Accompanying Letter: Educare*, 36, March 1990.

CORAD (1982) *Report by the Committee on Restrictions against Disabled People*, HMSO, London.

CROUCH, G., FORESTER, W. and MAYHEW SMITH, P. (1989) *Access in London: A Guide for those who have Problems Getting Around*, Robert Nicholson, London.

CROWLEY-BAINTON, T. (1987) 'Discriminating Employers', *New Society*, 27 Nov. 1987, pp. 14–16.

CSIE (1989) *Integration and Resource: Financing Mainstream Education for Children with Disabilities or Difficulties in Learning*, Centre for Studies on Integration, London.

—— (1989a) *The National Curriculum and Integration*, Centre for Studies on Integration, London.

DA (1975) *Poverty and Disability*, Disability Alliance, London.

—— (1987) *Disability Rights Bulletin*, Winter, Disability Alliance, London.

—— (1988) *The Financial Circumstances of Disabled People Living in Private Households: A Disability Alliance Briefing on the Second OPCS Report*, Disability Alliance, London.

—— (1990) *Disability Rights Handbook* (15th edn), April 1990–April 1991, Disability Alliance, London.

—— (1990a) *Social Security Bill: Government Proposals for Changes in Benefits for People with Disabilities*, Disability Alliance, London.

DANKS, S. (1989) *Integration of Children with Physical Disabilities into Ordinary Schools: Final Report*, Mid Surrey Health Authority, Epsom District Hospital, Surrey.

DARLINGTON, S. (1990) 'A View from the Teaching Profession', *Contact*, 64, Summer 1990, p. 22–23.

DAVIES, C. (1990) 'Channel For-ward', *Disability Now*, June 1990, p. 18.

DAVIS, K. (1986) *Developing our own Definitions — Draft for Discussion*, British Council of Organizations of Disabled People, London.

—— (1990) *Activating the Social Model of Disability: The Emergence of the 'Seven Needs'*, Derbyshire Coalition of Disabled People, Derbyshire.

—— (1990a) 'Old Medicine is Still no Cure', *Community Care*, 8 September, p. 14.

—— (1990b) 'The Crafting of Good Clients', *Coalition*, Derbyshire Coalition of Disabled People, Derbyshire.

—— (1990c) Personal communication.

DBC (1990) *Pre-Recorded Teletext Subtitles on TV*, Deaf Broadcasting Council, Coventry.

DCC (1986) *The Disability Project and the Seven Needs*, Derbyshire County Council Social Services Department, Derbyshire.

DCDP (1986) *The Seven Needs*, Derbyshire Coalition of Disabled People, Derbyshire.

—— (1990) 'Access Campaigners Face Gaol', *Newsletter*, Derbyshire Coalition of Disabled People, Derbyshire.

DE (1988) *Code of Good Practice on the Employment of Disabled People*, 2nd edn, Dep of Employment, London.

—— (1990) *Employment and Training for People with Disabilities: Consultative Document*, Dep of Employment, London.

DE JONG, G. (1983) 'Defining and Implementing the Independent Living Concept', in CREWE, N. and ZOLA, I. (eds), *Independent Living for Physically Disabled People*, Jossey-Bass, London.

DES (1980) *Special Needs in Education*, White Paper Cmnd. 72996, Dept of Education and Science, London.

—— (1983) *Young People in the Eighties: A Survey*, Dept of Education and Science, London.

—— (1986) *Report by HMI Inspectors on a Survey of Science in Special Education*, Dept of Education and Science, London.

—— (1988) *Report by HMI Inspectors on a Survey of Provision for Pupils with SEN in Secondary Schools in the London Borough of Richmond upon Thames*, Dept of Education and Science, London.

—— (1989) Circular 22/89. *Assessments and Statements of Special Educational Needs: Procedures Within the Education, Health and Social Services*, Dept of Education and Science, London.

—— (1989a) *Report by HMI Inspectors on a Survey of Provision for Pupils with Emotional/Behavioural Difficulties in Maintained Special Schools and Units*, Dept of Education and Science, London.

—— (1989b) *Report by HMI Inspectors on Educating Physically Disabled Pupils*, Dept of Education and Science, London.

—— (1989c) *Report by HMI Inspectors on the Effectiveness of Small Special Schools*, Dept of Education and Science, London.

—— (1989d) *A Report by HMI Inspectors: Provision for Primary Aged*

Pupils with Statements of Special Educational Needs in Mainstream Schools, Dept of Education and Science, London.
—— (1989e) *A Survey of Support Services for SEN*, Dept of Education and Science, London.
—— (1990) *Educational Statistics: Schools*, Dept of Education and Science, London.
DHSS (1987) 'Mental Illness and Mental Handicap Hospitals and Units in England: Legal Status and Statistics 1982–1985', *DHSS Statistical Bulletin* 2/87, HMSO, London.
DIG (1985) *An Introduction to the Disablement Income Group*, Disablement Income Group, London.
—— (1987) *DIG's National Disability Income*, Disablement Income Group, London.
DILLON, E. (1990) 'Reviews', *Access by Design*, 51.
DISABILITY BENEFITS CONSORTIUM (1990) *Government Paper: 'The Way Ahead' — Benefits for Disabled People: A Briefing from the Disability Benefits Consortium*, Disability Benefits Consortium, London.
Disability, Handicap and Society (1987) 'Editorial', 2, 1, 3–4.
Disability Now. (1990) 'Telethon is a Modern Day Freak Show', June, p. 3.
—— (1990a) 'Disability Groups Face Cuts', Sept., p. 1.
—— (1990b) 'Demonstrators Mentally Retarded'. Nov., p. 1.
—— (1990c) 'Government Job Logo', Nov., p. 3.
—— (1990d) 'Thousands Show at Demo', Dec., p. 28.
—— (1991) 'Motor Charity Slammed', Jan., pp. 1–3.
DoE (1987) *Housing and Construction Statistics*, March Quarter (Part 1), Dept of the Environment, London.
—— (1990) *Housing and Construction Statistics*, June Quarter (Part 1), Dept of the Environment, London.
—— (1990a) Circular 10/90: *House Adaptations for People with Disabilities*, Dept of the Environment, London.
—— (1990b) *The Building Regulations 1985 — Part M: Access for Disabled People*, Dept of the Environment, London.
DOUGLAS, M. (1966) *Purity and Danger*, Routledge and Kegan Paul, London.
DOYAL, L. (1980) *The Political Economy of Health*, Pluto Press, London.
DOYLE, C. (1988). 'Transport Handicap: its Causes, its Scale and its Effect', *International Disability Studies*, 10, pp. 84–5.
DPI (1981) *Proceedings of the First World Congress*, Disabled People's International, Singapore.
DPTAC (1989) *Public Transport and the Missing Six Millions: What Can Be Learned?* Disabled Persons Transport Advisory Committee, London.
—— (1988) *Making Buses More Suitable for Elderly and Ambulant Disabled People*, Disabled Persons Transport Advisory Committee, London.
DRIEDGER, D. (1989) *The Last Civil Rights Movement: Disabled People's International*, Hurst, London.
DSS (1990) *The Way Ahead: Benefits for Disabled People*, HMSO, London.

—— (1990a) *Disability Allowance: Assessment and Adjudication*, Dept of Social Security, London.

DT (1990) *Draft Directive on 'Mobility Improvement Measures for Workers with Reduced Mobility'*, Disability Unit, Dept of Transport, London.

—— (1990a) *The Orange Badge Scheme*, Dept of Transport, London.

DTWO (1987) *Getting the Right Balance: Guidance on Vehicle Restrictions in Pedestrian Zones*, Local Transport Note 1/87, Dept of Transport and the Welsh Office, London.

DUTTON, P., MANSELL, S., MOONEY, P., EDGER, M., and EVANS, E. (1989) *The Net Exchequer Costs of Sheltered Employment*, Dept of Employment, Employment Services, Sheffield.

DURRANT, P. (1983) 'Personal Social Work', in BRECHIN, A., LIDDIARD, P. and SWAIN, J., *Handicap in a Social World*, Hodder and Stoughton in association with Open University Press, Milton Keynes.

DYER, L. (1990) 'The Right to Work', draft article for *Open Mind*, unpublished at time of writing.

Employment Gazette (1990) 'Disabled Employees in the Public Sector', Feb., 98, ii, pp. 78–83.

ES (1988) *Code of Good Practice on the Employment of Disabled People*, Dept of Employment, Employment Services, Sheffield.

ETCHELL, L. (1990) 'No Go For Disabled People', *Contact*, 65, pp. 17–18.

EVANS, D. (1989) 'Section 28; Law, Myth and Reality', *Critical Social Policy*, Winter 1989, 27, 73–95.

EVANS, J. (1984) *Philosophy and Basic Principles of Independent Living in Seminar Report*, CEH, London.

EXPERT SEMINAR. (1989) 'Resolution', Rainbow Coalition, Strasbourg.

FAGIN, L. and LITTLE, M. (1984) *The Forsaken Families*, Penguin Books, London.

FINDLAY, B. (1990) 'Campaigning for Accessible Transport', *Contact*, 65, p. 33.

FINKELSTEIN, V. (1980) *Attitudes and Disabled People: Issues for Discussion*, World Rehabilitation Fund, New York.

FIELDER, B. (1988) *Living Options: Housing and Care Support Services for People with Severe Physical Disabilities*, Prince of Wales Advisory Group on Disability, London.

Forum. (1989) 'Leeds Access: 21 Years of Success', *Forum*, August, Leeds Forum of Disabled People and Equal Opportunities Unit, Leeds.

—— (1990) *A to Z of Groups*, Leeds Forum for Disabled People and Equal Opportunities Unit, Leeds.

FOSTER, K. J. (1990) *Self Identification of People with Disabilities Questions: Pilot*, Dept of Employment, Employment Services, Sheffield.

FRANEY, R. (1983) *Hard Times: The Tories and Disability*, Disability Alliance, London.

FRY, E. (1986) *An Equal Chance for Disabled People: A Study of Discrimination in Employment*, The Spastics Society, London.

—— (1987) *Disabled People and the 1987 General Election*, Spastics Society, London.

FRYE, A. (1990) 'Everybody Moving Together', *Contact*, 65, p. 14.

—— (1991) Personal communication.

FULCHER, G. (1989) *Disabling Policies: A Comparative Approach to Education and Disability*, Falmer Press, Basingstoke.

GALASKO, C. and LIPSKIN, C. (1989) *Competing for the Disabled*, IEA Health Unit, London.

GARTNER, A. and JOE, T. (eds) (1987) *Images of the Disabled: Disabling Images*, Praeger, New York.

GINSBURG, N. (1988) 'Institutional Racism and Local Authority Housing', *Critical Social Policy*, Winter 1988/9, 24, 4–19.

GLAD (1986) *All Change: A Consumer Study of Transport Handicap in Greater London*, Greater London Association for Disabled People, London.

—— (1988) *The Impact of Transport on the Quality of Life and Lifestyle of Young People with Physical Disabilities*, Transport Paper no. 2, Greater London Association for Disabled People, London.

GLENDINNING, C. (1986) *A Single Door: Social Work with Families of Disabled Children*, Geo. Allen and Unwin, London.

—— (1989) *After 16 – What Next? Services and Benefits for Young Disabled People* (6th edn), The Family Fund; Joseph Rowntree Memorial Trust, York.

—— (1990) 'Social Policy and Physically Disabled People in Great Britain 1980–1990', Paper Presented for 4th Sino-American-British Conference on Social Policy, 22–28 July 1990, Taiwan.

GMCDP (1989) 'Service Brokerage – The Conference', *Coalition*, Oct.

GOFFMAN, E. (1961) *Asylums*, Penguin, Harmondsworth.

GOODALL, L. (1988) 'Living Options for Physically Disabled People', *Disability, Handicap and Society*, 3, 2, pp. 173–94.

GOVERNMENT OF ONTARIO COMMUNICATIONS (1989) 'Equity in the Portrayal of the People of Ontario', *Government of Ontario Communications: A Guide for Executives and Managers*, Government of Ontario, Canada.

GRAHAM, P., JORDAN, D. and LAMB, B. (1990) *An Equal Chance or No Chance?* The Spastics Society, London.

GRAY, A., WHELAN, A. and NORMAND, C. (1988) *Care in the Community: A Study of Services and Costs in Six Districts*, Health Economics Consortium, University of York, York.

GREGORY, J. (1987) *Sex, Race and the Law*, Sage, London.

GRIFFITHS, R. (1988) *Community Care: Agenda for Action*, HMSO, London.

GROVER, R. and GLADSTONE, G. (1982) *Disabled People – A Right to Work?*, Bedford Square Press, London.

HAFFTER, C. (1968) 'The Changeling; History and Psychodynamics of Attitudes to Handicapped Children in European Folklore', *Journal of the History of Behavioural Studies*, 4.

HAHN, H. (1986) 'Public Support for Rehabilitation Programmes: The

Analysis of U.S. Disability Policy', *Disability, Handicap and Society*, 1, 2, pp. 121–38.

HANKS, J. and HANKS, L. (1980) 'The Physically Handicapped in Certain Non-Occidental Societies', in PHILIPS, W. and ROSENBERG, J. (eds), *Social Scientists and the Physically Handicapped*, Arno Press, London.

Hansard (1983) 11 Feb.

—— (1988) 12 Jan.

—— (1989) 6 June.

—— (1990) 16 Jan.

—— (1990a) 24 April.

—— (1990b) 22 May.

—— (1990c) 29 June.

—— (1990d) 25 Oct.

—— (1991) 1 Feb.

—— (1991a) 25 March.

HARP, W. (1991) Personal communication.

HARPER, M. (1990) 'Storm as Pub Bans Disabled Skittles Team', *Mail on Sunday*, 25 Nov. 1990, p. 14.

HARRIS, A. (1971) *Handicapped and Impaired in Great Britain*, HMSO, London.

HARRISON, J. (1987) *Severe Physical Disability: Responses to the Challenge of Care*, Cassell, London.

HASLER, F. (1991) 'The International Year of Disabled People', *Disability Now*, January, p. 5.

HCIL (1990) *HCIL Papers 1990*, Hampshire Centre for Disabled People, Hampshire.

HIRST, M. (1982) *Young Adults with Disabilities and Their Families*, Social Policy Research Unit, University of York, York.

—— (1984) *Moving On: Transfer of Young People with Disabilities to Adult Services*, University of York Social Policy Research Unit, York.

—— (1985) *Dependency and Family Care of Young Adults with Disabilities in the United Kingdom*, Child Care; Health and Development, 11, pp. 241–57.

—— (1987) 'Careers of Young People with Disabilities Between Ages 16 and 21', *Disability, Handicap and Society*, 2, 1, pp. 61–75.

—— (1990) 'Financial Independence and Social Security', *Child and Society*, 4, 1, pp. 70–84.

HMSO (1979) *Aspects of Secondary Education: An HMI Survey*, HMSO, London.

—— (1981) *The Education Act 1981*, HMSO, London.

—— (1988) *English House Condition Survey*, HMSO, London.

—— (1989) *Health and Personal Social Services Statistics for England 1989 Edition*, HMSO, London.

—— (1989a) *Working for Patients*, Cmnd. 555, HMSO, London.

—— (1989b) *Caring for People: Community Care in the Next Decade and Beyond*, HMSO, London.

—— (1990) *Efficiency, Scrutiny of Government Funding of the Voluntary Sector*, HMSO, London.
—— (1990a) *The Broadcasting Act: 1990*, HMSO, London.
—— (1990b) *A Guide to Fire Regulations in Existing Places of Entertainment and Like Premises*, HMSO, London.
—— (1991) *Social Trends 21*, HMSO, London.
HOBSBAWN, E. J. (1968) *Industry and Empire*, Penguin, Harmondsworth.
HOLDEN, G. (1990) 'RADAR's New Director: Bert Massie talks to Geraldine Holden', *Disability Now*, April, p. 7.
HOME OFFICE (1989) Circular LXN/89 177/1/2, 20 Dec.
HOOPER, E. (1990) 'Sex and Disability: More People Talk about their Setbacks and Successes', *Disability Now*, March, pp. 12–13.
HOUSE OF COMMONS BILL 208 (1990) *Compensation For Medical Injuries Bill*, House of Commons, London.
HOUSE OF COMMONS COMMISSION ON CITIZENSHIP (1990) *Encouraging Citizenship: Report of the House of Commons Commission on Citizenship*, HMSO, London.
HOUSE OF COMMONS SOCIAL SECURITY COMMITTEE (1990) *Community Care: Social Security for Disabled People 9th Report*, House of Commons, London.
HUGHES, S. (1990) 'Getting There — with BR', *Contact*, 65, p. 21.
HURST, A. (1984) 'Adolescence and Physical Disability. An Interactionist View', in BARTON, L. and TOMLINSON, S. (eds), *Special Education and Social Interests*, Croom Helm, London.
HURST, R. (1990) Minutes of British Council of Organizations of Disabled People Council Meeting held on 6 Jan.
HYMAN, M. (1977) *The Extra Costs of Disability*, Disablement Income Group, London.
IFF RESEARCH (1990) *Evaluation of Jobclub Provision for People with Disabilities*, Dept of Employment, Employment Services, Sheffield.
IFS (1990) *Poverty in Official Statistics*, IFS, London.
ILEA (1985) *Equal Opportunities For All?*, Inner London Education Authority, London.
ILSLEY, R. (1981) 'Problems of Dependency Groups: The Care of the Elderly, the Handicapped and the Chronically Ill', *Social Science and Medicine*, 15a.
INGELBY, D. (1983) 'Mental Health and Social Order', in COHEN, S. and SCULL, A. (eds), *Social Control and the State*, Basil Blackwell, London.
JONES, A. and LONGSTONE, L. (1990) *A Survey of Restrictions on Jobcentre Vacancies*, Dept of Employment, Employment Services, Sheffield.
JONES, K. *et al.* (1983) *Issues in Social Policy* (2nd edn), Routledge and Kegan Paul, London.
JONES, K. and FOWLES, A. J. (1984) *Ideas on Institutions*, Routledge and Kegan Paul, London.
JOWETT, J (1982) *Young Disabled People: Their Further Education, Training and Education*, NFER, Windsor.

KENNEDY, M. (1989) 'Child Abuse, Child Sexual Abuse', *Deafness*, 3, 2, p. 47.

KENT, A. and MASSIE, B. (1981) 'Significant Living Without Work', *Educare*, 12, pp. 31-5.

KENT, A., MASSIE, B., NEWMAN, B. and TUCKEY, L. (1984) *Day Centres for Young Disabled People*, RADAR, London.

KETTLE, M. (1979) *Disabled People and Their Employment*, RADAR, London.

KUH, D., LAWRENCE, C., TRIPP, J. and CREBER, G. (1988) 'Work and Work Alternatives for Disabled Young People', *Disability, Handicap and Society*, 3, 1, pp. 3-27.

LABOUR MARKET QUARTERLY REPORT (1990) 'Overview', Feb.

LABOUR RESEARCH (1990) 'Fit For Danger? — Facing the Health Test', *Labour Research*, Feb., pp. 17-18.

LADC (1983) *Leeds and District Committee for the Disabled*, Leeds Access for the Disabled Committee, Leeds.

LAND, H. (1988) 'Social Security and Community Care: Creating Perverse Incentives', in BALDWIN S., PARKER, G. and WALKER, A. (eds), *Social Security and Community Care*, Gower Press, Aldershot.

LANGAN, M. (1990) 'Community Care in the 1990s: The Community Care White Paper: Caring for People', *Critical Social Policy*, 29, Autumn, pp. 58-70.

LARGE, P. (1981) 'Enabling the Disabled'. Paper given to Royal College of Physicians, London.

—— (1990) 'Additional Costs of Disability'. Paper presented at the PSI Seminar on the Needs and Resources of People with Disabilities, held 3-4 Dec. at Policy Studies Institute, London.

—— (1990a) 'When Respite Care is not a Holiday', *Contact*, 63, Spring, p. 51.

LAURIE, L. (1991) *Report on the Conference on Housing, Independent Living and Disabled People 1990*, Shelter, London.

LEAH, J., BEATTIE, C. and DUTTON, P. (1990) *A Report on the Organization of Special Jobcentre Services for People with Disabilities*, DE, Employment Services, Sheffield.

LEAT, D. (1988) *Residential Care for Younger Physically Disabled Adults: The Research Reviewed*, HMSO, London.

LESBIAN AND GAY COMMITTEE (1990) *Disability Review*, March, 12, 1990.

LESTER, A. (1987) 'Forward' in PALMER, C. and POULTON, K. (1987), *Sex and Race Discrimination in Employment*, Legal Action Group, London.

LEVY, L. (1990) 'Out of Sight Out of Mind', *Marketing*, 18 January 1990, pp. 28-9.

LIGGETT, H. (1988) 'Stars are not Born: An Interactive Approach to the Politics of Disability', *Disability, Handicap and Society*, 3, 3, pp. 263-76.

LISTER, L. (1989) 'Social Benefits: Priorities for Distribution', in ALCOCK, P., GAMBLE, A., GOUGH, I., LEE, P., and WALKER A.

(eds), (1989) *The Social Economy and the Democratic State*, Lawrence and Wishart, London.
LONSDALE, S. (1986) *Work and Inequality*, Longman, Harlow.
—— (1990) *Women and Disability*, Macmillan, London.
LRT (1990) *London Taxicard Scheme for Disabled People: Information Booklet*, London Regional Transport, London.
LYNES, T. (1988) 'A Guide to the Social Fund', *New Society*, 83, 1319, 19–20.
McCART, M. (1991) 'South Bank Shut Out', *Disability Now*, Feb., p. 10.
McROBBIE, A. (ed.) (1989) *Zoot Suits and Second Hand Dresses*, Macmillan, London.
McCOLL, I. (1986) *Review of Artificial Limb and Appliance Centre Services* (Vols 1 and 2) DHSS, London.
McCRUDDEN, C. (1981) 'Institutional Discrimination', *Oxford Journal of Legal Studies*, 2, pp. 303–67.
McDONALD, P. (1991) 'Double Discrimination Must be Faced Now', *Disability Now*, March, p. 8.
McDOWELL, L. (1989) 'Gender Divisions', in HAMNETT, C., McDOWELL, L. and SARRE, P., *The Changing Social Structure*, Sage, London.
MACFARLAND, A. (1978) *The Origins of English Individualism*, Basil Blackwell, Oxford.
MACGEE, D. (1990) 'Kane Joins Attack on Disabled Student', *The Scotsman*, 9 May 1990, p. 7.
MAINSTREAM (1990) *Workmates: A Study of Employment Opportunities for Disabled People*, Mainstream, London.
MARSHALL, T.H. (1950) *Citizenship and Social Class*, Cambridge University Press.
MARTIN, J., MELTZER, H. and ELLIOT, D. (1988) *The Prevalence of Disability among Adults*, OPCS, London.
MARTIN, J. and WHITE, A. (1988) *The Financial Circumstances of Disabled Adults Living in Private Households*, OPCS, London.
MARTIN, J., WHITE, A. and MELTZER, H. (1989) *Disabled Adults: Services, Transport and Employment*, OPCS, London.
MASON, P. (1990) Personal communication.
—— (1991) Personal communication.
MASHAM, B. (1990) 'Disabled Access to the Gaols', *Prison Report*, 11, June 1990, p. 5.
MASSIE, B. (1988) 'Disabled People and Public Transport', *International Disability Studies*, 10, p. 92.
—— (1990) 'Comment: Ending the Battle for Mobility', *Contact*, 65, Autumn, p. 2.
—— (1990a) 'Moving Toward Accessibility', *Contact*, 65, Autumn, p. 6.
—— and KETTLE, M. (1986) *Employers Guide to Disabilities*, RADAR, London.
MECHANIC, D. (1964) 'Mental Health and Social Policy', Prentice-Hall, Englewood Cliffs, New Jersey.
MELVILLE, J. (1986) 'Sitting Pretty', *New Society*, 14 March 1986, p. 465.

MELTZER, H., SMYTH, M. and ROBUS, N. (1989) *Disabled Children: Services, Transport and Education*, OPCS, London.
MILLER, E. J. and GWYNNE, G. V. (1972) *A Life Apart*, Tavistock, London.
MIND (1989) *The Right to Vote*, MIND (North West), Preston.
MORGAN, D. (1989) 'Sterilisation and Mental Incompetence', *Bulletin of Medical Ethics*, 53, Sept./Oct., pp. 18–23.
MORRELL, J. (1990) *The Employment of People with Disabilities: Research into the Policies and Practices of Employers*, DE, Employment Services, Sheffield.
MORRIS, J. (1988) *Freedom to Lose: Housing Policy and People with Disabilities*, Shelter, London.
—— (1989) *Able Lives: Women's Experience of Paralysis*, Women's Press, London.
—— (1990) *Our Homes, Our Rights: Housing, Independent Living and Physically Disabled People*, Shelter, London.
—— (1990a) 'Wheelchair's Invisible Clamp', *Guardian*, 31 August 1990, p. 23.
—— (1991) Personal communication.
MOTABILITY (1990) *A Guide to Motability and How to Apply*, Motability, Essex.
NACABx (1990) *Assessing the Assessors: Medical Assessments for Disability Benefits*, NACAB, London.
NACABx (1990a) *Hard Times for Social Fund Applicants*, NACAB, London.
NAHA (1988) *Health Authorities Concerns for Children with Special Needs: A Report on a Survey of Health Authorities on the Implementation of the Education Act 1981*, National Association of Health Authorities, Birmingham.
NANTON, P. (1990) 'Professional Training and Passive Discrimination against Ethnic Minorities; A Review of Recent Evidence', *Critical Social Policy*, Summer 1990, pp. 79–84.
NCC (1991) 'Mobility Matters', National Consumer Council, London.
New Society (1985) 'Findings', 7 June, p. 370.
New York Times (1990). 'House Approves Bill Setting Rights for the Disabled', 23 May 1990, p. 18.
NICHOLS, V. (1991) Personal communication.
NUT (1991) *Guide-lines on Disability*, National Union of Teachers, London.
OLIVER, M. (1981) *Disablement in Society* (Unit 2 of OU course; The Handicapped Person in the Community), Open University Press, Milton Keynes.
—— (1983) *Social Work with Disabled People*, Macmillan, Basingstoke.
—— (1984) 'The Politics of Disability', *Critical Social Policy*, 11.
—— (1985) 'Discrimination, Disability and Social Policy', in BRENTON, M. and JONES, C. (eds), *The Year Book of Social Policy 1984–5*, Routledge and Kegan Paul, London.

—— (1987) 'From Strength to Strength', *Community Care*, 19 February.

—— (1989) 'Conductive Education: If it Wasn't so Sad it would be Funny', *Disability, Handicap and Society*, 4, 2, pp. 197–200.

—— (1990) *Disablement in Society: A Socio-Political Approach*, Thames Polytechnic, London.

—— (1990a) 'Speaking Out: Disabled People and State Welfare', paper presented at seminar 'The Needs and Resources of People with Disabilities', held 3–4 Dec. 1990 at Policy Studies Institute, London.

—— and HASLER, F. (1987) 'Disability and Self Help: A Case Study of the Spinal Injuries Association', *Disability, Handicap and Society*, 2, 2, pp. 113–27.

OLIVER, M. and ZARB, G. (1989) 'The Politics of Disability: A New Approach', *Disability, Handicap and Society*, 4, 3, pp. 221–40.

OLIVER, M., ZARB, G., SILVER, J., MOORE, M., and SAINSBURY, V. (1988) *Walking into Darkness*, Macmillan, London.

OUNSTED, D. (1989) 'The 1988 Housing Act: What does it Mean for People with Disabilities?', *Design For Special Needs*, 48, p. 15.

OUTSET (1987) *Public Attitudes toward Disabled People*, Outset, London.

OWENS, P. (1987) 'Community Care and Severe Physical Disability', Bedford Square Press, London.

PAGEL, M. (1988) *On Our Own Behalf*, Greater Manchester Coalition of Disabled People, Manchester.

PALMER, C. and POULTON, K. (1987) *Sex and Race Discrimination in Employment*, Legal Action Group, London.

PARKER, G. (1984) *Into Work: A Review of the Literature about Disabled Young Adults' Preparation for and Movement into Work*, Dept of Social Administration and Social Work Social Policy Research Unit, University of York.

—— (1990) *With Due Care and Attention: A Review of Research on Informal Care* (2nd edn), Family Policy Studies Centre, London.

PARKER, S. (1979) *The Sociology of Leisure*, Geo. Allen and Unwin, London.

PARRATT, D. (1989) 'The Disabled Persons Act 1986: Reality or Myth', *Contact*, vol. 60 (Summer), pp. 13–17.

PATTEN, C. (1990). 'Big Battalions and Little Platoons', 7th Annual Goodman Lecture Charities Aid Foundation.

PATTON, B. (1990) 'A Survey of the Disabled Students' Allowance', *Educare*, 36, March 1990, pp. 3–7.

PLUMB, L. (1990) *Access in Lothian: A Guide for Disabled People*, Plumb Promotions, Edinburgh.

PRESCOTT CLARKE, P. (1982) 'Organizing House Adaptations for Disabled People', Department of the Environment, London.

—— (1990) 'Employment and Handicap', Social and Community Planning Research, London.

PRESS, M. (1991) Personal Communication.

RAD (1991) *A Change in Approach: A Report on the Experience of Deaf People from Black and Ethnic Minority Communities*, Royal Association in Aid of Deaf People, London.

RADAR (1987) *Response to the Government's Proposals on Home Improvement Grants*, Royal Association for Disability and Rehabilitation, London.

RAE, A. (1990) 'Secretarial Address given at the BCODP Annual Conference', Nottingham University, 17 Sept.

RATZKA, A. (1988) 'Independent Living', *Vox Nostra*, p. 5.

REES, S. (1978) *Social Work, Face to Face*, Edw. Arnold, London.

REISER, R. and MASON, M. (1990) *Disability Equality in the Classroom: A Human Rights Issue*, Inner London Education Authority, London.

RNIB (1990) *Thomas Rhodes Armitage — RNIB's Founder*, RNIB, London.

—— (1990a) *Royal National Institute for The Blind*, TCS/C5004/Nov., Peterborough.

RNID (1990) *Submission to the Select Committee on the Televising of Proceedings of the House*, Royal National Institute for the Deaf', London.

ROBERTS, K., DENCH, S. and RICHARDSON, D. (1986) *The Changing Structure of Youth Labour Markets*, Dept of Employment, Employment Services, Sheffield.

ROBINSON, D. and HENRY, S. (1977) *Self Help and Health*, Martin Robertson, Oxford.

ROBINSON, I. (1987) *Re-evaluating Housing for People with Disabilities in Hammersmith and Fulham*, London Borough of Hammersmith and Fulham Special Needs Unit, London.

ROCK, P. (1988) 'The Carers' Movement: Dangers Ahead'. *CareLink*, Winter, pp. 4–5.

ROGERS, R. (1986) *Caught in the Act*, Centre for Studies on Integration in Education and the Spastics Society, London.

—— (1986a) *Guiding the Professionals*, Centre for Studies in Integration in Education and the Spastics Society, London.

ROTH, M. and KROLL, J. (1986) *The Reality of Mental Illness*, Cambridge University Press.

ROWE, A. (ed.) (1990) *Lifetime Homes: Flexible Housing for Successive Generations*, Helen Hamlyn Foundation, London.

ROWE, B. (1973) 'A Study of Social Adjustment in Young Adults with Cerebral Palsy', unpublished B.Sc dissertation, University of Newcastle-upon-Tyne.

ROYAL COLLEGE OF PHYSICIANS (1986) *Physical Disability in 1986 and Beyond*, Royal College of Physicians of London.

RUSSELL, B. (1948) *History of Western Philosophy*, Geo. Allen and Unwin, London.

RYAN, J. and THOMAS, F. (1980) *The Politics of Mental Handicap*, Penguin, Harmondsworth.

Same Difference (1989) *Adult Training Centres*, Series 3, Factsheet 1.

—— (1989a) *Insurance Quotes*, Series III, Factsheet 2.

—— (1989b) *The Sheltered Placement Scheme*, Series 4, Factsheet 1.
—— (1990) *Air Travel*, Series 5, Factsheet 4.
—— (1990a) *The Independent Living Fund*, Series 5, Factsheet 5.
—— (1990b) *People with Disabilities and the Arts*, Series 5, Factsheet 3.
—— (1990c) *Disabled People and Newspapers*, Series 5, Factsheet 6.
—— (1990d) *The National Access Organizations*, Series 5, Factsheet 8.
—— (1990e) *The Employment Quota Scheme*, Series 5, Factsheet 10.
SAPSFORD, R. J. (1981) 'Individual Deviance; The Search for the Criminal Personality' in FITZGERALD, M., MCLENNAN, G. and PAWSON, J. (eds), *Crime and Society: Readings in History and Theory*, Open University Press, Milton Keynes.
SCHLESINGER, H. and WHELAN, E. (1979) *Industry and Effort*, Spastics Society, London.
SCOTT PARKER, S. (1989) *They Aren't in the Brief*, Kings Fund Centre, London.
SCULL, A. (1978) *Museums of Madness*, Allen Lane, London.
—— (1984) *Decarceration* (2nd edn), Polity Press, London.
SEGAL, A. (1986) 'Push for Power', *New Society*, 23 April, 79, 1217, pp. 16–17.
SHEARER, A. (1981) 'A Framework for Independent Living' in WALKER, A. and TOWNSEND, P. (eds), *Disability Rights in Britain*, Martin Robertson, Oxford.
SIA (1987) *Comments on the Royal College of Physicians Reports on Disability*, Spinal Injuries Association, London.
SIMMONS, S. (1990) 'Examination Arrangements for Students with a Disability', *Skill*, National Bureau for Students with Disabilities, London.
SIMPSON, P. (1990) 'Education For Disabled Children — Today and Tomorrow', *Contact*, 64, Summer, pp. 9–11.
SJAC (1979) *Can Disabled People Go Where You Go? Silver Jubilee Access Committee Report*, Dept of Health and Social Security, London.
Skills Bulletin (1989) 'Defusing the Demographic Time Bomb', Winter 1989, 10.
SMITH, A. (1990) 'Opportunities for Students with Disabilities', Public Information Unit, Labour Party, London.
SMYTH, M. and ROBUS, N. (1989) *The Financial Circumstances of Families with Disabled Children Living in Private Households*, OPCS, London.
STONE, D. A. (1985) *The Disabled State*, Macmillan, London.
STOWELL, R. (1987) *Catching Up: A Survey of Provision for Students with Special Educational Needs in Further and Higher Education*, National Bureau for Handicapped Students, London.
—— and DAY, F. (1983) *Tell Me What You Want and I'll Get it For You — A Study of Shopping When Disabled*, Disablement Income Group, London.
STUBBINS, J. (1983) 'Resettlement Services of the Employment Services, Manpower Services Commission: Some Observations' in BRECHIN, A., LIDDIARD, P. and SWAIN, J., *Handicap in a Social World*, Hodder and Stoughton in association with the Open University, Milton Keynes.
SUTHERLAND, A. T. (1981) *Disabled We Stand*, Souvenir Press. London.
SWANN, W. (1988) 'Trends in Special School Placement to 1986; Measur-

ing, Assessing and Explaining Segregation', *Oxford Review of Education*, 14, 2, pp. 139–61.
—— (1989) *Integration Statistics: LEAs Reveal Local Variations*, Centre for Studies on Integration in Education, London.
—— (1991) *Variations Between LEAs in Levels of Segregation in Special Schools, 1981–1990: Preliminary Report*, Centre for Studies on Integration in Education, London.
TESTER, S. (1989) *Caring By Day: A Study of Day Care Services for Older People*, Centre for Policy on Ageing, London.
THOMAS, A. P., BAX, M. C. O. and SMYTHE, D. P. L. (1989) *The Health and Social Needs of Young Adults with Physical Disabilities*, Blackwell Scientific Publications, Oxford.
THOMAS, D. (1982) *The Experience of Handicap*, Methuen, London.
THOMAS, K. (1977) 'The Place of Laughter in Tudor and Stuart England', *Times Literary Supplement*, 21 Jan., pp. 77–81.
THOMPSON, P., BUCKLE, J. and LAVERY, M. (1989) *Not the OPCS Survey: Being Disabled Costs More Than They Said*, Disablement Income Group, London.
THOMPSON, P., LAVERY, M. and CURTICE, J. (1990) *Short Changed by Disability*, Disablement Income Group, London.
TOMLINSON COMMITTEE (1943) *The Tomlinson Committee Report on the Rehabilitation and Resettlement of Disabled Persons*, HMSO, London.
TOMLINSON, S. (1981) *Educational Subnormality: A Study in Decision Making*, Routledge and Kegan Paul, London.
—— (1982) *The Sociology of Special Education*, Routledge and Kegan Paul, London.
—— (1985) 'The Expansion of Special Education', *Oxford Review of Education*, 11, pp. 157–65.
TOOLEY, M. (1983) *Abortion and Infanticide*, Oxford University Press, New York.
TOPLISS, E. and GOULD, B. (1981) *A Charter for the Disabled*, Basil Blackwell, Oxford.
TOWNSEND, P. (1967) *The Last Refuge — A Survey of Residential Institutions and Homes for the Aged in England and Wales*, Routledge and Kegan Paul, London.
—— (1986) 'Democracy for the Poor', Forword in McCARTHY, M (ed.), *Campaigning for the Poor: CPAG and the Politics of Welfare*, Croom Helm, Beckenham.
TOZER, G. and PARSONS, J. (1989) *Evaluation of the Services Provided for People with Disabilities Outside the Disablement Resettlement Services*, Dept of Employment, Employment Services, Sheffield.
TREVELYAN, G. M. (1948) *English Social History*, Longmans Green, London.
UNDERSTANDING DISABILITY EDUCATION TRUST (1990) *Understanding Disability: Teaching Notes Produced by the Understanding Disability Education Trust*, Understanding Disability Education Trust, London.

UNITED NATIONS (1988) *A Compendium of Declarations on the Rights of Disabled Persons*, United Nations, New York.

UPIAS (1976) *Fundamental Principles of Disability*, Union of Physically Impaired Against Segregation, London.

VOADL (1990) Report to the VOADL Committee on 1 March by Mike Brothers, Voluntary Organizations for Anti-Discrimination Legislation, London.

WAGSTAFF, J. (1990) 'Getting Around London', *Contact*, 65, pp. 35–6.

WALKER, A. (1982) *Unqualified and Underemployed*, Macmillan/National Children's Bureau, Basingstoke.

WARBURTON, W. (1990) *Developing Services for Disabled People*, Dept of Health, London.

—— (1979) *Poverty in the United Kingdom*, Harmondsworth, Penguin Books.

WARD, L. (1987) *Talking Points: The Right to Vote*, CMH, n.p. (West of England).

—— (1990) 'Casting Aside', *Community Care*, 19 April, p. 16.

WARNOCK REPORT. (1978) *Special Educational Needs: Report of the Committee of Enquiry Into the Education of Children and Young People*, HMSO, London.

WATSON, G. (1989) 'The Abuse of Disabled Children and Young People', in STANTON, W. *et al.* (eds), *Child Abuse and Neglect: Facing the Challenge*, Batsford, London.

WHELAN, E. and SPEAKE, B. R. (1977) *Adult Training Centres in England and Wales*, National Association of Teachers of the Mentally Handicapped, Manchester.

Which (1989) 'No Entry'. Oct., pp. 498–501.

—— (1990) 'No Go'. June, pp. 347–50.

WILDING, P. (1982) *Professional Power and Social Welfare*, Routledge and Kegan Paul, London.

WILLIAMS, G. (1983) 'The Movement for Independent Living: An Evaluation and Critique', *Social Science and Medicine*, 17, 15.

WILLIAMS, I. (1989) *The Alms Trade: Charities, Past, Present and Future*, Unwin Hyman, London.

WILLIS, N. (1989) Letter to the British Deaf Association, Aug. 24.

WILLIS, P. (1985) *The Social Condition of Young People in Wolverhampton in 1984*, Wolverhampton Borough Council, Wolverhampton.

WOLFENSBERGER, W. (1980) 'The Extermination of Handicapped People in World War II', *American Journal on Mental Deficiency*, 19, 1.

—— (1989) 'Human Services Policies: The Rhetoric versus the Reality', in BARTON, L. (ed.), Disability and Dependence, Falmer Press, Basingstoke.

WOOD, P. (1981) 'International Classification of Impairments, Disabilities and Handicaps', World Health Organization (WHO), Geneva.

WOOD, R. (1990) 'Care of Disabled People', paper presented at seminar on 'The Needs and Resources of People with Disabilities', held 3–4 Dec. 1990 at Policy Studies Institute, London.

YATES, A. (1990) 'Multi-Generational Housing Cost Considerations', Appendix 9 in ROWE, A. (ed.), *Lifetime Homes: Flexible Housing for Successive Generations*, Helen Hamlyn Foundation, London.
YOUNG, P. (1987) *Mastering Social Welfare*, Macmillan, London.
ZOLA, I. (1981) *Missing Pieces: A Chronicle of Living with a Disability*, Temple University Press, Philadelphia.

ADDENDA

AUDIT COMMISSION. (1992) *Getting in on the Act: Provision for Pupils with Special Educational Needs, The National Picture*, HMSO, London.
BARNES, C. (1992) *Disabling Imagery: An Exploration of Media Portrayals of Disabled People*, British Council of Organisations of Disabled People.
—— (ed.) (1993) *Making Our Own Choices: Independent Living, Personal Assistance and Disabled People*, British Council of Organisations of Disabled People.
BEGUM, N., HILL, M. and STEVENS, A. (1994) *Reflections: Views of Black Disabled People on Their Lives and Community Care*, London, CCETSW.
BERTHOUD, R., LAKEY, J. and McKAY, S. (1993) *The Economic Problems of Disabled People*, Policy Studies Institute, London.
CARSON. S. (1992) 'Normalisation: Needs and Schools', *Educational Psychology in Practice*, vol. 1, no. 4. pp. 216–22.
CASEY, W., JONES. D., KUGLER, B. and WATKINS., B. (1988) 'Integration of Down's Syndrome Children in the Primary School: A Longitudinal Study of Cognitive Development and Academic Attainments', *British Journal of Educational Psychology*, no. 58, pp. 279–86.
COLERIDGE, P. (1993) *Disability, Liberation and Development*, Oxfam Publications, Oxford.
COOPERS AND LYBRAND. (1992) *Within Reach: Access for Disabled Children to Mainstream Education*, Coopers and Lybrand in association with the National Union of Teachers and the Spastics Society, London.
CUMBERBATCH, G. and NEGRINE, R. (1992) *Images of Disability on Television*, Routledge, London.
Department of Social Security. (1994) *A Consultation on Government Measures to Tackle Discrimination against Disabled People*, Dept of Social Security, Enable, Bristol.
GLENDINNING, C. and BEWLET, C. (1993) *Involving Disabled People in Community Care Planning: The First Report*, University of Manchester, Dept of Social Policy and Social Work.
GOODING, C. (1994) *Disabling Laws, Enabling Acts*, Pluto Press, London.
HONEY, S., MEAGAR, N., and WILLIAMS, M. (1993) *Employers'*

Attitudes towards People with Disabilities, Manpower Studies Institute, University of Sussex.

HEVEY, D. (1992) *The Creatures Time Forgot*, Routledge, London.

HUMPHRIES, S. and GORDON, P. (1992) *Out of Sight: The Experience of Disability, 1900–1950*, Northern House Publishers, London.

KESTENBAUM, A. (1993) *Making Community Care a Reality*, Independent Living Fund, Nottingham.

LAURIE, L. (ed.) (1991) *Building our Lives: Housing, Independent Living and Disabled People*, Shelter, London.

THE LAW SOCIETY. (1992) *Disability, Discrimination and Employment Law: A Report on the Law Society's Employment Law Committee*, London, Law Society.

LONSDALE, S. (1990) *Women and Disability*, London, Tavistock.

LUNT, N. and THORNTON, P. (1993) *Employment Policies for Disabled People: A Review of Legislation and Services in Fifteen Different Countries*, Sheffield, Employment Department.

MANNION, R. (1994) *Disabling Transport: Mobility, Deprivation and Social Policy*, Avebury, Aldershot.

OLIVER, M. and ZARB, G. (1993) *Ageing with a Disability*, University of Greenwich, London.

POTTS, M. and FIDO, R. (1991) *A Fit Person to be Removed: Personal Accounts of Life in a Mental Deficiency Institution*, Northcote House, Plymouth.

SMITH, S. (1992) *Wasted Opportunities: The Practice of Training and Enterprise Councils as Viewed by Training Providers and Advocates for Disabled People*, London, Spastics Society.

STEVENSON, O. and PARSLOE, P. (1993) *Community Care and Empowerment*, Joseph Rowntree Foundation, York.

SWAIN, J., FINKELSTEIN, V., FRENCH, S. and OLIVER, M. (eds) (1993) *Disabling Barriers – Enabling Environments*, Sage/Open University, London.

WADE, B. and MOORE, M. (1993) *Experiencing Special Education: What Young People with Special Education Needs Can Tell Us*, Open University Press, Buckingham.

WESTCOTT, H. (1993) *Abuse of Children and Adults with Disabilities*, National Society for the Prevention of Cruelty to Children, London.

INDEX